PRAISE FOR *DIY U*

"Anya Kamenetz brilliantly reveals the illogic and wasteful inequities of America's blind faith in higher education. Her book will be devastating for older people who still believe one more graduate degree is the road to personal success and a prosperous economy. Younger people will feel relief that someone has finally told the truth about their predicament. Kamenetz offers a radically different way to think about the future and she gives young people a more rational and promising way to think about theirs."

—WILLIAM GREIDER, bestselling author of *Come Home, America:*
The Rise and Fall (and Redeeming Promise) of Our Country,
and National Affairs Correspondent for *The Nation*

"A vibrant democracy depends on vibrant education. Anya Kamenetz shows a way to shake up education to release more potential at every level. The transition won't be easy for institutions mired in the past, but students will have more—and better—options in a world in which knowledge increasingly must bypass gatekeepers and find new paths."

—NAOMI WOLF, bestselling author of
The End of America and *Give Me Liberty*

"Kamenetz shows us 'higher education' as a crumbling facade. It doesn't work well or deliver on its promise. Meanwhile, a thousand alternative flowers are beginning to bloom and the means for any of us to educate ourselves have become available. Let's get on with it."

—JAMES MARCUS BACH, author of *Secrets of a Buccaneer-Scholar*

"A fascinating and provocative book."

—JOHN MERROW, Education Correspondent,
PBS *NewsHour,* and President, Learning Matters, Inc.

"Anya Kamenetz offers a thoughtful and much-needed call to rethink higher education in a world of spiraling tuition costs, a 50 percent college drop-out rate, and a growing understanding that the one-size-fits-all college model is broken. According to Kamenetz, it's high time to put student learning at the center of the educational process. This book is not only a smart and forward-thinking look at new and exciting trends in self-directed higher learning, it's also a smart resource guide for students and their families anxious to take their education into their own hands."

—DANIEL H. PINK, author of *Drive* and *A Whole New Mind*

"Anya Kamenetz is one of the best reporters and commentators on the millennial generation and its economic future. In *DIY U*, she offers a provocative, highly readable take on the growing challenge of ensuring an affordable college education, and she envisions an alternative path that would shake up the established order and radically transform how we learn."

—DAVID HALPERIN, Director, Campus Progress,
and Senior Vice President, Center for American Progress

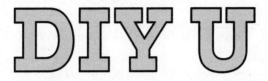

DIY U

Edupunks, Edupreneurs, and the
Coming Transformation of Higher Education

ANYA KAMENETZ

Chelsea Green Publishing
White River Junction, Vermont

FSC

Mixed Sources
Product group from well-managed forests, controlled sources and recycled wood or fiber

Cert no. SW-COC-002358
www.fsc.org
© 1996 Forest Stewardship Council

Preserving our environment
Chelsea Green Publishing Co. chose to print the pages of this book on recycled paper and saved these resources[1]:

energy	water	greenhouse gases	solid waste
34 million BTUs	48,526 gal.	10,076 lbs	2,946 lbs

Printed by **Webcom Inc.** on Legacy Hi-Bulk Natural 100% post-consumer waste.

ANCIENT FOREST™ FRIENDLY

106 trees were saved for our forests

[1] Estimates were made using the Environmental Defense Paper Calculator.

Project Manager: Emily Foote
Developmental Editor: Jonathan Teller-Elsberg
Copy Editor: Cannon Labrie
Proofreader: Robin Catalano
Indexer: Lee Lawton
Designer: Peter Holm, Sterling Hill Productions

Printed in Canada
First printing March, 2010
10 9 8 7 6 5 4 3 2 1   10 11 12 13 14 15

Our Commitment to Green Publishing
Chelsea Green sees publishing as a tool for cultural change and ecological stewardship. We strive to align our book manufacturing practices with our editorial mission and to reduce the impact of our business enterprise on the environment. We print our books and catalogs on chlorine-free recycled paper, using vegetable-based inks whenever possible. This book may cost slightly more because we use recycled paper, and we hope you'll agree that it's worth it. Chelsea Green is a member of the Green Press Initiative (www.greenpressinitiative.org), a nonprofit coalition of publishers, manufacturers, and authors working to protect the world's endangered forests and conserve natural resources. *DIY U* was printed on Legacy Natural, a 100-percent postconsumer, recycled paper supplied by Webcom.

Library of Congress Cataloging-in-Publication Data
Kamenetz, Anya, 1980-
   DIY U : edupunks, edupreneurs, and the coming transformation of higher education / Anya Kamenetz.
     p. cm.
   Includes bibliographical references and index.
   ISBN 978-1-60358-234-6
   1. Education, Higher--United States. 2. Educational change--United States. 3. College costs--United States. 4. Alternative education--United States. I. Title.

   LA227.4.K36 2010
   378.73--dc22

                                            2009054136

Chelsea Green Publishing Company
Post Office Box 428
White River Junction, VT 05001
(802) 295-6300
www.chelseagreen.com

CONTENTS

ACKNOWLEDGMENTS

This book is all about the power of sharing ideas freely. There's a long list of open minds and generous hearts who shared theirs with me so I could share mine with you.

Thanks to Megan Lynch for originally suggesting this topic. Thanks to Margo Baldwin, Jonathan Teller-Elsberg, and everyone at Chelsea Green for being amazing editors and publishers. Thanks so much to my agent, Katinka Matson, and the Brockman family, all of whom have put a lot of faith in me over the years. A huge shout-out to the whole team at *Fast Company*—especially to Bob Safian and Will Bourne, Editors of the Year in more ways than one—for helping these ideas bloom, and giving me the gift of time.

Thanks to my parents, Moira Crone and Rodger Kamenetz, and sister Kezia for being my champions and my best readers. Thanks to all the brilliant and busy folks who read chapters for me and returned invaluable feedback: Dustin Boyer, Jackie Delamatre, Mike Dover, Michael Horn, Julia Monturo, Linda Rosenbury, Luke Swarthout, and Suzanne Walsh. Thanks to the edupunks—especially Jim Groom and David Wiley—for sharing their mysterious ways, and to everyone else who spoke with me. I also have to thank my personal learning network—the Twitterers, bloggers, Facebook friends and Google Reader contacts who cheered me on through this process and give me interesting things to think about every day. Zara Kessler, you are a rock star, and I couldn't have done this without you.

Adam, thank you for being my partner in life and in infinite dinner-table conversations that end in Googling something. I love you and a bowl of soup.

Thanks finally to all of the educators out there who are working tirelessly to help their students become who they want to be. This book is for you.

INTRODUCTION

Almost nine out of ten American high school seniors say they want to go to college.[1]

This is a new historical fact. For most of the thousand years or so since it was invented, a university education was thought to be suited only for a tiny group—a ruling class or a subculture of scholars. Since World War II, this country has turned it into not only a mass-market product but the best hope of achieving a middle-class income. Sending your kids to college is now part of the American Dream, just like homeownership; and just like homeownership, it's something we have been willing to go deeply into hock for.

Faith in the universal power of higher learning is at the heart of modernity. From enhancing our basic humanity to preserving culture, economic and technological development to social equality, and redressing ills from global warming to AIDS, there are very few needs for which more education has not been prescribed. As H. G. Wells famously put it, "Human history becomes more and more a race between education and catastrophe."[2]

Warranted or not—and I'll argue that it's been overstated—this belief is the closest thing we have to a world religion. And it is winning converts at unprecedented speed. People around the world are demanding more education as a human right and as a pathway out of poverty. In 1900, about half a million people worldwide were enrolled in colleges. A century later the number was 100 million.[3] According to a 2009 report by the United Nations Educational, Scientific and Cultural Organization (UNESCO), there are 150 million students today enrolled in some kind of education beyond high school, a 53 percent increase in less than one decade.[4]

That number represents more than one in four college-aged young people worldwide.[5] The growth has touched even the most impoverished and war-torn countries. Sub-Saharan Africa, the world's poorest region, has 5 percent of its young people enrolled in higher education, which is roughly equal to what the United States had in the 1920s. It's also the lowest participation rate on the planet.[6] UNESCO concluded that there's no foreseeable way enough traditional universities could be physically built in the next two decades to match the demand. Young people worldwide are caught between the spiraling cost of college and an apparently bottomless hunger for it.

Meanwhile here in America, the birthplace of mass higher education, our faith is no longer moving mountains. Since the 1970s, our educational attainment has stalled while the rest of the world is roaring ahead. About 30 percent of high school students drop out,[7] and almost half of all college students don't graduate, so only a little over a third of Americans end up with any kind of college degree. For centuries the world's most educated nation, we've fallen behind ten others. Unlike citizens of every other rich country except Germany, Americans in their late teens and early twenties are no more educated than older generations.[8]

President Obama is clear on the problem. In his first address to Congress, he promised: "We will provide the support necessary for all young Americans to complete college and meet a new goal: By 2020, America will once again have the highest proportion of college graduates in the world."[9]

Obama has appointed some wonderful advocates for students to the Department of Education. His administration has backed great proposals, like increasing the Pell Grant, cutting corporate subsidies out of the student-loan program, simplifying the federal student-aid application process, and raising funding for community colleges. But nothing on the table is addressing the underlying issues that make tuition rise, nor the capacity problems and leaks in the system.

What's to be done about dropout rates approaching 50 percent[10] and outstanding student-loan debt that currently totals over $730 billion,[11] or $23,200 per graduating senior in 2008?[12] At first, I stood with progressives who say the federal government should increase grants and rein in the parasitic student-loan business. But while the student-loan industry has been part of the problem, and more grants are part of the solution, there is more to this story. College tuition has been outpacing inflation for decades. Between 1990 and 2008, tuition and fees rose 248 percent in real dollars, more than any other major component of the Consumer Price Index.[13] Raising the Pell Grant doesn't address this underlying problem. Constant transfusions of public money help keep the patient alive but do not stop the bleeding.

Metaphors aside, the higher-education system has a lot in common with another great challenge our country is confronting: health care. Colleges, like hospitals, have little incentive to conserve resources or compete on price. They can actually gain prestige by raising tuition. They shift costs to students to make up for gaps in state funding, and then hand out grant money to the applicants they want the most, not the ones who need the most help. Community colleges dedicated to serving the poorest get a fraction of the public money that goes to flagship state universities. One in five of the nation's eighteen million college students took at least one online class by the fall of 2006, according to a study by the Sloan Consortium,[14] but technology hasn't yet changed the prevailing model or brought down costs in higher education as it has for so many other industries.

As a top higher-education policy aide told me, "We are just tinkering around the edges." And an Obama appointee (who also did not want to be identified) agreed that the nation is highly unlikely, given current tactics, to reach Obama's target, which would essentially mean doubling the numbers who graduate within one decade. The National Center for Education Statistics released a report in September 2009, estimating that college enrollments will increase by just 13 percent by 2018, to 20.6 million, at a time when the U.S. population is projected to increase by 14 percent.[15]

This isn't good enough. The claims we make on behalf of formal education are at times exaggerated. On its own it is no panacea. And there's a dangerous confusion between ends and means—between growing educational institutions and advancing the cause of learning itself. Yet the power of learning, while mysterious, is real. America can't remain a global economic powerhouse while it slides to the middle of the heap in education. Nor can we grapple with the challenges we face as a global community without meeting the world's burgeoning demand for education. There are two basic options the way I see it: fundamentally change the way higher education is delivered, or resign ourselves to never having enough of it.

The good news is that all over the world people are thinking big about how to change higher education. Brick, stone, and marble institutions with centuries of prestige behind them are increasingly being joined by upstarts, both nonprofit and for-profit, and even more loosely organized communities of educational practitioners and apprentices. The open education movement started at the Massachusetts Institute of Technology in 2001, when the school decided to put its coursework online for free. Today, you can go online to MIT Open Courseware and find the full syllabi, lecture notes, class exercises, tests, and some video and audio for 1900 courses, nearly every one MIT offers, from physics to art history. As of late 2009, 63 million people and counting have raided this trove.[16]

Open educational content is just the beginning. Want a personalized tutor to teach you math or French? A class that's structured like an immersive role-playing game? An accredited bachelor's degree, in six months, for a few thousand dollars? A free, peer-to-peer Wiki university? These all exist today, the beginnings of a complete educational remix. Do-It-Yourself University means the expansion of education beyond classroom walls: free, open-source, vocational, experiential, and self-directed learning.

This opening world presents huge questions about the true nature of a college education. The university is over a thousand years old, older than modernity itself. On American soil it has grown like Katamari Damacy, the Japanese video game where a magical "clumping spirit" snowballs around the world collecting everything in its path until it attains the size of a star. The latter-day "multiversity," as it was dubbed by University of California president Clark Kerr in 1963,[17] clumps teaching with research; vocational and technical education with liberal arts; sports, clubs, and parties with intellectual life; accreditation and evaluation with mentoring and friendship. For students "college" means very different things at different times: the place to grow up, be out on your own, make friends, take leadership roles, prepare for and find a good job, and even learn.

Technology upsets the traditional hierarchies and categories of education. It can put the learner at the center of the educational process. Increasingly this means students will decide what they want to learn; when, where, and with whom; and they will learn by doing. Functions that have long hung together, like research and teaching, learning and assessment, or content, skills, accreditation, and socialization, can be delivered separately.

Here are four trends guiding this transformation:

1. *The 80/20 Rule.* This book is not, for the most part, about Harvard and Yale. They have gotten plenty of ink already. Most of the growth in higher education over the next century will come from the 85 percent of students who are "nontraditional" in some way—older, working adults, or ethnic minorities. They will increasingly attend the 80 percent of institutions that are nonselective, meaning they admit the vast majority of applicants. This includes most mainstream public universities as well as community colleges and for-profit colleges, which saw the most growth between 2002 and 2006.[18]

   For-profit colleges are the only U.S. institutions that are seriously committed to expanding their numbers, community colleges already enroll half of all undergraduates, and both disproportionately enroll the demographic groups that dominate the next generation of Americans: Hispanics, all other minority groups, first-generation college students. Some of the boldest thinking is happening in these "nontraditional" institutions. Concerns about quality and affordability in the new mainstream of higher education have to be addressed head-on.

2. *The Great Unbundling.* Universities have historically combined many social, educational, and other benefits in one-stop shopping. Increasingly, some of these resources (e.g., faculty time) are strained, while others (like written course content) are approaching a marginal cost of zero.

   As it has with industries from music to news, the logic of digital technology will compel institutions to specialize and collaborate, find economies of scale and avoid duplications.

   Books can be freed from the printed page, courses freed from geographical classrooms and individual faculty, and students will be free from enrolling in a single institution.

   Stripped-down institutions that focus on instruction or assessment only, or on a particular discipline or area, will find larger and larger audiences. The most cutting-edge sciences and the most traditional liberal arts can both flourish in a specialized, concentrated, and technologically enhanced setting. I have seen professors elevate the craft of teaching rhetoric, composition, and critical thinking itself to new heights using social media and applying cutting-edge research about learning.

3. *Techno-hybridization.* No, it's not mutant robots from outer space. According to Department of Education research, a blend of technology-assisted and traditional class instruction works better than either one alone. This blending can occur with institutions enrolling students on campus or off, in classrooms or online—studies have shown that students do a better job collaborating online if they meet in person even once.[19]

4. *Personal Learning Networks and Paths.* There will likely still be plenty of demand for the traditional collegiate experience, but as only one of many options and entry points. People who graduate from high school at eighteen and go straight through four years of college are already a tiny minority of all young Americans, around one in ten.[20] Pulling America out of its educational slump requires designing programs flexible and supportive enough to reach the 44 percent of students who currently drop out of college and the 30 to 35 percent who drop out of high school. These programs have to provide socialization, personal development, and critical-thinking skills, not just job training.

Self-directed learning will be increasingly important. Already, the majority of students attend more than one institution during their college careers, and more than half seek to enhance their experience with an internship. In the future, with the increasing availability of online courses and other resources, individuals will increasingly forge a personal learning path, combining classroom and online learning, work and other experiences.

Open education pioneer Alec Couros at the University of Saskatchewan talks about assembling personal learning networks that include mentors, colleagues, media sources, books, and collections of links. The existing system will be challenged to come up with new forms of accreditation,

transfer credits, and certification so that the value of this
work can be recognized by potential employers and others.

Education is an essentially conservative enterprise. If we didn't
believe that one generation had something important to transmit
to the next, we wouldn't need education. So changing education
makes people really, really nervous. In a shakeup, the current elites
have the most to lose. So much of the present-day value of a college
degree is based on centuries of accumulated reputation. Real reform
will mean a system that is judged and judges its graduates on quality
of results, not on names alone.

Traditional educators raise concerns that are legitimate even
when they are self-interested. There's no good way to measure the
benefits of the old-fashioned face-to-face educational model; there's
worry that something important will be discarded in the race ahead.
More fundamentally, no one knows if it's possible to extend the
benefits of higher education to the majority of a population without
diluting its essence. For one thing, no two people can agree on what
that essence might be.

Still, in an ideal world, opportunities to stretch your abilities, test
your personal mettle, follow your natural curiosity, and jam intellectually with friends, colleagues, and mentors—all the good stuff
that is supposed to happen in college—would be more open to
more people at all ages and transition points in life. Traditional
colleges will continue to find plenty of eager applicants who want
the experiences only they can provide. The 80 percent of American
college students who currently attend nonselective institutions will
have many more options, and so will the majority of young people,
those who drop out or who never apply. Tuition costs would reach
sane levels due to increased use of technology, true competition, and
better-allocated federal and state incentives. This would lower one
of the most important barriers to educational access. By modifying
the economics of the nation's second largest industry, we would save
money, and tap the resources and energy of a whole new generation
to tackle challenges like building a greener society, expanding the
middle class, creating better jobs, and providing people with health
care. Alternatives to the four-year bachelor's degree would become
more visible and acceptable, which might help bridge one of the

biggest social divides in American life. Whether these incipient changes will lead to that kind of positive transformation, however, still hangs in the balance.

This book is organized in two parts. Part one is about how we got here. Chapter 1, "History," traces the development of the college-for-all myth, which grew along with the rest of the American Dream. Chapter 2, "Sociology," looks at the assumptions about human capital and meritocracy that need to be addressed if we are to build a system that works for everybody. Chapter 3, "Economics," gives the reasons behind the cost spiral.

Part two is about how we get there from here. Chapter 4, "Computer Science," is about the full spectrum of technological applications within existing institutions, from the incremental to the radical. Chapter 5, "Independent Study," discusses the expansion of education beyond classroom walls and covers vocational, experiential, and self-learning. Chapter 6, "Commencement," talks about which of these changes are inevitable, which will take hard work, and what the transformation of the university might mean for the future of humanity. Chapter 7, "Resource Guide for a Do-It-Yourself Education," is for the student who wants to hack her own education.

DIY U is about how America can get better at guiding all its young people toward supporting themselves, helping others, and living lives of awareness. It's an argument for rethinking higher education to take advantage of the tremendous opportunities of the times we're living in. And it's a guide for individuals. No matter your age or background, you can use this book to find learning experiences that match your needs, to pursue the good life, and make the world a better place.

part one

HOW WE GOT HERE

one

HISTORY

In a faraway colony, one in a thousand people—mostly young, rich, white men—are sent to live in isolated, rural Christian communes.[1]

Some are pious, learned, ambitious; others are unruly younger sons with no other prospects. The students spend hours every day in chapel; every few years, the entire community is seized by a several-days-long religious revival. They also get into lots of trouble. In their meager barracks they drink, gamble, and duel. They brawl, sometimes exchanging bullets, with local residents, and bother local women. Occasionally they rebel and are expelled en masse or force administrators to resign. Overseen by low-paid clergymen too deaf or infirm to control a congregation, hazed by older students, whipped for infractions of the rules, they're treated like young boys when their contemporaries might be married with children. And, oh yes, they spend a few hours a day in rote memorization of less than a dozen subjects.

This was the typical eighteenth-century American college, loosely modeled on England's Oxford and Cambridge, which date back to the thirteenth century. Nine colleges were founded in the colonies before the Revolution, and they're all still in business: Harvard, William and Mary, Yale, Princeton, Columbia, Penn, Brown, Rutgers, and Dartmouth.[2]

For universities, history is authority. It's no accident that America's most prestigious institution, Harvard, is also its oldest, or that some of the oldest organizations of any kind, worldwide, are universities.[3] Most colleges invoke a sense of continuity that may or may not have any support in the historic record.

Two periods of upheaval in the history of American higher education shed light on the situation today—a time of "catastrophic angst," according to a writer in the trade publication *Inside Higher Ed*.[4] The first was the emergence of the modern university, beginning in the 1860s. The second was the invention of mass higher education after World War II.

"Our country is to be a land of colleges," Reverend Absalom Peters, a friend of colleges including Williams and Amherst, remarked in 1851. Toward the end of the nineteenth century, Frederick Rudolph writes in *The American College and University: A History* (1962), England had four colleges for a population of 23 million, while the state of Ohio alone had thirty-seven colleges for a population of 3 million.[5] Unlike countries around the world that quickly put all their universities under centralized state control, the United States evolved a unique diversity of large and small, public and private institutions. At first, colleges multiplied because each Protestant denomination in each colony wanted its own. Reformers founded separate colleges for women, blacks, even Indians. Founding or growing a college was always useful to someone, somewhere, whether local political leaders, philanthropists, subcultures, sects, or ethnic groups. Colleges were built to further these interests—student demand was always secondary.

With so many supporters, colleges had many different functions. In the words of Ivy League father Ezra Cornell in the mid-nineteenth century: "I would found an institution where any one could study any thing."[6] Was college supposed to make people more pious or richer? Stoke the flames of the eternal classics or push forward the frontiers of scientific exploration? Be practical and technical or abstract and theoretical? Concern itself chiefly with minds or with the whole person, emotional, spiritual, and physical? Direct itself toward a small elite, or be democratic and educate everybody? The answer tended to be yes, yes, yes. As Henry S. Pritchett of the Carnegie Foundation wrote in 1929, "From the exposition of esoteric Buddhism to the management of chain grocery stores . . . [the American university] offers its services to the inquiring young American."[7]

Any college that trumpets its "centuries-long tradition of academic excellence," however, is lying. Colonial colleges were established long before high schools, so they often filled classes with barely literate fourteen- or fifteen-year-olds. Throughout the nineteenth century, "Nowhere were really challenging intellectual demands being placed upon [students]," Rudolph states flatly, and as late as 1904, "Dean Briggs of Harvard announced his preference for 'moderate intelligence'," preferring well-mannered and well-rounded gentlemen to grinds.[8] Along with low standards, there was "little emphasis on completing degrees" well into the nineteenth century, writes University of Kentucky historian John R. Thelin in his 2004 book *A History of American Higher Education*, something of a sequel to Rudolph's work.[9] Students felt free to leave after a year or two of classes. The current college dropout rate of nearly 50 percent is actually pretty good by historic standards. Only a handful of colleges have ever done better.

When I read books and articles that disparage today's college students as "The Dumbest Generation,"[10] I can only shake my head. There is no vanished tradition of serious scholarship. Classes in pre–Civil War era colleges were pretty dull. The official course of study in colonial colleges was a pallid imitation of the fourteenth-century English and European curriculum, which itself was a shallow and error-riddled reconstruction of the intellectual achievements of Aristotle, Plato, and Socrates.[11]

One of the biggest historical fictions about college is that it purveys some kind of unbroken academic tradition: "the liberal arts," "core curriculum," "the classics" or "the canon." Today's definitions of the liberal arts tend to emphasize elements like critical thinking, clear writing, and deep, layered reading of texts. These are all important skills for an age awash in information. They have little to do with anything taught in the old days. From the 500s through the 1800s, in Europe and later in America, the major pedagogical methods were memorization and recitation. Students sometimes offset the boredom by founding debating and literary societies, like Phi Beta Kappa in 1776. In the decades to follow, such groups played host to radical thinkers like Ralph Waldo Emerson.[12] The less intellectually inclined ignored their classes and rushed to private tutors at the end of the semester to cram their way through exams.[13]

The "liberal" arts were dubbed that in classical times because they were the necessary basis of knowledge for free men, as opposed to slaves. Their order was fixed by the 500s: the trivium or "three" of grammar, rhetoric, and dialectic, and the quadrivium or "four" of arithmetic, geometry, astronomy, and music.[14]

Hugh of St. Victor (1078–1141), scholasticus of the abbey of St. Victor in Paris, in his work *De Studio Legendi* (On the Art of Studying) lays out the then-trendiest academic ideas on the seven arts:

> Philosophy is subdivided into theory, practice, mechanics and logic. Theory divides into theology, physics and mathematics, this latter into arithmetic, music and geometry; practice has three subdivisions: a solitary, a private and a public part (ethics, economy and politics). Mechanics subdivides into weaving, arms, navigation, agriculture, hunting, medicine and theater. Logic has two parts: grammar and the art of reasoning (ratio disserendi); this latter can work toward a threefold goal: certainty (demonstratio), probability and sophistry.[15]

Got that? Music is part of math. Weaving, medicine, and theater are all part of mechanics. St. Victor would certainly be confused to see a modern course catalog with its thousands of listings and hundreds of disciplines. Which is not to discount his learned efforts, only to underline the point that courses of study, as small selections from the vast and constantly evolving store of human knowledge, can only pretend to be fixed, logical, comprehensive, or traditional.

Nineteenth-century college life sounds pretty depressing. Most colleges were underfunded, stuffy, and conservative. They struggled with a general lack of demand from students. In 1825 Harvard professor George Ticknor wrote, "There is, at this moment, hardly a father in our country, who does not count among his chief anxieties, and most earnest hopes, the desire to give his children a better education than he has been able to obtain for himself."[16] Although this piety wouldn't raise eyebrows today, Ticknor was greatly exaggerating if he implied that most parents back then dreamed of getting their kids into Harvard. The election of the backwoods common man Andrew Jackson to president in 1828 fed a recurring American disdain for book learning, and hundreds of colleges folded in the following decades. There were plenty of opportunities on the frontier; no need for an ambitious boy to go to college. The best estimates put college enrollment at less than 1 percent of sixteen- to twenty-five-year-old men in the early 1800s, and just 1.75 percent of that group fifty years later.[17]

To draw even that many, Rudolph points out, colleges never charged students the full cost of maintaining the institution, subsidizing them with state money and donations much as they do today. Tuition was sometimes subject to last-minute discounting to fill up classes just before the beginning of the school year. "Colleges could either pay professors to teach or they could pay their students to enroll. They chose the latter course because it was the only way they could achieve the enrollment that justified their existence."[18]

Maybe there was some truth to Ticknor's words, though, because higher education did keep growing. On the eve of the Civil War, Vermont senator Justin Smith Morrill introduced the 1862 Morrill Act, signed into law by President Lincoln. Morrill, the self-taught son of farmers, was an advocate of universal education, even for women and former slaves.

Under Morrill's "Act Donating Public Lands to the Several States and Territories which may provide Colleges for the benefit of Agricultural and Mechanical Arts," more than seventeen million acres of public lands were sold to endow new state colleges. Over the next century sixty-nine American universities were founded with the proceeds of this and the second Morrill Act of 1890. These federal land-grant institutions would enroll one in five college students by 1955.[19]

There is no such thing as a fully private institution of higher learning. Every American college, going back to colonial times, has enjoyed public support. One-fourth of Massachusetts' annual tax levy went to start up Harvard, for example.[20] Today, the University of Phoenix, the largest example of a so-called market-driven institution, is also the largest recipient of federal student aid. But the establishment of colleges that were explicitly, rather than incidentally, public in the 1860s changed the nature of American higher education. There was a new focus on democracy in admissions and practicality in curriculum. States established "agricultural and mechanical" schools (like Texas A&M) with the purpose of developing the rural economy. Courses in agronomy, horticulture, and plant pathology joined philosophy, logic, and rhetoric.

At first, the people who were supposed to benefit from these new universities couldn't see the point of them. The so-called professors of agriculture were effete German specialists in botany and land-scaping, who knew far less about the practicalities of farming than the few near-illiterate boys who turned up. One rural newspaper called the new University of Illinois a "dude factory"—not compli-mentary. Soon, though, public universities established agricultural experiment stations that bore real results, fighting livestock diseases and boosting crop yields. The innovations weren't just confined to the fields. Mining, railroads, and bridge building demanded engi-neers. Manufacturing needed chemists and materials scientists. The expansion of the public school system brought a growing demand for teachers, mostly women, to be trained in the so-called normal schools, as well as expanding the supply of qualified college appli-cants. These years also saw the inception of the for-profit "career college." In the 1850s, H. B. Stratton and P. R. Bryant founded a chain of fifty schools, starting in Buffalo, New York, to teach short-hand, bookkeeping, and the use of the newfangled mechanical typewriter, primarily to women, who were not welcome at many colleges.[21]

"Vocational and technical education had become a legitimate function of American higher education," writes Rudolph, "and everywhere the idea of going to college was being liberated from the class-bound, classical-bound traditions which for so long had defined the American collegiate experience."[22] The Ivy League adapted to the example being set in the hinterlands; Harvard, in 1887, dropped its entrance requirement for Greek in favor of a new elective system that allowed students to choose more of what they studied.[23]

The enterprise turned to an entirely new justification: students were there to discover new knowledge, not just to repeat what was written in old books. Rudolph talks about a tension that arose in the nineteenth century between empirical and scholastic traditions.[24] Any time you are learning established information—names, facts, figures, ideas thunk by thinkers before you—that's scholastic learn-ing. Empirical knowledge, on the other hand, comes from direct experience and experimentation. Americans tend to emphasize the importance of empiricism, new discoveries, and the scientific method. The funny thing is that the empirical depends on the scholastic. Last year's discoveries are this year's history. It's essential to learn what's come before, so that, as Isaac Newton said, you can stand on the shoulders of giants. The university, then, continuously expands its territory by adapting and assimilating the empirical into the scholastic.

The old English-style colleges had focused on preparatory courses of study in a rural, residential setting. The German university was a looser-knit urban community of independent scholars.[25] It combined research with teaching, awarded advanced degrees for many years of study, and guaranteed academic freedom for both students and professors. America in the nineteenth century developed what Thelin calls a hybrid model with elements of both.[26] The American university has undergraduate residential liberal arts programs, plus graduate faculties of arts and sciences, and often a teaching college and law, medical, and engineering schools to top it off. Great universities are federations of independent fiefdoms, each struggling to grow and competing for resources.

The new universities amassed private endowments, installed prominent presidents, and built marble halls with rows of imposing columns, housing well-equipped laboratories, circulating libraries, and observatories. Gilded Age millionaires stepped up to fund them, even though they themselves were often self-taught. Cornelius Vanderbilt once remarked that "If I had learned education I would not have had time to learn anything else," yet he gave $1 million to found Vanderbilt University in Tennessee.[27] Leland Stanford was a railroad baron; Ezra Cornell made his money in telegraphs. Tufts University, outside Boston, accepted a founding gift from P. T. Barnum, of Barnum & Bailey Circus; their mascot became Jumbo the elephant. The ultimate tycoon, oil man John D. Rockefeller, built one of the prototypes of the new hybrid model, the University of Chicago. In 1876, financier Johns Hopkins founded the first American research university in Baltimore, with the largest-ever charitable bequest of any kind to that date, totaling $7 million (well over $130 million in today's dollars). Although the original vision was to grant graduate degrees only, Hopkins was persuaded to accept undergraduates as well.

Still serving less than 5 percent of the young white male population, and far fewer of everyone else, universities nevertheless evolved into a popular institution for the first time in the nineteenth century.

Rudolph writes in his loftiest tone, "College-founding was under-
taken in the same spirit as canal-building, cotton-ginning, farming,
and gold-mining. . . . All were touched by the American faith in
tomorrow, in the unquestionable capacity of Americans to achieve a
better world." In keeping with the rise of the world's biggest capi-
talist economy, Americans presumed academic prestige was a trad-
able good like any other. "We can bring the president of Oxford
University here by offering a sufficient salary," bragged a delegate to
California's constitutional convention in 1849.[28] Today's for-profit
colleges best capture this traditional expansionist attitude, and they
still tend to be based far from coastal power centers: the University
of Phoenix, for example, founded in Arizona.

With the rise of the university, the social status of university
teachers rose significantly. Harvard sociologist Christopher Jencks
called this the Academic Revolution in his groundbreaking 1969
study of the same title. No more would classes be taught by lowly
clerics struggling on poverty wages. University professors formed
their own professional association, which issued an influential
"Declaration of Principles" in 1915 calling for academic freedom
and tenure. University professors were newly celebrated as scholars and rewarded for doing original research. Their loyalty was to a
discipline, not to a particular institution, and they became experts
consulted on questions of the day.

The new professors taught differently. Recitation gave way to the
"sage on the stage" lecture model. They chose pet topics for small
seminars. Partly responding to professors' interest in the company
of more serious students, colleges raised admissions standards when
possible and added graduate programs. In 1863 Yale granted the first
legitimate American PhD (fake ones from diploma mills had been
available for decades).[29]

Universities didn't just professionalize professors; they profes-
sionalized other professions. It's not necessarily what you know, but
whom you know, that makes you a professional. Professionals band
together to decide what official hoops others have to jump through
to be allowed to join their ranks. Law, medicine, and the clergy have
professional traditions stretching back to medieval times. Since the
nineteenth century, more and more occupations have profession-
alized—teaching, social work, dentistry, architecture, accounting,

physical therapy, dentistry, naturopathy, massage therapy, to name a few. Each has established its own schools, contributing to the growth and power of the university.

Thelin names Thorstein Veblen as a prototype of the new professor.[30] Teaching at both the University of Chicago and Stanford, he gained national fame with his theories about the "leisure class" and "conspicuous consumption," popularizing the still-nascent field of sociology. In his 1918 book *The Higher Learning in America: A Memorandum on the Conduct of Universities by Business Men*, Veblen turned his critical eye on the great university itself. He hated vocational courses, calling the new business schools the "broadest and baldest example [of] the supercession of learning by worldly wisdom," and sniping at the age's educational entrepreneurs as "captains of erudition" (like captains of industry, only more hypocritical). In a diatribe against the democratic expansionism of the hybrid model, he writes:

> Educational enterprise of this kind has, somewhat incontinently, extended the scope of the corporation of learning by creating, "annexing," or "affiliating" many establishments that properly lie outside the academic field and deal with matters foreign to the academic interest,—fitting schools, high-schools, technological, manual and other training schools for mechanical, engineering and other industrial pursuits, professional schools of divers kinds, music schools, art schools, summer schools, schools of "domestic science," "domestic economy," "home economics," (in short, housekeeping), schools for the special training of secondary-school teachers, and even schools that are avowedly of primary grade; while a variety of "university extension" bureaux have also been installed, to comfort and edify the unlearned with lyceum lectures, to dispense erudition by mail-order, and to maintain some putative contact with amateur scholars and dilettanti beyond the pale.[31]

Housekeeping! Dilettantes! Barbarians (and women) at the gates! Despite his case of the vapors, Veblen was himself part of the movement to push academics out into the broader world. He advocated for a "technocracy"—a society run like a machine by trained experts such as himself appointed into high places. Today, despite grumbles, the technocracy is ascendant. Most people accept the suitability of, say, Obama's appointing a cabinet consisting of 40 percent Ivy Leaguers, or even of taking love advice from "Dr. Phil."

Universities were markedly different from the other emerging large organization in the early twentieth century, the corporation. There was no single chain of command or unifying vision; they were more like cities, with many competing interest groups. Take Stanford, founded in 1891. Leland Stanford and his wife were primarily interested in building an enormous, Frederick Law Olmstead–designed memorial to their dead son, using as much sandstone as possible. The president, David Starr Jordan, wanted to make Stanford into the Harvard of California. Faculty members like Veblen wanted to advance their disciplines and equally their personal reputations. The students, the immediate excuse for the college being there? They had their own ideas too. The motivations of the typical college student all the way back to the 1700s would be pretty familiar to the majority of today's freshmen: to make friends, have fun, get a little polish, and prepare for careers.

Religion loosened its grip on campuses beginning in the nineteenth century, and campuses developed their own distinct subculture, chronicled in popular music, newspapers, magazines, and books like the 1871 bestseller *Four Years at Yale*. Literary and debating societies yielded popularity to singing groups. The phrase "Alma mater" originally referred to a campus anthem. The age-old college pastimes of drinking and carousing found a love match with the new diversions, fraternities and sports. The first college football game took place on November 6, 1869, between what is now Rutgers and Princeton. (Rutgers won, 6-4.)

At first barely tolerated by administrations, sports unexpectedly grew into the one single element that most endeared colleges to the public. Alumni fans built grand stadiums. In the 1920s, Thelin writes, nuns across the nation exhorted Catholic schoolchildren to pray for Notre Dame's Fighting Irish; their football fans were known as "subway alumni," some of whom actually gave money to the college, even though their only connection was over the radio.[32]

Although college still touched a small percentage of Americans personally, middle-class people in the early twentieth century did increasingly aspire to send their children there. As a college guidebook proudly stated in 1928, "In this last decade, higher education has become such a fetich in America that all the youth of the country, rich or poor, from the cities and the farms, fit or unfit, are seeking the roads that lead to the universities. To each one, or to his parents, a college degree is a stamp of social superiority, its lack, a social stigma. Each one believes that it is a magic key to happiness, success, and riches."[33] That's probably something of a self-serving exaggeration, but it is true that after World War I enrollment picked up, from 250,000 nationwide, or less than 5 percent of the eighteen-to twenty-year-old male population in 1917, to 1.3 million and 15 percent of that population by 1937.

That was the year that *Life* magazine could repeat as a truism, "This faith [in the benefits of higher education] is a cornerstone of any democratic philosophy, the very pith and kernel of what writers since Jefferson have called the American Dream."[34]

If that "magic key to happiness" stuff sounds like an advertising slogan, it's no accident. We had so many colleges that relentless boosterism and campaigning was needed to drum up demand. As the Carnegie Foundation reported back in 1911: "In no other civilized country do institutions of higher learning compete for students. Nowhere else are the allurements and advantages of the colleges' training so advertised. College education in America is a commodity that is sold somewhat after the manner of life insurance and patent medicine." Like life insurance, the wisdom of the investment rests on chance; like patent medicine, the ingredients and effectiveness are varied at best.[35]

The growing faith in universities reinforced, and was reinforced by, the growing influence of all large institutions. The mid-twentieth century was the era of the military-industrial complex and mass media. Large corporations, nonprofits, and government bureaucracies increasingly dictated the life of the "organization man." Universities had characteristics of all three. World War II drew the nation's universities, emblems of local and state pride, into closer partnership with the federal government. The Manhattan Project and the 1958 National Defense Education Act signaled a new era in federally supported research.

Between 1940 and 1960 there was a hundredfold increase in federal grants to universities, the majority going to just a handful of the largest research universities.[36] In 1958, Clark Kerr became the president of the University of California, the nation's exemplar of a large and centrally planned university system. His 1963 classic *The Uses of the University* talked about the "federal grant university" that was increasingly aligned with a national, not just a state or local, mission, and the great "multiversity" that could be all things to all people.

Universities' usefulness during the war encouraged President Roosevelt to sign the American Servicemen's Readjustment Act, the "GI Bill," in 1944. Rather than be unleashed on the job market all at once, the veterans would get a chance to decompress on campus. More than two million returning soldiers took advantage of the free ride, which nearly doubled college enrollment in one decade. Both my grandfathers were among them; one studied accounting and the other pharmacy, good examples of the practical moneymakers that many vets gravitated toward.

Responding to the heightened demand, colleges and universities increased their admissions and marketing staffs, as well as their reliance on accrediting bodies and standardized testing, as Nicholas Lehmann describes in his book *The Big Test.* The federal government, which was directly bankrolling large numbers of students for the first time, wanted quality control over both colleges' "products" and their "customers."

College had been long been a popular aspiration. Now it got closer to a popular expectation, for men and women, whites and blacks. In the optimism and prosperity of the 1960s, an unprecedented federal taxpayer commitment was made toward subsidizing college for the largest-ever generation in the name of international competitiveness and a newly complex knowledge economy. "It means that a high school senior anywhere in this great land of ours can apply to any college or any university in any of the 50 states and not be turned away because his family is poor," proclaimed Lyndon B. Johnson on the signing of the Higher Education Act of 1965.[37] The act, with the 1972 additions of the Pell Grant and the Guaranteed Student Loan, created permanent federal financial aid programs that would become the largest single source of tuition money. The

Higher Education Act was one of the most popular provisions of the War on Poverty; it grew into what Stanford sociologist Mitchell Stevens has called America's most impressive, revered, and successful welfare program. With this step, Johnson was redefining opportunity. A college degree was now the passport to the middle class. Yet the promise had its limits—foreshadowing today's crisis.

One problem was a recurring ambivalence about making college a truly broad social entitlement. From the 1600s on, colleges had enrolled a small number of rich elites, joined by a tiny percentage of the poor who were extremely smart, ambitious, or just lucky. Social progressives periodically charged that the country was wasting talent. In 1935, for example, a study showed that 57 percent of young men with above-average income and high test scores attended college, while only 13 percent of their poorer classmates with the same test scores went there.

Still, when college attendance hovered around 15 percent of the relevant (young, white, male) population, there were many other ways for talented people to succeed. President Franklin D. Roosevelt gave America universal old-age insurance and health care for the poor and elderly, but he balked at universal higher education. He grumbled in 1939: "I am sick and tired of having a lot of long-haired people around here who want a billion dollars for schools, a billion dollars for public health. Just because a boy wants to go to college is no reason we should finance it." Whether a woman should be funded to go to college was not yet a question in the 1930s.

In fact, eventually it was the demands of women, African-Americans, Native Americans, and Hispanics for equal educational access that strained liberal promises to the breaking point. The City University of New York is a telling example. In the 1960s blacks and Latinos made up less than one-fifth of all students at the city's public-college system, and most were confined to a non-baccalaureate track. The same colleges that had offered the city's Jews and other immigrant groups important opportunities for advancement in the 1930s were frustrating the dreams of a new generation. In the spring of 1969, students at CUNY's City College staged a campus takeover, hanging a banner that proclaimed the school that had once been known as the "Harvard of the poor" to be "Harlem University." Student activism and community support led the state Board of

Higher Education to vote swiftly to open CUNY admission for the first time to all city high school graduates. However, only a few years after the college was fully integrated, in 1976, CUNY imposed tuition for the first time. It seemed that citizens could support free education, or open education, but not both.[38]

The second problem with the 1960s expansionist campaign was that as higher education became a mass product, it was in danger of being McDonald's-ized. No more great universities were founded in the twentieth century to equal the Harvards and Yales of the seventeenth and eighteenth centuries, or the Chicagos and Stanfords of the nineteenth. The expansion of the 1960s and 1970s occurred instead in two ways. State universities grew in enrollment from the thousands to the tens of thousands. Too often they scaled up by watering down, depending increasingly on large lecture courses and part-time instructors. On the other hand was the multiplication of what Jencks in *The Academic Revolution* terms "anti-university" colleges.[39] These types of schools were Veblen's nightmare, diluting pure scholarship while relentlessly annexing and expanding the academic mission.

There were about 200 small two-year colleges in the United States as of World War II. They introduced night classes and short courses to serve students who were older, working, or parents. Public community colleges opened at the rate of one a week between the mid-1960s and the mid-1970s. They got larger too—the average size was 500 students in 1940 and 2,500 by 1965, when 1 in 5 students were enrolling there. Enrollment in 1950 in public two-year colleges was 168,043; it had doubled by 1960 to 393,553, and by 1970 it was 2.1 million.[40]

The biggest knock on community colleges has historically been that they offer low-quality, low-standards education. In practice, expanding educational access has always meant lowering the entry bar to meet the students where they are academically. When colonial colleges were founded in New England, the history books say, academic standards were almost nonexistent; when the agricultural and mechanical schools opened in the Midwest, standards were lowered; when the GI Bill admitted two million vets, standards fell yet again. You'd be surprised that college students can parse *The Cat in the Hat* at this point.

In my mind, the real concern with the growth of community

colleges is social, not academic. As colleges started to be more centrally planned and state funded, the divisions between them hardened, which damaged their historic role as a path to social mobility.

California was, as *Life* magazine put it in 1948, "a Show Place for Mass Education."[41] Clark Kerr, longtime president of the University of California, earned his own magazine cover on *Time* for his "Master Plan" of 1960.[42] Under the plan, the University of California, with its flagship at Berkeley, would have the exclusive right to grant doctorates and admit the state's top eighth of high school graduates. The California State University campuses could award only master's degrees, and could admit the top one-third of high school grads, plus transfer students. Community colleges, awarding only two-year degrees, served everybody else. California enrolled half its freshmen in community colleges by the sixties, the same proportion seen nationwide today.[43]

Soon, states like New York and Michigan were adopting similar plans. In 1970, with Kerr as chair, the Carnegie Commission came up with its famous classification system that, for the first time, graded all of the nation's colleges by a single rubric: (1) doctoral-granting institutions, separated into five grades depending on how heavily they invested in research; (2) comprehensive colleges (those that grant master's degrees); (3) liberal-arts colleges (more or less selective); (4) two-year institutions; and (5) freestanding professional schools.[44]

Nicholas Lehman describes the grandly named Master Plan as a moment of "strategic brilliance" on Kerr's part.[45] Henceforth, colleges that enrolled the brightest students, as measured by standardized tests, would also get the most money, enroll the most graduate students, run the biggest research projects, and have the most prestige. And all of this would be enforced by state law.

Strictly separating colleges by function and type seems like a fine, organized thing to do. But it triggers a natural tendency among college leaders to try to move up the ranks and be eligible for more cash from federal and state governments, not to mention alumni. Whenever and wherever they could, normal schools became state teachers' colleges, became state colleges, became state universities. The best proxies for prestige are spending per student and selectivity, both of which drive up costs. The perception, and sometimes the reality, has been that colleges for the poor must be poor colleges.

As the colleges above them in the Carnegie rankings keep stretching for more and more resources, community colleges battle stigma and invisibility. They have less fundraising capacity, and fewer strong advocates, whether among alumni, religious, cultural, or political leaders. They offer undergraduates no straightforward means to a four-year degree, which requires transferring; no exposure to research or graduate education, and fewer of the intangibles of collegiate life like leadership opportunities, cultural activities, dorms, sports, or frats. In the fall of 2009, a sitcom titled *Community*, featuring Chevy Chase, premiered on NBC, illustrating all of the worst perceptions about community colleges. The premise is that a high-flying lawyer who lied on his résumé must be humbled by doing time in a community college. The show's tagline is "a halfway house for losers."

In *The Academic Revolution*, Jencks suggests that two-year colleges serve an important purpose within the academic universe: precisely to segregate. President Lowell of Harvard admitted in the 1960s: "One of the merits of these new institutions will be [the] keeping out of college, rather than leading into it, [of] young people who have no taste for higher education."[46] Was it really true that America's poor, immigrants, and minorities had no taste for Harvard? Or Harvard that had no taste for them?

Four-year institutions naturally seek higher academic standards and the prestige of exclusivity. The American middle class wants to make sure their children have a place in college, any college, believing it's a "magic key to happiness." Community colleges fill in the gaps by taking all comers, yet the product they offer is generally acknowledged to be a substitute for the real thing.

Today, when community colleges are tasked with becoming the front line of access, it's troubling to think that they've always been better at keeping kids out of college than at moving them through. Tracking is difficult, but the National Center for Education Statistics estimates between one and five and one in ten people who enroll in community college actually complete a degree. Granted, part of the reason is that the colleges serve hobbyists, retirees and people who just want to pick up a specific skill. Still, even first-time, full-time freshmen of similar economic backgrounds fare much worse in community colleges than four-year colleges.[47]

One more reason for the expansion of community colleges in the 1960s and early 1970s was political. Nixonian law-and-order conservatives hoped educating young people while they lived at home would keep them quieter than sending them away to school. The nation had recently been riveted by scenes of campus unrest, which peaked with the four students shot by National Guard troops at Kent State in Ohio.

It's hard to realize now just how seriously people took campus radicalism. Mass media for fifty years had focused on college students as trendsetters, and student leaders like Mario Savio at UC Berkeley capitalized on the sense that "the whole world is watching." They marched on Washington, but they also addressed their protest to their universities themselves, as representative of the "establishment" of large organizations that put people second. The counterpart to peace protestors burning their draft cards was the computer punch card that some college students clipped to their lapels as a symbol of the bureaucratic indifference of the technocracy. In his famous speech on the steps of Berkeley's Sproul Hall in 1964, Savio compared the university to a factory and students to the raw materials.

> [We] don't mean to be bought up by some clients of the university, be they government, business, or organized labor ... we're human beings! ... There's a time when the operation of the machine becomes so odious, makes you so sick at heart, that you can't take part, you can't even passively take part, and you've got to put your bodies upon the gears and upon the wheels, upon the levers, upon all the apparatus, and you've got to make it stop![48]

The radicals, it turns out, did succeed more than they would have wished to in sabotaging the "knowledge factory." They alienated politicians, older alumni, and the nation at large. Popular support for college and college students never fully recovered to its midcentury high. Ronald Reagan made the University of California a major punching bag of his 1966 campaign for California governor, with the encouragement of FBI director J. Edgar Hoover, who saw campus peace activists as dangerous subversives.[49]

"This presents the bureau with an opportunity to . . . thwart the ever increasing agitation by subversive elements on the campuses," Hoover noted in a memo.

"They are spoiled and don't deserve the education they are getting," Reagan said on the stump about University of California students.[50] Upon taking office he managed to have UC president Clark Kerr fired and proposed instituting tuition at the UC colleges for the first time. Reagan's career as an enemy of higher education extended to the White House; he ran for president on a proposal to disband the just-founded Department of Education. "During the 1980 presidential campaign, Ronald Reagan dubbed the fledgling Department of Education 'President Carter's new bureaucratic boondoggle.'"[51]

Written as the dust of campus takeovers had hardly cleared, *The Academic Revolution* predicted that student rebellion and the "generation gap" would be the major source of reform in the higher-education sector in future decades. Student democracy did lead to some important changes. Student activism brought about new courses of study like ethnic- and gender-studies departments, enhanced women's athletics and clubs under Title IX starting in 1972, and led to disability accommodations and mental health services. But the student-as-radical meme didn't last. When I was writing my first "Generation Debt" pieces in the *Village Voice* in 2004, students had long since reverted to the historical norm of being primarily concerned with campus social life, personal identity, and their future careers. They lived quietly (or, at least, nonrevolutionarily) in riot-proof dorms, those Soviet-style concrete relics that dot campuses across the country. Faculty who remembered the halcyon days of 1960s student activism through a haze of pot smoke bemoaned this attitude as apathy. Instead, I see a resigned pragmatism reinforced by the new phenomenon of student debt, which raises the risk to students to do anything that might interfere with their ability to graduate and get a good job.[52]

Between the end of World War II and the 1970s, the college system had expanded greatly, nearly to its current size. Tuition was still rising more slowly than family income, and was free for in-state students at hundreds of community colleges and state institutions. The Pell Grant was introduced in 1972; a few years later the maximum grant peaked at over 80 percent of the cost to attend the average state university.[53] More minorities and low-income students were making it to college than at any time in the past. In 1972, 49 percent of high school grads enrolled immediately in college, the highest percentage to that date (influenced by the Vietnam draft with its student exemption).[54]

"By the early 1970s one could say that America 'had it all,'" writes Claudia Goldin and Lawrence Katz in *The Race between Education and Technology*.

> Each generation of Americans achieved a level of educa-
> tion greater than the preceding one, meaning that the aver-
> age adult had considerably more education than his or her
> parents. The nation's economy was strong. Its people were
> sharing relatively equally in its prosperity regardless of their
> position in the income distribution. Racial and regional
> differences in educational resources, educational attain-
> ment, and economic outcomes had narrowed substantially
> since the early twentieth century. Upward mobility with
> regard to education characterized American society.[55]

What's happened in U.S. higher education over the past forty years looks like a slow loss of momentum. On the bright side, enroll-ment keeps growing, both absolutely and as a percentage of all high school graduates. The number of undergraduates more than doubled from 7.4 million in 1970 to 18.2 million in 2007, according to the National Center for Education Statistics.[56] Two-thirds of all high school graduates now enroll in college immediately. And women now make up more than half of all undergraduates.

On the darker side, though, although the relative economic return to college has increased, that's largely because the supply of graduates has stagnated and the salaries of noncollege graduates have fallen sharply. High school graduation rates, which rose dramatically throughout the twentieth century, plateaued in 1970 at 70 percent.[57]

College-going continues to rise, but more slowly, and graduation rates have fallen slightly since the 1970s. Just 30 percent of young people today get a four-year college degree, and another 8 percent get a two-year degree or less, putting America now behind ten other countries.[58] What's more troubling, our younger workers are now no more educated than older workers. When it comes to college attendance, gaps between rich and poor, blacks and whites, and Hispanics and whites have actually widened.[59]

Starting in the 1980s, for reasons explored in chapter 3, tuition rose much faster than family income and inflation. Federal aid has grown, but not as fast as tuition; the Pell Grant now pays for less than a third of total costs at an average state institution. Around two-thirds of undergraduate students take on debt to get through college, with an average graduating debt of $23,200 in 2007–2008.[60]

Looking at the history of American colleges and universities convinces me that many aspects of the current so-called crisis in higher education are actually just characteristics of the institution. It has always been socially exclusionary. It has always been of highly variable quality educationally. It has always had a tendency to expand. It may be because we keep asking more of education at all levels that its failures appear so tremendous.

Still, the United States does seem to have reached an impasse given escalating demand for higher education, spiraling costs, and limited resources. Unlike the 1860s and unlike the 1960s, there is little national will to grow our way out of this problem by founding more colleges or spending much more money on the ones we do have. Is this merely one more symptom of national decline? Have we hit some kind of natural limit for an educated population? Or is there a mismatch between the structures of the past and the needs of the present?

John Meyer has an explanation. A stooped, white-bearded professor emeritus of sociology at Stanford University, Meyer graduated from Indiana's Goshen College in 1955. He's the foremost living authority on the sociology of the university. "Higher education is, and has been, the central cultural institution of the modern system," he told me, which makes the sociology of higher education something like the king of sociologies. Talking to him is like getting Gandalf himself to explain the legend of the rings.

Universities, Meyer argues, have multiplied worldwide in the twentieth century by teaching, practicing, and spreading universalism, or "the idea that local reality can be understood in universal terms." I didn't realize that I was a universalist, but I am, and you probably are too. Universalistic principles form the all-but-invisible warp upon which the carpet of global civilization is woven. From individual examples (an apple falling on the ground), we expect that universal principles (gravity) can be derived and used to measure, predict, and control the outcome of events. Hypotheses about the world can be deduced from observation and tested through repeatable experiments. For Meyer, these beliefs add up to nothing less than a "rationalistic religion" that has supplanted the old mystical religions. The university's "hidden curriculum," he says, has always been teaching its own importance.

Is it fair to call these principles a religion? It's certainly true that when you reduce rationalism to its essence, you get a set of axioms that can only be taken on faith. To expose the esoteric nature of universalism in education, Meyer points to the idea of an exchangeable academic credit: the notion, honored by universities around the world, that one unit of algebra in Kentucky can somehow be equated to a unit of lute-playing in Bulgaria, just like a dollar can be changed into a Bulgarian lev. "The idea is that your value in the mind of a rational god is a standardized thing in this world."

The rationalistic god, says Meyer, is a jealous and devouring god. "It must be growing, advancing, enlarging, accumulating, till the end of time," as Philip Lindsley, nineteenth-century president of the University of Nashville, wrote.[61] Or as Jefferson mused in his 1818 "Report for the Commissioners of the University of Virginia": "And it cannot be but that each generation succeeding to the knowledge acquired by all those who preceded it, adding to it their own acquisitions and discoveries, and handing the mass down for successive and constant accumulation, must advance the knowledge and well being of mankind, not infinitely, as some have said, but indefinitely."[62] This is the Katamari Damacy problem. As human knowledge grows, so does the university. The scholastic digests the empirical; the frontier of the empirical moves forward. It is America's, and the world's, final frontier.

American popular culture flaunts its disdain for the merely academic. Yet academia still holds the reins in our complex society. In fact, as American media and politics get more lowbrow, erudition sometimes seems even more like a power relegated to a priestly class.

It was generally acknowledged that a misplaced faith in economic expertise created the crash of 2008, yet even more economics experts, including the former president of Harvard, were brought in to fix it. An African-American man with several Ivy League degrees can get elected president in this country, but would we elect someone who's never graduated from college? Someone largely self-taught, like Abraham Lincoln, Thomas Jefferson, Andrew Jackson, or Benjamin Franklin? Impossible.

Meyer has called education a cargo cult for the way its rituals, from caps and gowns to Latin and parchment diplomas, have been adopted around the world, believed to bring all good things—economic development, cultural progress, social justice. We all know there are times when book learning doesn't stack up to street smarts. The paradox, and the reason I find it hard to say we should entirely throw off the yoke of the rationalistic religion, is that education in the abstracting model actually does bring benefits to life in the real world. Those farm boys in Wisconsin and Michigan started going to college not just to learn how to plant soybeans better, but because they found it prepared them to go to the city and get into business. It is difficult to gain power, and therefore money, in our hard-driving, materialistic society unless you concern yourself at least a little bit with the abstract, non-immediate, and nonmaterial. "Useless"—or at least not immediately useful—knowledge is the real soul of a liberal education. It's also true, on balance, that access to education tends to enhance people's sense of personal possibility and freedom.

However, as aspirations toward, and for, higher learning grow, the model of inexorably growing bureaucratic institutions of formal education is under extreme pressure. "Our learning institutions, for the most part, are acting as if the world has not suddenly, irrevocably, cataclysmically, epistemically changed—and changed precisely in the area of learning," as Cathy N. Davidson and David Theo Goldberg write in *The Future of Learning Institutions in a Digital Age*. Universities may be on the brink of a phase change from something monolithic to something more fluid: a sea of smaller, more specialized and diverse institutions offering a greater variety of learning opportunities, a cloud of ideas, texts, and conversations.

This evolution may not be as difficult as it seems. Universities grew up literally in the shadow of the medieval cathedral, and they have always been a lot like churches. Late into the nineteenth century, in many colleges, a student spent as much time in chapel as in class. The president of Trinity College in 1868 wrote in his diary, "Without religion a college is a curse to society," and an Amherst professor in the 1800s remarked, "To have prayed well is to have studied well."[63]

Well, even in America, the churchiest of the rich countries, regular worship attendance has dropped from 40 percent as recently as the 1960s to less than 25 percent today.[64] Opportunities to explore spirituality are many and diverse; it's just that most people no longer feel the need to visit a large, stone building for hours every week, submit to the authority of a cleric, and listen to some garbled Latin or Hebrew in order to connect to a higher power. I have to wonder if organized higher education could someday go the way of organized religion—not to disappear, by any means, not even to diminish in absolute size, but to cede its place at the very height of human thought and center of daily action.

– two –

SOCIOLOGY

In March of 2008 I boarded a Hudson Line Metro-North train to
visit Dutchess Community College, 100 miles north of New York
City. The train stayed close to the river as hawks circled overhead.
When I arrived on the snowy, wooded hillside campus, though, the
distance from the city felt more isolating than peaceful. I shared
a lunch of potato chips on Styrofoam plates with a half-dozen
students. They talked about their struggles to balance classes with
full-time jobs and child care. Several were making their second or
third try at college. Women outnumbered men, who seemed especially adrift. Whites, blacks, and Latinos sparred over the campus's
scarce resources. Military recruiters visited often. In the fall of that
same year, six months after my visit, two banks that had served the
students with federal and private student loans abruptly pulled out,
saying the credit crunch forced them to tighten lending standards.
Leaving students scrambling for financing, the move was a vote of
no confidence in the opportunity offered at Dutchess, a school that
calls itself "one of the best community colleges in New York State
for academic excellence and the success of our graduates." The
cognitive dissonance between the ever-present message of "College
is your path to success" and the gloomy prospects on and off campus
was taking its toll; the college had recently held an event for disaf-
fected students titled "Why Are You Here?"

Chapter 1 told the story of the academic revolution—a century
of expansion of higher education in the United States and around
the world. That revolution remains unfinished. Our country has not
transitioned from mass to universal, or even majority, higher education. The sticking points are class and race. "The only way to reach
the numbers we need in order to be internationally competitive is

to improve equity," Bob Shireman, a longtime student advocate and founder of the Project on Student Debt, whom Obama appointed deputy undersecretary of education, tells me. "Increasing access means reaching the kids who are hard to reach—the low-income and underrepresented minorities who are not completing college at the same rates."

Our existing higher-education system, which ranks private above public, research university above teaching college, bachelor's above associate's degree, liberal arts above vocational and technical education, reinforces these historic inequities. Americans endorse equality of opportunity, yet we also embrace living in a competitive meritocracy where the most gifted and hardworking in particular areas get richly rewarded. The two values often come in conflict. Putting our faith in the power of the four-year college degree to both raise earning power broadly and reward individual talent has allowed us to relieve that conflict, but only temporarily, and at great cost. That's why transforming the structure of higher education is a political cause.

The view of higher education as an investment can be traced to a 1964 book by University of Chicago economist Gary Becker.[1]

Human Capital argues that individuals in a knowledge economy invest in education—and society invests on their behalf—to raise their future value in the labor market, just as if their minds were plots of land that they were cultivating. The analogy of a return on investment is invoked to explain the wide gap in salaries by level of education, which has persisted for the past hundred years and emerges in countries around the world. In 2005, according to the Bureau of Labor Statistics, the bars stacked up perfectly: PhDs earned an average of $1,555 a week; those with a BA took home $978; "some college" without a degree netted $645; high school graduates with no college got $583; and high school dropouts earned less than a fourth of those at the top, just $426.[2]

This payoff is why most people want a degree, and why in 2008–9, taxpayers spent $117 billion on federal higher-education aid.[3] We also direct proportionally more private resources, both family funds and philanthropy, toward higher education than any other developed country,[4] and we have never rationed places in college or tracked students as many other countries do. Instead, we encourage every American to shoot for the sheepskin. The purpose is to offer talented young people a way to bootstrap themselves out of poverty, a beloved, bipartisan American formula for success. "If you don't complete something beyond high school you're working poor and you're not going to escape that. That's the general rule," is how Dewayne Matthews, vice president for policy and strategy at the Lumina Foundation, a private foundation dedicated to expanding college access, sums up the prevailing wisdom. The Lumina Foundation is one of the most prestigious and innovative in higher-education policy (funded from the sale of USA Group, a student lender). Their "big goal" is to boost the numbers of Americans with a post-secondary credential from 36 percent to 60 percent by 2025.

Starting during the campaign in 2008, President Obama adopted this target too. He's repeatedly called for America to once again lead the world in college attainment, specifically by graduating five million more people from community colleges in order to "provide Americans of all ages a chance to learn the skills and knowledge necessary to compete for the jobs of the future."[5]

That sounds good, but what does it really mean? Will spending more time in community college classrooms really make Americans, and America as a whole, better off?

Throughout the twentieth century, the relationship of education to wages has traced a U shape.[6] In 1915, the "wage premium" was just where it was in 2005. Those with a college degree or more earned 60 percent more than those with a high school degree or less. For the next eight decades, that advantage to a diploma narrowed, bottoming out at 30 percent in 1950—a college degree was worth half as much, relative to a high school degree, in 1950 versus 1915. It remained at roughly that level for the next thirty years. Starting in 1980, college grads gained a bigger edge, and the relative value of their degree rebounded until it passed 1915 levels again around 1995.[7]

During the 2008 recession, I heard from plenty of college graduates worried about the lasting market value of their degree. Economists, however, assume that the demand for college grads is always growing, thanks to the forward march of technology that today requires store clerks, farmers, and auto mechanics to be conversant with computers. The swing in the relative value of a college degree thus can be chalked up to changes in supply. Between 1915 and 1940, the number of college graduates grew much more quickly than it had before, so their degrees were worth less. After 1980 the reverse was true. America entered its current slump in educational attainment, adding college grads less quickly than it had before—2 percent a year compared to the earlier rate of 3.19 percent. The United States and Germany are the only two rich countries today where younger adults are no more educated than middle-aged adults.[8] The value of a degree in the U.S. job market has gone up in the last generation because, relatively speaking, credentialed adults have gotten scarcer.

There are other important factors determining the wage premium besides the simple supply and demand of educated workers. During World War II, for example, a major manufacturing mobilization and a shortage of male civilian workers increased the number of high-paying factory jobs for high school graduates. The rise of the union movement throughout the early twentieth century also helped create an economy of unprecedented equality, where a man with only a high school diploma could support a family in the middle class. That situation has long since reversed itself. Since the 1970s, Richard Rothstein, research associate at the left-leaning Economic Policy Institute, has found "perhaps as much as a third of the growth in the wage disparity between high school and college graduates has been caused by a falling minimum wage and a decline in unioniza-tion."[9] Wages diverged once again toward the end of the twenti-eth century, until America had arrived at a second Gilded Age with CEOs making hundreds of times what their front-line workers took home.[10] In sum, the United States had a more equal society at midcentury not only because the Higher Education Act led to a swift increase in college enrollment, but also because stronger unions and the effects of the War on Poverty allowed the rising tide to lift all boats. The evidence doesn't suggest that more education alone can return us to this state.

Unfortunately, education alone has been the program, more or less, since the 1970s. Stanford sociologist Mitchell Stevens has called federal higher-education aid America's most ambitious social welfare program. "We don't call it welfare—heaven forbid! That's one of the reasons it's so popular. But if you think of welfare as a means of redistributing social resources or public wealth, there's no question this is a primary method in the post–World War II era," Stevens says.

"In the twentieth century the federal government worked system-atically to allow as many people as possible to lead middle-class lives. Obama's proposal for a majority of Americans to get a degree by 2025 is only an extension of a fifty-year-long federal government commitment to feeding prosperity through access, by investing in campuses and putting money in college students' pockets in the form of grants and federally subsidized or guaranteed loans." This is Becker's human-capital theory at work: invest in our young people and they will yield a return both for themselves and for the nation at large.

The problem is that it hasn't worked. In the decades since a BA became the primary visa for entry into the middle class, the middle class has only gotten smaller. We often hear about the $1 million average lifetime income premium for a college diploma.[11] But if you look at median incomes by education since 1970, there's no increas-ing return to a college degree to go with the increased cost. There's a steep decline in the incomes of less-educated workers combined with flat or declining income for more-educated workers. That is, the noncollege penalty is rising, not the college reward.[12]

The most recent recession drove that point home. In June 2009, the *New York Times* reported on teenagers in Ohio adjusting to the bankruptcy of car giant General Motors, one of the originators of the informal pact between business, government, and organized labor that allowed CEO Charles Wilson to say in the 1950s, "What's good for GM is good for the country."

> "Before, kids would say, 'I don't need to go to college. I can go to work with my dad at G.M. and have a good life,'" said Carol Romie, the chief guidance counselor at West Carrollton High School in this blue-collar Dayton suburb. "With G.M. closed, that's not an option nowadays."
>
> Brandon Abney, a newly minted high school gradu-ate, would have loved to work at the G.M. truck plant in Moraine, a neighboring suburb, but it closed last December. So he is enrolling in an 18-month college program to become a firefighter. "After what happened at G.M., you have to go to college to find a job," he said.[13]

Leave aside the question of whether firefighting ought to require a college degree at all. "The collapse of a union-supported family wage for working people has changed all the rules of the game," Stevens comments. "If college is a welfare program, it's a welfare program for which all the rewards require you to graduate from high school. You have to make a high academic baseline to get into this game."

In other words, college as a welfare program is ability-tested, not means-tested. It's available to those who by some combination of talent and circumstance happen to score well on the right tests. "College for all was a great idea when it was an aspirational goal," says Stevens. "College was about improving your circumstances. It wasn't about creating a baseline of survival. What does it mean if college is the only avenue to a decent living in this century? That's the conversation we're not having nationally."

Education is an important value. Yet we may be approaching the limits of what human-capital policy can do all by itself to create both a just society and a powerful economy. A four-year college degree is still a good investment for the individual who is academically prepared, has the external resources and internal fortitude to finish that degree, and who is also interested in working in a field that requires that degree. But the current official strategy of trying to cram more of our least-prepared young people into our most resource-deprived institutions, with the absence of any other components of a welfare state or investment in quality job creation, and hoping it somehow makes America into a more broadly prosperous country is not likely to work. The reasons why range from the supply, demand, and institutional factors observed by Goldin and Katz, to the theory of human capital itself.

In the first place, there's no evidence that we have the real commitment of resources needed to expand access to higher education. As a rough approximation, "doubling the shares who graduate means spending twice as much money," Dr. Anthony Carnevale, director of the Georgetown University Center on Education and the Workforce, who's been working at the intersection of the workforce, education, and employment policy for almost three decades, tells me. Higher education, he points out, is already a $320 billion economic sector. "Where does the next $320 billion come from?

There are fantasies that we'll do it with computers, or find $320 billion worth of savings and efficiencies in a $320 billion budget. It's a loaves and fishes speech."[14]

In fact, the end of the first decade of the twenty-first century is an atmosphere of historic scarcity with regard to the state budgets that are the most important source of funding for higher education. Suzanne Walsh at the Lumina Foundation says, "Almost every public institution has been told by their state legislatures and governors, 'We want more grads able to participate in our state economy.' In no state are they being told, 'and we'll give you more money to do that.'"

Charles Reed is the chancellor of the California State University system, the largest public university system in the country and the global template for mass higher education for more than fifty years. When I interviewed him over e-mail in the spring of 2009 (his assistant said he was too swamped to schedule a phone interview) his situation sounded truly dire. UC president Mark Yudof had called for—and eventually passed—a staggering 32 percent increase in tuition; at the start of the fall term, student and faculty groups across the state staged walkouts in protest.

"In the more than forty years that I have been involved in higher education and politics, I have never seen an economic meltdown such as the one that we are currently experiencing," Reed wrote me.

> At the state level, we have gridlock as legislators try and figure out how to close what is estimated to be a $24 billion deficit in California. We were cut $100 million in 2008–9, and are expecting a $584 million cut to the state's overall support of the California State University for next fiscal year. The legislature's inability to pass a timely budget has increased the severity of the cuts to the system, and shortens the amount of time we have to prepare. I have said publicly that this is the end of the Master Plan for Higher Education in California. The days of unlimited access and free tuition to California's public universities are truly over.

The end of the Master Plan. That's a sobering statement, for, whatever its shortcomings, the Master Plan was once the crown jewel of a shining national public commitment to higher education for the majority of citizens.

Let's say America did somehow find a way over the next decade to double the numbers of those with a degree. The new degree holders might be disappointed. They'd flood the market, competing with each other, and their wages could well go down, as happened in the first half of the twentieth century. Although demand for college grads has been steady for a century, just as with any investment, past performance is no guarantee of future results. In fact, after growing for decades, the wage premium for a college degree stayed flat throughout the years 2000–2009.

One reason is that new technology puts different kinds of jobs at risk. Earlier technological waves of industrialization and mechanization mostly replaced low-wage manual work; high-tech and high-speed global communications can do more. David Autor, an economist at MIT, has published several papers about the "hollowing out" of the distribution of work activities and wages. High-level problem solving, professional and managerial jobs, which constitute about 30 percent of the workforce, are difficult to automate. So are hands-on manual jobs like waiter or home healthcare aide, which are about 15 percent of the workforce. Midlevel white-collar jobs that involve typing, bookkeeping, answering phones, filing, and the like, which used to pay decently and require some college, have become easier to replace with either computers or lower-priced foreign workers operating over a fast broadband connection. At the bank, for example, there is still demand for personal financial advisors, but your basic bank teller has largely given way to the ATM.[15]

As the nation gets more educated, the credentials necessary to get the really good jobs might just keep on inflating. Already, people with graduate degrees earn more than plain old BAs; people with technical majors earn much more than liberal arts grads. When I visit wealthier private colleges and public universities today, the students tend to take it for granted that the goalposts are already moving down the field. They expect to go on for a law degree or an MBA or at least a specialized master's in order to get the kind of job they want. The same thing happened at the turn of the last century. Back then, a high school degree could score you an office job. A huge increase in the high school graduation rate between 1910 and 1940—from 9 percent to over 50 percent—did away with that. These days, high school grads have a much smaller edge over high school dropouts in the job market.[16]

Because of the diversification of the workforce, the up-skilling of outsourcing, and credential inflation, college is becoming a riskier investment. In the last three decades, income and wage inequality among different college grads has risen faster than income inequality among Americans overall, and volatility of income has risen too. A couple of years out of college and working as a freelance writer, I was earning literally one-hundredth as much as my former classmate was taking home from a hedge fund—and only one of us was inflating the bubble of global economic meltdown.

Trying to educate the majority of citizens now for the "jobs of the future" may or may not be feasible. This raises theoretical questions with human-capital theory itself, going back to the discussion in chapter 1 about what really defines the university experience. Does it really follow that education makes minds more valuable? How could that possibly work?

The seminal work critical of human-capital theory, dating from the inception of mass higher education, is Christopher Jencks' 1972 study *Inequality: A Reassessment of the Effect of Family and Schooling in America*. Drawing on four years and $800,000 worth of research ($4 million in today's dollars), Jencks and his colleagues at Harvard's Center for Educational and Policy Research found a startling lack of correlation among factors like test scores, grades, family background, income, and job performance. They concluded that there wasn't much evidence "that equalizing the amount of time people spend in school is an effective way of equalizing anything else," and so, "giving everyone the same amount of schooling and the same credentials would not make them more alike or equalize their bargaining power when they sought jobs."[17]

This is a point worth repeating: equal education doesn't necessarily mean an equal chance. College-educated women, though they make up a majority of all students today, still earn less on average than their male classmates. College-educated blacks still earn less than college-educated whites; up to one-fourth of graduates of historically black colleges default on their student loans within two or three years, compared to less than 10 percent of all graduates, which suggests they have a harder time reaping the rewards of their degrees.[18]

Poor students are overrepresented at colleges with fewer resources, like Dutchess; they have to work more hours while in school, take longer to finish, and are more likely to drop out. About half of college students in the United States graduate within six years; for low-income students it's closer to 25 percent.[19]

A 2006 study found that the highest-achieving students from high-income families—those who earned top grades and took all the AP courses—are nearly four times more likely than low-income students with the same academic accomplishments to end up in a highly selective university.[20]

In his 1987 essay collection *The Economics of Education and the Education of an Economist*, eminent British economist Mark Blaug takes a "jaundiced" look at human-capital theory, among many other "fads" to which he says economics is "as susceptible as dressmaking." Like Jencks, Blaug found it was no use trying to single out the economic return on education alone. "Better-educated people have better-educated parents, come from smaller homes, obtain financial help more easily, live in cities, are better motivated, achieve higher scores on intelligence and aptitude tests, attain better academic grade records, gain more from self-education, and generally live longer and are healthier," he writes. "To put it very bluntly, clever and/or middle-class children get more schooling than stupid and/or working-class children, and later they earn more simply because they have had all the advantages in life, of which more education is only one and not even the most important one."[21]

It makes sense that a college degree all by itself may not be able to make up for all else that is lacking in someone's background, or for good old racial or gender discrimination. Still, the degree confers a pretty robust advantage for individuals, compared to not having one. Jencks and his fellow researchers presented the signaling hypothesis to explain this. They wrote: "The relationship between educational attainment and occupational status derives primarily from the fact that schools certify people who were different to begin with." The signaling hypothesis, which Blaug calls "the acid that corroded my confidence in human capital theory," says that the really valuable work of a college happens in the admissions office. The idea that the value of college is all in the packaging is supported by the "sheepskin effect"—two years of college after high school raises your income, but not as much as if you earn a two-year associate's degree.

People like me who have been to college tend to agree that it has intangible benefits. Still, it's hard to define what the value-add might be across the widely varying instances of what we call college. I spend four years writing papers on Melville while my roommate is synthesizing proteins—what could our experiences possibly have in common that make us suitable for employment in middle management? There's no wide agreement on how to measure "liberal arts" or "critical thinking" or "decision making" or the other skills that college purports to teach. John Meyer might say that the supposed transferability of these intangible elements through the sacrament of face-to-face classroom time and dorm-room bull sessions is part of the hocus-pocus side of the university's "rationalistic religion."

Blaug argues that the return on higher education emerges because these credentials are available to only a small minority of society. It's a racket, pure and simple. "Much of the higher earnings is not a return on education but a monopoly rent on (1) the scarcity of parents who can afford to educate their children well and (2) the restrictions to members permitted into a profession which existing members have a financial interest in maintaining scarcity."[22] Doctors, nurses, teachers, lawyers, accountants, speech pathologists—the list grows over time, it never shrinks—have raised barriers of entry into their ranks, requiring attendance at specialized colleges as well as their own private licensing procedures. By restricting the numbers who enter, they cut down on the competition and can charge more for their services.

The nation's top colleges seem to assent to the signaling hypothesis when they agree to rate themselves by how selective they are— that is, how many people they reject, the SAT scores of entering students, and so on. That's like Weight Watchers advertising that they only take skinny people. If elite schools really subscribed to the value-added, human-capital theory, wouldn't they instead advertise how good they are at improving the very low SAT scores of entering students? Wouldn't they say, "We can take absolutely anyone and use our proven teaching methods to turn them into Swarthmore or Pomona material?" (For-profit colleges, which make their money on inclusivity, not exclusivity, do tend to make these kinds of value-added marketing claims.)

The signaling hypothesis says that whatever work earns you the diploma doesn't really matter. College is nothing more than an elaborate and expensive mechanism for employers to identify the people who were smarter and harder workers and had all the social advantages in the first place, and those people then get the higher-paying jobs. Now that it's illegal to discriminate in employment by race, ethnicity, gender, religion, or sexual orientation, judging people by where and how much they went to school is just about the only acceptable form of prejudice left.

Let's be clear. When you shuck off the signaling effect and the sheepskin effect and the social-sorting effect, I believe, higher education still retains some irreducible value, a pearl inside the oyster. It may be very difficult to define, but its power over individuals and populations is too real to be ignored.

Ideally, the system would change to discount or control for those extraneous effects as much as possible. By definition, if we want a majority of the population to be able to take advantage of the benefits of post-secondary education and training, we need to get better at recognizing the value of education that's not socially exclusive. In order for that to happen, those who have managed to "win" in the system as it's currently set up need to discover a little humility about that fact. Fundamentally, educated people, myself included, are lucky that the thing we happen to do well is something society values. We need to be open to different ways of measuring the value of everyone's contributions.

The "big lie" theory of the college imperative is that it helps Americans swallow an unfair system. The rhetoric of merit masks a much messier story where people succeed based on a combination of personal background, innate talent, perseverance, social obstacles, and their luck with the myopic screening processes of various institutions along the way. Or as educational reformer John Holt wrote in his 1976 screed *Instead of Education*: "Poverty is not a reading problem and better reading won't solve it, and it is a cruel lie to pretend that it could or will."[23] Crafting a more equitable system requires not only helping more kids read better, but rewarding and honoring different kinds of success.

Inequality is a given under capitalism. It's especially harsh when government does little through taxation to ensure a floor of financial security for all. When there aren't enough good jobs, high salaries, or benefits to go around, making education the measure of who gets the goodies has a distinct advantage. It seems more objective to be able to point to someone's standardized test scores or grades and say: It's not because you're black, it's not because you're poor. You didn't get it because your number is such-and-such, and sorry—you must be this tall to ride.

The 2009 appointment of Sonia Sotomayor to the Supreme Court brought these issues to the national stage. One of her most controversial decisions involved testing and race. In 2003, the New Haven, Connecticut, fire department decided to implement a written test to determine future promotions. But of those who took the test, no African-Americans and only two Hispanics scored high enough to make the cutoff. So the fire department threw the test out. Some of the white firefighters who had passed the test sued the city, claiming reverse discrimination. Sotomayor's opinion in the federal Second Circuit upheld the city's right to abandon the test in order to avoid claims of discrimination by minorities, but it frustrated critics that she didn't take the opportunity to address the underlying constitutional issues. Is it permissible for an employer to pick and choose qualifying tests based on which groups are able to pass them? If so, the tests must be pretty arbitrary in the first place. Justice Sotomayor's own background makes an interesting counterpoint to this case. Although her rise from public housing in the South Bronx to the Supreme Court was upheld nationwide as a shining example of American meritocracy, she herself tells a somewhat different story. She has said publicly and repeatedly that her acceptance to Princeton and Yale Law School would have been "highly questionable" if not for affirmative action initiatives, now out of favor, which bent the rules to let her in to the elite schools even though her test scores were lower than those of her white classmates.[24] Sotomayor's subsequent career speaks for itself. What does it say about the fairness of our higher education system that the most elite colleges in the country wouldn't have been able to identify her talent based on her academic record alone?

Dr. Carnevale, at the Georgetown Center for Education and the Economy, gave me the best insider rundown I've heard of the real relationship between education, economics, and politics; of why it's so hard for Americans to talk about differences between people and to fund choices for everyone. "It's really pretty clear that access to post-secondary education or training pretty much determines whether or not people will make a successful transition from the dependency of youth to independent adulthood, and that's a very new fact," he said in a rumbling voice. Invoking the signaling hypothesis, he continued: "In the American system employers use post-secondary training as a sorting device for hiring. For the most part access to education gets you through the door, gets you earnings and authority. . . So in the end, you have the whole population headed for college and most of them don't get through."

Carnevale has worked in the House, in the Senate, and for the AFL-CIO. He was named by President Clinton to chair the National Commission on Employment Policy and by Bush the younger to work on a similar commission, and he's also advised President Obama. Under Clinton, Carnevale was caught up in the sticky politics of trying to advocate paths other than four-year college. Clinton signed the 1994 School-to-Work Opportunities Act to expand work-based learning and partnerships with employers. But key provisions of the bill—including the use of the word "apprenticeship"—were weakened in Congress. "We took it to the Hill and the people who care about poor people and minorities said to us, 'Look. There are two education systems in America: one where people go to college and live happily ever after and the other, where people don't, and struggle. The worst thing that can happen is that we have two systems *that work*, because we all know who's going to be in the *other* one.'" In other words, explicit vocational tracking is a no-no even if the outcomes for poor people are better, because they enshrine social divisions in law, something Americans have always been wary of doing. "In the end the truth is the public rejected the idea," of school-to-work, says Carnevale. "In all the focus groups, we asked people: do you think everybody needs to go to college? Seventy to eighty percent said no. But what we forgot to ask, and asked a few years later, was, Should *your* kid go to college? Eighty-five percent said yes."

That kind of thinking has built a winner-take-all system where the penalties for losing are as harsh as they've ever been. "Ninety-four percent of high school students *think* they're going to college," says Nancy Hoffman, an advocate for vocational programs at a nonprofit organization called Jobs For the Future. "We're good at encouraging people to go to college compared to other countries. The problem is that we are much less successful than we should be, given the amount of money we're spending, in moving people through the system. We do not have a good system for transitioning people into secure career and technical education, or in making sure that it's a good investment once they get there. That is very much stigmatized in this country. We've adopted a rhetoric of 'four-year college for all.'"

We punish young people, especially poor kids and minorities, for failing out of the academic system, instead of holding the system accountable for failing them. In the exact same period of time that the United States has fallen behind in educational attainment, we've built more prisons, until we now have more people incarcerated than any other nation in the world. Prisons are the photographic negative of colleges. They are packed with the exact same young men of color who are missing from classrooms. Instead of growing human capital, imprisonment depletes it—fracturing families, reducing ex-inmates' earning and employment potential, taking away voting rights, and damaging health. The state of California, which has more prisoners than any other state in the country, spends only 40 percent as much per public university student as it does per prisoner.[25] The university system underwent massive budget cuts in 2009, with the effect of turning away a projected 300,000 students.[26] More cuts are on the horizon for the 2010–11 school year and beyond.

"It's a question of priorities," Martha Kanter, deputy undersecretary of education, formerly chancellor of the Foothill–De Anza Community College District in Los Altos, California, told me. "We pay for what we want to pay for. So, for example, in California we have built prisons. Every time I see a prison go up, I think, you know, that's my school that didn't happen."

So what is to be done? I have three suggestions.

1. Allocate funds for access

There's an argument to be made—for example, by American Enterprise Institute conservative Richard Vedder in his book *Going Broke by Degree: Why College Costs Too Much*—that public universities are fundamentally regressive, since the working class and middle class pay taxes to support universities, but it's more affluent students who most consistently use them. (Upper-middle-class students even get more federal and state tuition support than poorer students, who tend to attend less expensive colleges.) This turns on its head Stevens' idea of college as America's most popular welfare program; it looks more like an antiwelfare program. Rudolph, in *The American College and University*, documents this sentiment going back quite a ways. In 1825 the governor of Kentucky thundered against its public university: "The State has lavished her money for the benefit of the rich, to the exclusion of the poor . . . the only result is to add to the aristocracy of wealth, the advantage of superior knowledge."[27] Vedder suggested ceasing all public support of higher education, but even he conceded this is "unlikely to occur in the near future."[28]

For both practical and moral reasons, centuries of tradition of public support for higher education are worth continuing. However, public resources should be targeted to the greatest public needs.

The major reason that aid, whether federal, state, or institutional, is failing to make college more broadly affordable is that it often goes to the wrong people. Colleges that serve rich students get more federal and state money than colleges that serve poor students. And even within the same institution, colleges give out more money to rich kids than to poor kids.

Colleges may have a public-spirited intention of offering discounted slots to poor but deserving students. But they also want to attract a mix of high academic achievers, athletes, and artists, which they do by offering merit discounts. And they need enough out-of-state, international, and affluent students who can pay a full ride to subsidize the others.[29] The art of balancing all these interests is known as "enrollment management."[30]

Once a student has been admitted, financial aid officers review their Free Application for Federal Student Aid, a 106-question form with exhaustive—some feel, intrusive—information about family income, taxes, and assets.[31] Then they present the student a package combining federal aid like the Pell Grant, state scholarships, and institutional aid. Although federal money is given out on the basis of income, colleges have no obligation to give out the total packages in such a way that they maximize access for low-income students.[32]

"Engines of Inequality," a 2006 report by the Education Trust, a national education advocacy and policy organization, reviewed the financial aid decisions of a selected group of state flagship and major research universities. In 2003, this group spent $171 million on aid to the poorest students—those whose families made less than $20,000 a year. At the same time, they spent $257 million on financial aid for the richest students, from families earning more than $100,000 a year. To look at it another way, between 1995 and 2003, grant aid from those same public universities to students from families making $80,000 or more increased 533 percent, while grant aid to families making less than $40,000 increased only 120 percent.[33]

These ratios need to be reversed. Federal aid like the Pell Grant should come with matching requirements from both the institution and the state. In order to get the funds, colleges should be able to show that they are increasing their percentage of Pell-eligible students who are accepted and persist to graduation. Several people, like Century Foundation fellow Richard D. Kahlenberg, have proposed this type of class-based affirmative action.[34]

States, too, should direct more resources to institutions that enroll needier students. According to the Delta Cost Project's analysis of Department of Education data, between 2002 and 2006, "The fastest growth in enrollment has occurred in those institutions with the least resources and with the greatest evidence of actual spending cuts in the last few years—the public community colleges. In 2006, these colleges enrolled about 6 million students, more than any other institutional group, and the average [cost per student] was less than $10,000, an amount less than any other type of college or university."[35]

Expanding access to higher education begins at community colleges, where, as described in the last chapter, fully half the nation's college students attend, though public community colleges receive on average one-third the resources per student of public research universities.

I visited the southeast campus of the Houston Community College System in the fall of 2008. HCCS is the fourth-largest community college system in the United States. It serves a diverse population with roughly equal proportions of whites, blacks, and Hispanics, and even 5 percent international students. Enrollment grew from 36,000 in 2001 to 87,000 in 2007, on six different campuses. Tuition in fall 2008 was just $837 for students who lived in the district. The campus I visited was housed in a repurposed Home Depot, set on a giant parking lot in strip-mall-land. Everyone there was incredibly nice and incredibly harried.

The college is not just Texas-size, it's ambitious too. My visit was part of an annual event sponsored by the Honors College, which is an attempt to create a richer academic experience within the school for well-qualified students and to help them transfer to a four-year college. The students who greeted me included Ayesha Mela, who came to this country from Pakistan at the age of two, the youngest of five children. She has doe eyes and blunt-cut bangs that make her look like a brunette Daphne from *Scooby-Doo*. Her mother left both her homeland and her husband behind in order to seek better educational opportunities in America, particularly for Ayesha's oldest sister, who has special needs. "It's really ingrained into us, the importance of education," she says. "When my mother was growing up, all the girls in her family weren't pressured to pursue education—that was more of a men's thing. But now, in our generation, education is crazy." Ayesha graduated in the top of her class at a public high school and came to live with her sister in Texas. But in her second year, without warning, the honors scholarship was defunded. Ayesha didn't even find out until her tuition bill was due. "The dean said, didn't you get my e-mail four months ago?" Ayesha's issue was less about the tuition itself than the cost of books, her car, which kept breaking down (the campus isn't well served by bus routes), food, and clothing. She had to decide whether to take out more loans, get a job, or even take time off school. She was particularly upset because she had already changed her class schedule, foregone an internship, and cut back on work hours to have more time to study in order to keep the scholarship.

Wick Sloane describes himself as an "embedded" professor at Bunker Hill Community College in Boston, Massachusetts, where he teaches writing—including a midnight class for students who work both day and night—and writes about teaching. His columns appear in the trade publication *Inside Higher Ed*, and he is also the author of a pamphlet, *Common Sense,* advocating the abolishment of the four-year bachelor's degree. He's an MBA whose lifelong interest in education led him to take the position of chief financial officer at the University of Hawaii in 2001. "That was when I saw how the federal policies totally screw poor students," he says. "That's when I realized how big the problem was. . . . Actually educating the poor is not seen as a top purpose by anyone. And that's where I just fell in love with community colleges. You see these people who are showing up after hour-long commutes and working two shifts. They have such motivation. . . . There are 6.5 million of them, they're just as smart as everyone else, and almost nobody's speaking up for them."

According to an analysis by the Institute for College Access and Success, in 2007–8, just over half of all students at public and private four-year colleges with documented financial need had a gap between their package of loans, grants, and work study and what their family could reasonably afford. At community colleges, the figure of those with unmet need was much higher: 80 percent had unmet need, and their needs averaged over $5,000. Partly this is because lower-income students seem more reluctant to take out student loans. Partly this is because, like HCCS, these schools have limited state, federal, and institutional funds for grants.

Sloane suggests one simple change that can help students like Ayesha. "Many people think, and I might have been guilty of it, that we need $25,000 per year per student and that's what it takes to get through college. But really it's very often $50 problems that knock them out: a car breakdown, a dental bill, a changing shift in their job. So really helping these students, as a policy matter, is a lot cheaper than people think." Central New Mexico Community College in Albuquerque is one that's tried this approach: the "Rust Opportunity Assistance Fund," established with half a million dollars by private donors in 2005, provides emergency grants to students who submit a personal statement and recommendation. According to *Inside Higher Ed*, the students who got these funds in 2008 were 26 percent more likely to stay on for the next semester.

2. Support many paths to success

It's time to aggressively demystify the college degree and to say more loudly that four-year college is not for everyone: not in the name of limiting choice, but in the name of expanding it. Unless and until we fix our public schools, eradicate poverty and all forms of social disadvantage, we need a higher education system that works for the youth we've got. That means supporting appropriate training programs for important jobs like firefighters, police officers, the trades, and the service and hospitality industry.[36]

An Obama proposal, the $12 billion American Graduation Initiative, passed the House in the fall of 2009 and had a good chance of succeeding in the Senate in 2010. The proposal, which will be paid for by cutting all subsidies to student lenders, calls for 5 million more community college graduates by 2020. It creates a system of competitive grants to encourage various reforms, all aimed at streamlining the path between high school, college, and the workplace. These include school-to-work programs, dual enrollment at high schools, better remedial programs, and better counseling.

The Obama administration has done more to promote community colleges than any in recent times, and these are the right policies. But in order to succeed where the Clinton administration and previous administrations have failed, they should heed Carnevale's warning. They must address head-on the dissonance between the rhetoric of "college for all" and the reality of one-year certificate programs at underfunded community colleges, and they should streamline the transition from one piece of the system to another. The administration acknowledges that a lack of knowledge of how to navigate the system is a primary barrier to access. This is not the time to be vague or polite.

"We struggle for words," says Bob Shireman at the Department of Education. "You may have noticed the president's remarks about 'at least a year of college.' We get pushback on that because people are picturing one year at some liberal arts college. That's not really what the intention is of that one year." The same equivocation happens in community college course catalogues where remedial courses—now called "developmental" courses—are often not clearly distinguished from the credits that are transferable to a four-year college. "They don't want to stigmatize," says Cecilia Rouse, a Princeton economist who represents education and labor on President Obama's Council of Economic Advisers. "It's difficult figuring out through course catalogues how you craft together a program. One English class is transferable, another is a basic skills class." The state of Ohio has a course-transfer policy that should be a model for the country; a "universal course equivalency system" compares courses taught at all publics, privates, and two-years within the state, in order to smooth transitions, and students have a guaranteed right to equitable treatment in transferring credits.

Public high schools can be part of the path to success when they include vocational training. Public-policy research organization MDRC has found that career academies can significantly raise future wages, specifically for young men in underserved populations.[37]

Urban Assembly is an excellent example.[38] It's a nonprofit that runs twenty-two small public schools serving 7,400 students in the New York City area. Each school is organized around a theme, most of which relate directly to careers, such as justice, sports, design, and construction. The Harbor School even runs a small oyster farm on Governor's Island. Students in the career-focused schools must complete a four-week internship. The school arranges the jobs and supports students with special coaching on how to use computers, how to dress for the office, how to stand up straight and look people in the eye. Laura Gagne, an outreach coordinator, told me that the jobs help students connect their studies with the future they learn to imagine for themselves.

The nonprofit has an explicit commitment to see their students go out in the world and succeed. It tracks them from freshman year through college and into careers. It doesn't screen for test scores; its kids are 95 percent African-American and Latino, and predominantly low-income. Yet 85 percent graduate, and 90 percent of graduates are accepted by colleges, three-quarters of which are four-year colleges. By comparison, the average in New York City public high schools is a 58 percent graduation rate and 38 percent college-acceptance rate.

Amazing numbers, but I was surprised when Gagne told me the Academy has had internal discussions about whether their emphasis on 100 percent college attendance is too rigid for their students. They have been given a chance to prove their ability to achieve. If they want to take that confidence and become a paralegal, a court reporter, a police officer, a medical technician, an electrician, a musician, a construction foreman, an entrepreneur, who's to say that that is the wrong choice?

And what about young people who simply don't do well in traditional classes? It takes hard work to create a program that can draw them out. Public Allies is one.[39] The Americorps-funded nonprofit identifies young people with "passion" and leadership potential and places them in ten-month apprenticeships with nonprofits in their own communities. They work four days a week, earning a $15,000 stipend plus benefits, and spend the fifth day together doing training based on a simple idea. "Everyone leads," says executive director Paul Schmitz. "Leadership is an action everyone can take, not a position few can hold." This is not some kind of apple-polishing stint for graduates of elite schools. Two-thirds of Public Allies' recruits are minorities, and only half have college degrees when they join in their teens and early twenties. Nor—and this is important—is the purpose of the program getting them into college. Since the inception of Public Allies in 1992, over 80 percent of the 2,500 alumni have continued careers in the nonprofit sector. Of those alumni who go to college afterward, many do it part-time while they keep working; the credential is not an end in itself but is in the service of their life mission.

"If there's a pipeline to public leadership, a lot of programs are building a piece that doesn't extend to communities," says Schmitz.

> Martin Luther King or Cesar Chavez wouldn't have gotten into those programs. So there need to be more pipelines. I'm having lunch tomorrow with an alumnus of ours who worked in a deli and, in his words, smoked a lot of pot. One day someone hung a Public Allies poster in the deli and he took it down because it was exactly what he was looking for and he didn't want anyone else to see it. He began a career advocating for people with disabilities. Today he's the executive director of the National Alliance on Mental Illness in Wisconsin.

A lawyer named Michelle Obama served as the founding executive director of Public Allies Chicago from spring 1993 until fall 1996, and later on their national board of directors. Paul Schmitz was on the Obama transition team, and he and other advocates of service have every reason to be pleased. On April 20, 2009, Senator Edward Kennedy, in his last Senate appearance, presided over the signing of the Edward Kennedy Serve America Act, which expands federally funded national service from 75,000 to 250,000 slots by 2017. Public Allies itself is expanding from its current 600 yearly participants in eighteen cities, to 1,000 in thirty cities by 2012.

National service is a cute kitten of a policy—everyone loves it. But what intrigues me is how a program like Public Allies can work as a substitute for a four-year college degree. It reaches young people who aren't necessarily successful academically, who might otherwise be stigmatized as dropouts and relegated to dead-end jobs, but who do have a drive to succeed. It connects them with a community of people pursuing meaningful careers. All this and the one-year program costs just $8,000 per person for recruitment, training, and all other overhead. Not counting the $15,000 stipend, which the nonprofits say their participants more than earn through their work, that's cheaper for taxpayers than a year at a public university, and it's a hell of a lot cheaper than a year in prison for a young person whose life goes down the wrong track.

Schmitz cautions that growing programs such as his will take care. You can't mass-produce on demand an ethos of community commitment, relationships with local organizations, or supportive alumni. He says of the Obama administration, "I think they realize you have to think broadly of the term higher education. Expanding the University of Chicago by 10 percent isn't going to reach those goals. I think that national service is seen as a way to create incentives and opportunities for more people to get that access."

3. Fix the economy, not just education

If a four-year college degree is your only hope of getting a good job, and a flimsy hope at that, the problem is not that there aren't enough people with four-year degrees. The problem is that there aren't enough good jobs, whether blue-collar or white-collar. Richard Rothstein at the Economic Policy Institute has written:

The number of available jobs (including those that require college education and those that do not) depends upon the size and growth of the economy, affected in turn by . . . the strength of consumer (public and private) demand and credit availability. Education reform cannot influence such factors. Yet while this truth is obvious in today's economic crisis, at other times many observers forget it and assert a fiction: that if more students graduated from college as attractive job candidates, more would find highly skilled jobs requiring college education.[40]

Or as Kevin Carey of the progressive thinktank Education Sector puts it to me: "We shouldn't think education is the only thing to worry about. SEIU [Service Employees International Union] has successfully organized hotel workers in Las Vegas for good wages and benefits. A hotel maid doesn't need a college degree, she needs a union. Nor do I think we have to choose between investing in educational opportunities and having other means by which people get fair wages and better benefits."

As long as America makes expanding access to college the centerpiece of all our efforts to improve equality and prosperity, we will never, ever get there. The 2008 recession gave way to another so-called jobless recovery, where companies rebuilt productivity and profits while continuing to squeeze jobs, wages, and benefits.[41]

Even jobs that require a college degree increasingly do not offer traditional middle-class trappings like full-time hours, health care, retirement security, or a path to advancement. Heck, college students can see that even their own instructors, people who have sacrificed their entire lives on the altar of education, are increasingly cobbling together part-time adjunct jobs at poverty wages and without benefits.

Solving this problem requires a movement. More progressive taxation. Universal healthcare. Better laws to guarantee benefits such as paid vacation and family leave. And strong support of the right to organize, with laws like the Employee Free Choice Act, so workers can fight for their fair share of corporate profits. This kind of social justice work will increase access to better opportunities for a decent living for all Americans, regardless of how many years of education they manage to get.

At the same time, we can continue to increase access to education itself by opening up the institutional structure of education, offering more mix-and-match, smaller-scale options, self-directed and self-contained courses of study where people are able to follow their interests—informed by knowledge of what career options are out there, and which fields have good prospects down the road. People also need new ways to communicate their achievements and success so that they can be recognized by peers and potential employers—"signaling" without the "sheepskin."

The good news is that there's a great deal of this kind of innovation going on inside and outside the higher-education establishment. They range from technologies to improve educational quality while reducing its costs (chapter 3) to myriad alternatives to the four-walled classroom and social networks that allow students and graduates to present portfolios rather than diplomas (chapters 4 and 5). These innovations offer the chance of breaking the iron links between how much money colleges spend, how exclusive they are, how prestigious they are, and especially how successful their students are. To truly progress in education, and in our society as a whole, we need to redirect our resources and energy from institutions toward individuals.

three

ECONOMICS

On October 15, 2008, Hofstra University in Hempstead, Long Island, held the final presidential debate of the election season.[1]

That morning, Brian Lehrer, the friendly, bearded host of a popular New York City public radio show, invited me and a few others to the campus to talk about higher education before a live student audience.[2] Hofstra happens to be in the worst value-for-money quadrant in higher education: private, yet nonelite. It charged $39,455 in tuition, fees, room and board in 2009–10, but it's third-tier in the *US News and World Report* rankings, with so-so national name recognition. Hofstra's president, Stuart Rabinowitz, told the *New York Times* that the debate, held at a cost of $3.5 million (underwritten by private donors), was "priceless advertising" to raise the college's national profile and attract more applicants.[3]

Lehrer played a clip of then-candidate Barack Obama talking about his and Michelle's student loans for law school—debts that lingered until Obama published his first best-selling book in 1995.[4]

He then asked some of the students about their own debt. A freshman named Nick said, "When my six-month grace period is up, I will have to make $94,000 a year in order to pay my loans back in ten years. That's not even realistic unless I become the next Tom Cruise out of college." He cracked a grin, adding, "With all these cameras here, if I look good, I might be able to afford that."

College provost Herman Berliner, a balding man with rimless glasses, then had the thankless task of defending the college's high, and steadily increasing, tuition. The case he made inadvertently revealed the real reasons colleges keep raising their tuition, and why increasing federal aid won't be enough to make college affordable.

"We've been going up about 6 or 7 percent a year," he said,

> but you really have to put that in context. If you have
> many classes that have only fifteen or twenty students, if
> you provide students with a lot of additional services, very
> different than when I went to college in terms of counsel-
> ing and advisement, a host of other co-curricular activities,
> a recreation center that really is as fancy as any athletic
> club. . . . The students are looking for all those extras, a very
> personal education, and a small student-faculty ratio. . . .
> They're looking for a fully textured experience. The expec-
> tations have gone up tremendously, and we're doing every-
> thing we can to meet those expectations.

The bottom line, Provost Berliner argued, is that young people don't have a choice but to buy what he's selling. "They will be primarily in dead-end jobs unless they pursue a college education."

The high price of college has become a trope of contemporary life, the plot of movies and books, the refrain of blogs, Web sites, and Facebook groups. Young people sell themselves in all sorts of ways to pay for school. The *New York Times Magazine* reported in 2008 that Seeking Arrangements, a personals Web site that sets up "sugar daddy" relationships between older, rich men and younger women, pays to have its ads pop up on Google when someone searches for the phrases "student loan," "tuition help," or "college support."[5] In 2007, twenty-two-year-old Natalie Dylan put her virginity up for auction at the Bunny Ranch, a legal brothel in Nevada. The Sacramento State graduate told Howard Stern she wanted to use the money to pay for a master's degree in Marriage and Family Relations.[6]

Lurid examples aside, concern about rising tuition is not misplaced. Traditional colleges are trapped in an unsustainable cost spiral. In the 1940s and 1950s, according to *The Race between Education and Technology*, college tuition rose more slowly than household income, and in the 1950s through 1980 they rose at about the same rate. Since 1980, tuition at both private and public colleges has soared relative to both inflation and family income. College tuition and fees leaped 439 percent from 1982 to 2007, after inflation.

"Higher Education May Soon Be Unaffordable for Most Americans," read a headline that topped the *New York Times* most e-mailed list for weeks in December 2008.[7] The story drew on a report by the National Center for Public Policy and Higher Education that the average four-year *public* university cost more than one-quarter of the median American household income, up from 18 percent at the start of the decade.[8] For the poorest one-fifth of Americans, public university tuition cost 55 percent of their income. The report graded each state on the affordability of its public higher-education system, taking into account not just state median incomes, but aid programs and the amount of loan debt that students take on. California passed with a C-minus; every other state failed.

Higher education isn't supposed to be a luxury good. Up until the 1970s, our higher-education system expanded close to its current size while remaining broadly affordable. The stagnation in enrollment and completion since the 1970s has coincided with unprecedented tuition bloat. The cost spiral is a key reason that the ideal championed by Lyndon Johnson and every president since—to extend entrée to the middle class by making college available to all who qualify—has never come to pass.

There are many explanations for rising tuition. Some people look at market fundamentals, others at the effects of subsidies including loans, and still others focus on the perks wars between schools desperate to market themselves like consumer products. Each explanation has its validity, each appeals to a different constituency, and each calls for a different approach to a solution. But everyone who takes the cost crisis seriously says that colleges must change how they're run in order to solve it.

Let's start with supply and demand. College graduates earn about 67 percent more than nongrads and have an easier time finding jobs.[9] Combine that with the social advantages of the degree and a near-continual increase in the number of young people, and the demand for college just keeps growing.[10] If you reduce the question of tuition to this simple supply-and-demand argument, you are likely to maintain there is little to be done, as colleges continue to charge what the market will bear (although that logic sounds pretty mercenary in contrast with the high-minded mission statements of the most expensive private colleges). This is a convenient line of reasoning for those who favor doing nothing—like conservatives who don't care for spending taxpayer money on access for minorities and the poor, or college administrators who don't want to mess with business as usual, except to ask for more federal aid. But it's not the whole story.

Supply and demand, for one thing, can be manipulated. "There's a system bias: this is imperfect information economics," says Rick Mattoon, an economist at the Federal Reserve Bank of Chicago and an expert on the economics of higher education. Markets function best when both buyers and sellers are well informed. When either side is missing information, prices are likely to be too low or too high. In health care, for example, comparison shopping is difficult because patients lack expertise about the relative benefits of various treatments. In the case of education, too, Mattoon argues, "There's very little transparency. The schools have all the power. As an applicant you have to tell them everything about your financial situation, your ability to pay for the education, and they tell you nothing about their cost of supplying it. It's even worse than an airline," where people sitting in adjoining seats may have paid very different fares. "In higher ed everyone is paying a radically different price for the same good. . . . If you want to get suspicious about it, it's cartel behavior."

College administrators don't like being referred to as a cartel, a group that colludes to set prices. Their preferred excuse for raising tuition is their own operating costs, especially wages. Provost Berliner alluded to this when he mentioned Hofstra's small class sizes and its counseling and advisement services. At first this seems convincing, since three-quarters of a typical college budget goes to salaries. Wages, particularly for skilled workers such as college professors, do tend to rise faster than other components of the cost of living that make up inflation. In a seminal 1966 study, Princeton economists William Bowen and William Baumol used the analogy of a string quartet to explain the "cost disease" of rising prices for skilled-labor-intensive enterprises like education, health care, and the arts. The wages of string musicians have increased since the nineteenth century, they wrote, but it still takes the same number of musicians the same amount of time to play a Beethoven string quartet. That is, productivity for musicians has not risen. The same was true, Baumol and Bowen later argued, for professors, who earn more than they did in the nineteenth century yet spend the same amount of time delivering lectures and grading papers as they did then.[11]

"It's a nice theory; it's not entirely true," says Jane Wellman. She is the executive director of the Delta Project on Postsecondary Costs, Productivity and Accountability, and she's been working on educational policy for thirty years. In 2009 her organization released a widely cited, detailed breakdown of spending patterns at universities, using data that all institutions report to the Department of Education.[12]

In Wellman's view, almost everything Provost Berliner told those students was wrong, beginning with the idea that small class sizes are the foremost reason for cost increases. "There's a whole host of common misconceptions about college cost that are rebuttable," she says, and one is "that it's impossible to control costs without compromising quality because the dominant driver is faculty labor." First of all, she says, "the majority of labor costs are not faculty labor costs. These are huge organizations with large academic support services." Her organization found that there's actually been faster growth in staff positions that have nothing to do with teaching than in faculty positions—departments like marketing, fund-raising, alumni relations, and enrollment management.

"Secondly, if you look at institutions holding the line on spending in higher ed, the place where they are doing the most to contain costs is on the faculty side." Colleges have figured out how to cut labor costs over the past thirty years by relying on graduate students and adjuncts—academic temps who have no benefits, no hope of tenure, and are paid a pittance. In 1975, according to the American Association of University Professors, the majority of all teaching staff at American degree-granting institutions, 57 percent, were full-time and either tenured or tenure-track, while 30 percent were part-time. By 2003, nearly half were part-time and just 35 percent were tenured or tenure-track.[13]

This pattern holds true even at the most prestigious and expensive private institutions. I spoke to an adjunct at Hofstra. She earned just $10,000 a year for a full-time teaching load—a quarter of what each of her students was paying.

Wellman points out that there are really two different stories in college costs. "There's been quite consistent spending within much of the public sector," particularly the 80 percent of institutions that are public, primarily serve their regions, and are nonselective. "Where spending has gone up has been at selective, research, and national universities—those that are operating at the high end of the food chain, competing for resources like students, research dollars, and reputation." Hofstra, she says, is one of those institutions in that 20 percent. "They've made a choice to pursue a business model that allows prices to go up to accomplish a goal of greater selectivity and prestige."

Our national debate over health care, which is trapped in a cost spiral very similar to the one in higher ed, has made many Americans more aware of the fact that a simplistic, supply-and-demand model of markets doesn't always hold true. In the real world, more competition doesn't always drive down prices, especially when there is a lack of transparency about real prices and costs, and a lot of public subsidies flowing into the market. Under these conditions, competition can lead to greater expenditures on marketing and features that don't contribute directly to the quality of the product or service, driving up the prices for everyone.

As discussed in chapter 1, American colleges have always advertised themselves and competed energetically. It's a natural outgrowth of having such a diverse and crowded higher-education field. Still, in the last few decades, the competition has stepped up to a new level. As college went from an elite bastion to a mass ambition, individual campuses have begun to market themselves as national brands. This is the cost factor that gets the most press, and the media has reinforced the competition. The first edition of the *US News and World Report*'s famous annual college rankings came out in 1987, exposing colleges across the country to students who in previous generations might have just headed for their state school. Institutions with more ambitious leaders started hiring marketing and branding consultants to refresh their images and expand their reach. Between 1996 and 2005, according to one report, 532 of the nation's 4,000-odd accredited colleges went through a rebranding process.[14]

This was largely a wave of regional state colleges, teachers' colleges, and technical schools styling themselves "universities," adding new programs, expanding their physical plants, recruiting on a national basis for students, and hiring. For example, Beaver College in Western Pennsylvania wrote on its Web site about its 2001 name change to Arcadia University: "This school is a far different place than it was at the time of its founding in 1853 as a small women's college in Western Pennsylvania's Beaver County. We now boast nationally ranked programs and nationally recognized faculty, and we are a recognized leader in international education." And of course, the old name was too embarrassing to Google.

Licensing extends far beyond sweatshirts to bottled water, credit cards, even a line of signature fragrances created by a company called Masik to evoke the intoxicating scents of big football schools like Auburn and Tennessee. Salaries for star faculty have risen as more and more colleges tried to compete with private industry, especially for professors in business, economics, and science departments. Campuses got an upgrade, with fancy food courts, dorms, gyms, and stadiums crowding the glossy brochures. Colleges installed rock-climbing walls (Middlebury), served organic food (Yale), and gave every student a free iPod (Duke). This is the "textured experience" idea that Provost Berliner presented as being "much fancier than when I went to school." When you talk to administrators about this stuff, there's a sense that it's out of their hands. "We're spending $16 million on a brand-new dining hall which will not improve the quality of education one little bit," Paul LeBlanc, president of Southern New Hampshire University, told me. "When families come to an open house, they spend a lot of time complaining about the sticker price: 'This is really expensive, and by the way do you also have singles available for freshmen, and do you have a food court in that new dining hall?' We're in an arms war."

Private schools often set the tone, but public schools have felt the pressure too. "There is a trickle-down that occurs everywhere," says Wellman. "Institutions that don't play that game feel more impoverished compared to the Ivy League. It sets a tone that affects the whole industry."

Nominally independent colleges like Hofstra may argue that they have a right to pursue whatever students they want without outside interference, though to the extent that they accept federal subsidies and tax breaks, that right conflicts with the public good. When public universities get caught up in the perks game, however, the offense to the public interest is even clearer. In March 2009 I visited the University of Tennessee at Knoxville. Eight students met me for dinner; they ordered $3 baked potatoes and side salads, and peppered me with informed, indignant questions.

The college had just announced a 5.7 percent budget cut and a 6 percent tuition increase. Italian, Russian, German, art history, religious studies, geology, public administration, and materials science and engineering were all on the table for "discontinuance." One young woman had just come from a meeting with her advisor; she had been forced out of the fall classes she needed to graduate on time with a French degree owing to cuts. Her choices were switching majors, or adding another semester or even another year, which would crank up her student-loan debt by another few thousand dollars.[15] Simultaneously, a giant, multiyear renovation to the football stadium was still underway, funded by alumni donors, to the tune of $200 million.[16] "I just can't even look at that thing," said a tall, blond senior, a humanities major headed for the Peace Corps. "They're taking my money, for my education, and spending it on sports."[17]

Kevin Carey, the policy director of the think tank Education Sector, has done some very smart research on the rationale behind the college cost spiral. It was from him, in fact, that I first heard the term "cost spiral." Carey used to work for the progressive Center on Budget and Policy Priorities, so I know he's not ideologically opposed to government funding public goods. As an assistant state budget director for education in the state of Indiana, he used to administer government funding decisions. He's well qualified to diagnose the attitudes feeding the tuition spiral. He explains the basis of the problem: "It doesn't cost the colleges anything to increase prices." The public institutions on which most students rely are competing with private nonprofits and for-profits that charge four times more.

> It's the public universities which have been increasing
> prices the most on percentage terms. If the market rate for
> tuition is $20,000 a year, and the government is subsidizing
> you so you can charge $5,000, going from $5,000 to $6,000

is still a good deal [for the students]. College and university administrators are very rational, very smart, they're self-interested like anyone. And all the incentives that currently exist incent them to raise prices. There are no incentives that make them want to hold prices stable or lower them other than their relationships with public policy makers and state governments.

Those relationships haven't been strong enough to do the trick. Most countries have a centralized, nationally administered system of overwhelmingly public institutions. In America, a diverse ecosystem of public and private, nonprofit and for-profit institutions each has great freedom to pursue its own institutional goals. Our system has created some of the best universities in the world. Unfortunately, Carey argues, its diversity is exaggerated. For-profits are proliferating to try to cover specialized market niches, including the exploding sector of affordable, bare-bones instruction. Community colleges, as mentioned, are straining at the edges with inadequate public support. But too many institutions out there are trying to do one, very expensive thing. "In the end, there is only one status ladder in higher education," Carey says. "Everyone wants to be Harvard."

If they were brands, a big chunk of the best-known American colleges would be more like a Four Seasons or a Starbucks than a McDonald's or a Wal-Mart. They try to compete on exclusivity and the quality of the experience, not on price. Affordability can actually hurt colleges. A marketer in the higher-education field who asked to remain anonymous told me a story about one of his clients, a regional state college in the South. Prospective students were looking at its price tag and concluding that its offerings were far inferior to the flagship state university, since the price was closer to that of a community college. The college took the least-resistance path of raising prices in order to remain competitive.

The crazy thing is that in the absence of real information about value, families and students encourage this kind of behavior by how we compare colleges. As Carey has pointed out, 25 percent of *US News & World Report* rankings come from peer ratings, which is a measure of reputation within the sector. The other 75 percent of the rankings come from either direct or proxy measures of spending per student and exclusivity. That means if a college wants to rise in the rankings, the logical thing to do is to raise tuition while accepting fewer applicants. If College A increases tuition, thus spending more on each student, making it harder for poor students to attend and turning more students away, they look more elite and desirable. If College B figures out a way to do more with less and cuts tuition, allowing them to offer slots to more applicants, they lower spending per student and become less selective. College B's ranking goes down relative to College A.

Bob Morse, research director at *US News*, has been working on their college rankings full time since they started in 1987, and he defends their validity. "We're constrained by the data available," he says. "Currently it's not possible on a comparative basis to measure outcomes or learning or student engagement or what is really going on in the classroom." There is a National Survey of Student Engagement, but only four hundred out of thousands of colleges share their results publicly on *USA Today*'s Web site, and the qualitative results are not particularly easy to rank or compare. There is no accepted standard for measuring productivity in higher education— the amount of learning that takes place for each dollar we spend.

As more and more public colleges try to crowd into that elusive top 20 percent, no one is minding the affordability store. "Public Colleges Get a Surge of Bargain Hunters," the *New York Times* reported in March 2009.

With the recession and new concerns about student loans, applications were up double digits in 2008 at public institutions coast to coast. The story wasn't about states worrying how they're going to serve everybody who qualifies with a good college education at a good price. Instead, it was an uncritical look from the point of view of the administrators, who are taking advantage of the bumps in enrollment to groom their campus's standing. The *New York Times* article described one example:

> Over the last decade, enrollment in the SUNY system [as a whole] has grown by 20 percent. But officials at [the New Paltz campus] do not want to grow, and instead see the swelling applicant pool as a way to further refine its status and student body. In the last five years, the college

has winnowed the student-to-faculty ratio to 14 to 1, from 17 to 1; more than two-thirds of courses are taught by full-time faculty members today, compared with 50 percent a decade ago. . . . Officials say they are determined not to diminish the quality of student life by expanding enrollment at their liberal-arts college beyond the current 6,000 undergraduates.[18]

Here's an institution that provides the best public college experience in the state of New York, and they don't want to grow? They refuse to serve more qualified students? Yes, it's laudable that they're concerned with maintaining quality for the students they have, but we're talking about a public institution, supported with taxpayer money. Does the library decide it doesn't want to lend more books? Does the post office decide it doesn't want to deliver mail to more addresses? What's going on here?

It's easy to beat up on colleges that seem more concerned with buffing their reputations than with serving the public. But Wellman is careful to point out that most public institutions don't exactly fit Hofstra's model. Her research shows that "for public institutions over the last fifteen years, the primary reason tuition has gone up has not been because the institutions are spending a lot more money," on marketing, food courts, or other frills. "It's because states have reduced public subsidies, and colleges are responding by shifting revenues to students rather than by cutting costs."

The primary dynamic driving tuition increases that affect the most vulnerable students is cost-shifting, a game of hot potato between states and the federal government. To understand how this works, it helps to remember that college doesn't cost what you pay for it. Except at for-profit colleges, tuition has never reflected the full cost of attendance. Francis Wayland, a reformist president of Brown University, lamented this fact in 1842: "We cannot induce men to pursue a collegiate course unless we offer it vastly below its cost, if we do not give it away altogether."[19] The United States has an unusual system of funding to go along with its unusually large and diverse system of higher education. Although we spend more per head on postsecondary education than any other country, our *public* spending per student (grants and subsidies) is slightly below the

rich-country average.[20] The balance is made up by private donors
and family money. Tuition and fees, state and local appropriations,
endowment income, and federal funds (roughly in that order) are
the dominant sources for college operating budgets, according to
the Delta Cost Project; and alumni and donor gifts, bond revenues,
and federal and state capital-outlay appropriations are the dominant sources for capital budgets. Most of this money comes with
earmarks of one kind or another. The rise in tuition thus consists
of a rise in the cost of running educational institutions, plus a shift
toward tuition and away from other sources of revenue.

Federal and state governments have always collaborated in subsidizing public universities, and it makes sense for both of them to
pitch in. Federal land grants provided the baseline funding to found
public universities, and Congress has granted them further money
in the service of broader national goals like medical and defense
research. State charters established public institutions and legislatures
continue to control them for the purpose of economic development
in each state. However, with the creation of large federal student-
funding programs like the Pell Grant and the Stafford Loan in the
1970s, the federal government became a major source of tuition
payments as well. The temptation grew for states to practice cost
shifting.

State governments have long since figured out that they can save
money in tough times by cutting funding to universities and hiking
tuition. State subsidies per full-time-equivalent higher-education
student hit a twenty-five-year low in 2005.[21]

In some cases, dating back to then governor Reagan instituting tuition at the University of California in the 1960s, hostility
from conservative state legislators toward liberal-leaning university
faculty has paved the way for cutbacks. In other cases, it's a matter
of political convenience. Families may grumble at tuition increases,
and some members of the middle class may get squeezed out, but
overall enrollment is usually not affected, and students bring with
them more federal money to make up the difference. It's like passing
a backdoor tax.

The Delta Cost Project concluded that colleges have pursued a
clear strategy of cost shifting over the past decade. "Between 1995
and 2006, the dominant revenue pattern across public institutions

was the growing dependence on tuitions as a primary source of revenue. . . . By 2006, students in public research universities were covering close to half of their educational costs, up from about 39 percent just four years earlier. . . . While tuition increased 29.8 percent among public research universities between 2002 and 2006, [non-research spending per student] only rose 2.5 percent."[22]

When the economy is good, colleges expand facilities and programs, and raise tuition. When the economy goes sour, state subsidies atrophy and tuition again goes up. The 2008 recession is no exception. Higher education has become a safety valve for state budgets facing cutbacks. For example, the City University of New York, the city's public college system, saw a 13 percent increase in freshman enrollment in the fall of 2008, followed closely by a 15 percent tuition increase announced in the spring of 2009.[23]

Cost shifting helps explain why the Pell Grant used to cover more than 80 percent of the average public university's tuition, and it now pays for less than a third. It explains why federal aid appropriations have grown every year, yet affordability peaked in the 1970s. And it explains why the college affordability measures proposed thus far by the Obama administration, to increase the Pell Grant and make it an entitlement, introduce new tax credits for higher education, and raise federal student-loan limits, may not make college more affordable in the long run. Dewayne Matthews of the Lumina Foundation says, "The public has engaged in enablement of these bad behaviors on the part of colleges. It sounds like a traditional Republican point of view—whenever we raise Pell Grants you just raise tuition. But honestly, that seems like a pretty accurate and reasonable accusation. Government has helped create that co-dependence," where universities are hooked on federal money.

Cost shifting is closely related to another major explanation for the rise in tuition—let's call it the bureaucratic argument. This is the observation that whatever goods or services are most subsidized by the government will tend to rise the most in cost. Peter Stokes is a consultant with Eduventures, the McKinsey of the collegiate world. (The very presence of educational management consultants, of course, constitutes its own evidence for bloat.)

"Like a lot of industries that depend on the government, colleges have few incentives to innovate," he says. "Whether you're a defense contractor, a state university, or an elite private college you're going to be getting hundreds of millions of dollars in research grants. It's comfortable that way. You look at any industry—everybody wants the government for a customer."

At colleges the normal interplay of market forces is disrupted by a constant buffer of state and federal funds in the form of grants and loans to students and budgetary appropriations to schools. This river of cash makes institutions less concerned than they should be about efficiency, and makes students and families less concerned than they should be about prices.

Informed observers who are neither hostile to higher education as a field nor beholden to its current way of doing business agree that colleges seem allergic to cost cutting. Carol Twigg, the president and CEO of the National Center for Academic Transformation, has been a higher-education expert for twenty years and worked with hundreds of institutions through NCAT's course redesign program, which is described in chapter 4. "Educators think the solution to not enough money is simply to find more money," she says. "Not many in higher education seem to care about reducing costs." Nancy Hoffman is with Jobs for the Future, a think tank with a long history of innovative approaches to human-capital problems. She says we have an allocation-of-resources problem. "It's not the problem that too few dollars are spent, but there's the wrong incentive for how to spend them, and the result is too great an expense for families with too little degree attainment." Kevin Carey says, "In general, the policy response has been if college is more expensive, let's give students more money to pay for college."

I used to take the standard progressive point of view on higher education, believing that the answer to the college cost problem was simply more public money. The Obama administration has largely taken this stance as well, increasing the Pell Grant and introducing new college tax credits and guarantees for student loans. But, Carey says, that's just not going to work. "There is no amount of money that the federal government . . . can put into student aid programs that can't be absorbed by colleges and universities increasing their tuition."

At Hofstra, Provost Berliner (poor Provost Berliner!) made clear that he did not like the notion of having to address costs one bit: "The idea of controlling costs is, I think, very bad because our costs are to a great extent added services we provide to our students. . . . Do we stop adding services that our students demand? I think that becomes an artificial constraint that doesn't make sense." By that logic, if you charged a million dollars a year, you could provide unlimited added services that students might also learn to "demand": a personal masseur and chef, horse-and-carriage rides to class. Calling price an "artificial constraint" is akin to saying that money is no object. In what universe is this true? The academic universe, apparently, where cost cutting has few natural champions.

For families, too, subsidies cushion tuition increases. According to the College Board, the average total charges at a public four-year university in 2009–10 were $15,213, but the average student at those colleges received $5,400 in grants and tax benefits, and some received far more. So net price was closer to $10,000. Between 1993 and 2004, aid increased so rapidly that the net price of college to the average student, after inflation, at a four-year public university actually fell slightly despite large annual tuition increases, although since 2004 it has climbed back up. Despite that dip, the overall growth in the cost of college has far outpaced the growth of federal subsidies for three decades. More ominous for access, the form of tuition subsidy has changed.

The liftoff of college tuition into the stratosphere in the past thirty years, and especially the past decade, is concurrent with, first, the rise of student loans, and later the secondary market for loans that saw them repackaged into attractive, government-backed securities for investors. Student-loan volume more than doubled in the past ten years, from $44.6 billion to $94.5 billion annually.[24] Student loans now make up the majority of all tuition aid. More than two-thirds of undergraduates are taking out student loans, and the ability to finance tuition through loans and home-equity lines of credit has made families less sensitive to tuition increases—a vicious cycle that leads from rising tuition to increased debt loads back to rising tuition, and so on.

Just as the securitized mortgage market contributed to a historic run-up in the cost of housing over the past decade, the securitized student-loan market fed increases in tuition. Edmund Andrews wrote a riveting story in the spring of 2009 for the *New York Times*

Magazine about the junk mortgage that nearly ruined him. He quoted his lender as saying "I am here to sell money."[25] When you have an army of money salesmen deployed to a particular economic sector, the result, as we have seen, is likely to be a quick run-up in prices.

Like any industry that exists by federal fiat, student lenders became a potent political force that lobbed great gobs of money onto the plates of influential lawmakers. Sallie Mae and another student lender, Nellie Mae, were the two largest contributors to the 2004 campaign of former House majority leader John Boehner.[26] Their special interest was greater student indebtedness. Their nefarious deeds supplied me with plenty of red meat as a reporter between 2004 and 2007. The most important favor the lenders won was a broad exemption from bankruptcy protection, which traps students in an unrelenting obligation if they default. In 1998, Congress legislated that federal student loans could not be canceled in bankruptcy except in cases of "undue hardship," which basically requires you to be a destitute paraplegic.

College financial aid offices, the most important place for students to get help figuring out how to pay for college, were also the lenders' most important marketing channels. Lenders were implicated in a major crackdown on for-profit colleges in the early 1990s. Student-loan defaults peaked in 1992 at 22 percent, and proprietary schools accounted for nearly half of all defaulters, although they were the source of just a fifth of all loans.[27]

Undaunted, lenders colluded with more reputable colleges as well. A sweeping nationwide investigation by New York State attorney general Andrew Cuomo found in 2007 and 2008 that lenders offered financial aid offices at colleges like Columbia and UT Austin special perks and kickbacks in exchange for marketing their loans more aggressively to students through "preferred lender lists."[28]

Not content with the profit margins offered by federally guaranteed student loans, lenders sometime in the 1990s introduced a new product: the "private" or "alternative" student loan. These were not too different from putting tuition on your credit card: they carried rates as high as 18 percent, much higher than a federal student loan, and they didn't have grace periods or other borrower-friendly policies. What's worse, private student loans, just like federal student loans, came under bankruptcy exemption in 2005, becoming $50,000 unsecured lines of credit that you can never, ever walk away from.

In the days of loose and easy credit, private student loans were much easier to get than federal student loans because students didn't have to fill out the long, confusing FAFSA form and share personal information. Over the past decade, student loans soared from 7 percent to a quarter of all student loans. While federal student-loan volume was increasing at 7 percent per year, private student-loan volume was increasing at 27 percent each year![29]

Most students who take out private loans have better options to pay for college. Private student loans are marketed directly to students, and disproportionately used by those at for-profit community or technical schools—students who probably would be eligible for income-based grants and subsidized federal student loans if they could get through all the paperwork.[30] In the fall of 2006, Barnard College tried a simple experiment. For any applicant who wanted to take out private loans, they required her and her parents to have a single conversation with a financial aid officer. That one change led to a drastic 73 percent drop in private-loan volume. Ninety-eight students took out a total of $1,559,385 in private loans in 2005–6, while thirty-nine students took out just $414,889 in private loans in 2006–7. There was only a moderate increase in parents borrowing PLUS loans to make up for it; most parents probably also dug deeper into their savings or resolved to tighten expenses instead, collectively saving over a million dollars in debt and what would have been nearly another million dollars in interest at typical rates over the life of the loans. This is at a prestigious private university where parents are probably educated and relatively financially savvy, but they still needed the disadvantages of private loans to be spelled out to them.

In 2005 I talked to a young man named Tony Allwein from Lebanon, Pennsylvania, who headed to Iraq after an Army recruiter told him his student loans would be taken care of if he enlisted. Unfortunately, Allwein didn't read the fine print: the $19,000 he borrowed to attend the Pennsylvania College of Technology, a public technical college, was all in private loans, which the military doesn't cover. He would have been eligible for Pell Grants and federal student loans if he'd understood the financial aid process better, or if his college, which processed his loans, had taken the time to explain the difference between private and federal loans.[31]

The insanity of the private loan market is part of the excesses of the entire credit industry in the past few years. Think about it: Large banks falling all over themselves to offer tens of thousands of dollars to seventeen-year-olds who merely enrolled in any accredited college, anywhere. Student loans formed their own credit bubble that looks something like a smaller version of the mortgage bubble. In the 2008 credit crunch, nearly two hundred lenders pulled out of the federal student-loan program, often abandoning the very community college students who have the greatest need for funding. The Treasury Department made a $260-billion line of credit available to prevent greater disruption in funds to students. A March 2008 report by the National Consumer Law Center found ten significant parallels between the growth of the private loan market and the mortgage crisis. "The question is whether a similar crisis [to the mortgage crisis] is on the horizon for student loan borrowers."[32]

The student-loan bubble probably doesn't have the potential to create the kind of global meltdown that the mortgage bubble did, because student loan–backed securities weren't as widely traded throughout the global economy, and because the overall market is smaller. But for a decade or more to come, student-loan burdens will continue to impair millions of individuals' ability to establish strong economic futures, and to do their part to pull the economy into recovery. The effects of inflated tuition, just like the effects of inflated house prices, will be felt for decades as well.

Today about $598 billion of federal education loans and about $132 billion of private student loans are outstanding, for a total of roughly $730 billion. In the most recent economic downturn, more borrowers are falling behind on their loan payments. The percentage of school leavers who defaulted in the first year their loans were due edged up from 5.2 percent to 6.7 percent in the 2008 fiscal year. Several years out of school the default rate gets worse. Alan Collinge, an activist with the group Student Loan Justice and the author of *The Student Loan Scam*, is a defaulted borrower himself. "It's an obvious and compelling comparison" between student loans and the mortgage crisis, he writes. "I would say that in the student-loan realm, the lack of bankruptcy (and other consumer protections) combined with a far more naive and vulnerable borrower) led to an even 'wilder west' in terms of lax oversight, inflation, and 'lenders gone wild' (and a much higher default rate as well. . . . MUCH higher)."

Collinge collects the worst stories of graduates with trouble repaying loans that can snowball to four, five, even ten times their value with fees and penalties.

"I am a single mother, currently unemployed," writes "Petra" in a representative tale on the Student Loan Justice Web site.

> I graduated from law school in 1986 with a little over $45K in federally guaranteed student loans. I moved to Illinois and began making regular payments on my loans as required. In 1990, I lost my job due to the market crash and began defaulting on my loans. . . . I have been chased around and abused by the Department of Education (DOE) and its agents for the past 20 years. A $45,000 loan has now "grown" to an astronomical sum of $152,000 and I receive letters and phone calls almost weekly threatening legal action and seizure of assets. This agency is worse than any collection firm I have ever had the misfortune of dealing with.[33]

Without bankruptcy as a last resort, those with unmanageable student-loan debt have few options. Collinge points out to me a Department of Education audit published in 2003, during a time of economic expansion, well before the financial crisis. For loans taken out in 2000, the Department of Education estimated a 19 percent default rate for all four-year students, a 30 percent rate for all two-year students, and a shocking 44 percent rate for for-profit college students.[34] Millions of student-loan borrowers in default means millions of people with ruined credit, difficulty saving, and little forward economic momentum.

The good news is that it looks as though the student-loan insanity may be calming. With the American Graduation Initiative, President Obama stands a good chance of accomplishing something that was first tried by President Clinton in 1993: cutting off federal subsidies to student lenders altogether, and supplying all subsidized federal

loans through the Direct Loan Program, where students borrow
directly from the Education Department. This move would save up
to $87 billion in corporate subsidies over the next ten years, money
that would be used for Pell Grants and community colleges. By
kneecapping the student-loan industry, it removes a powerful force
in favor of indebtedness. Another set of important student-loan
reforms went into effect in July 2009. Income-based repayment,
which allows graduates to adjust their payments based on their
income, and Public Service Loan Forgiveness, which repays loans
for people going into nursing, teaching, social work, and a variety of
other public service careers, bring our student-loan programs more
in line with those in many other countries, making payments more
affordable for graduates in need.[35]

This is great. But it doesn't address the bankruptcy exclusion, nor
the abuses of the private loan market. Federal student-loan borrowing jumped by an unexpected and dramatic 25 percent in the 2008–9
academic year as other sources of funding, like parents' home equity
loans, dried up. As tuition and fees keep rising, public-university
students typically face gaps of $10,000 a year between what their
families can afford and their cost of attending school. There has been
some tightening of credit standards, and some private lenders have
stopped lending, but students are still looking to borrow.

Unchecked student loans may not be the best way to subsidize
the cost of college, but that doesn't mean we shouldn't subsidize it at
all. Higher education is a public good deserving of public support.
Broadly accessible higher education contributes to broadly shared
prosperity. Subsidies should be designed and targeted to benefit the
public. The increasing cost of college tuition, and the affordability gap, comes down to a clash of priorities. Our society professes
the goal of making a quality higher education accessible to anyone
who's qualified, willing to work hard, and sacrifice. But colleges have
different goals. As institutions, they want to perpetuate and aggran-
dize themselves; to grow in budget, operations, and staff. They want
to get better at what they do, they want to do more, and they want
to improve their reputations.

The cost spiral is unsustainable—better to halt it by intentional
and judicious application of the brakes, rather than waiting for it to
hit a wall. Not only tuition, but colleges' operating costs, must come

down. Belt tightening has been in vogue recently. Endowments for colleges lucky enough to have them are way down due to the collapse of the financial markets—Harvard and Yale, the top two endowed colleges, each lost 30 percent. The need for student aid is unprecedentedly high, and state budget cuts are deep.

Students and families, too, are ready for a change. College has gotten so expensive that it's forcing a shift in how we measure the value of a college degree. Rather than be abjectly willing to pay whatever it takes, or to take cost as a proxy for quality, families are far more likely today to act like smart consumers and make comparisons based on price versus a few years ago. *SmartMoney* magazine put out a survey in December 2009 that serves as a useful counterpoint to those *US News* rankings. This one compared the published cost of a four-year degree to the average salaries of graduates. The public institution Texas A&M scored number 1, with a payback more than two and a half times that of Harvard. And the state universities of tiny Delaware and Rhode Island scored higher than every Ivy League school.

"The system works the way it has worked since World War II," says Suzanne Walsh, who in her job with the Lumina Foundation works with states to improve "educational productivity," a new concept, by helping colleges and universities to be more effective and efficient with the dollars they have and actually comparing outlay of funds to educational outcomes, such as the cost per degree granted. "I think it's at a breaking point. . . . I suppose one of the moments in the timeline that we should be watchful of is the year there isn't any more stimulus money. The next two years, maybe we're okay. But what happens in year three? If you run a state, your order of priorities is K–12, then the roads, then hospitals, then public works. Higher ed is fifth at best."

One answer, says Kevin Carey of Education Sector, is that we need to change how we evaluate what a good college is.

> Roughly 80 percent of all students attend a college that admits the majority of applicants; community colleges or open-access four-year colleges. These institutions will never be famous research universities; they weren't built to be famous research universities. We have to give them a way

to be good at what they were meant to do, to accomplish
their mission—not to produce Nobel Prize winners or
educate the elite but to provide a high quality education to
students who are middle class or lower income. Give them
a way to compete where they can become more efficient
and not be penalized for it.

If public universities and colleges don't figure out ways to cut
costs, they will increasingly cede territory to for-profit colleges.
So-called proprietary schools, which rely on tuition to both cover
their operating costs and turn a profit, already enroll about 9 percent
of college students; they run 28 percent of all two-year colleges. In
the 2007–8 academic year they collected over $16 billion in federal
loans, grants, and campus-based aid.[36] For-profits have been the fastest-growing sector in higher education for more than a decade, and
their annual growth rate doubled to 17 percent during the 2008
recession.

In the late 1980s, for-profit colleges, then better known as trade
schools, were a nationwide scandal. Newspaper reports, TV hidden
cameras, and a Senate investigation found that some did their recruiting outside welfare offices and homeless shelters, collected tuition
money from the federal government, and offered useless courses or
outright folded overnight. Fifteen hundred of the nation's then four
thousand trade schools lost accreditation, and the feds tightened
regulations. Trade schools polished up their image too; the National
Association of Trade and Technical Schools renamed itself the Career
College Association and began million-dollar lobbying campaigns.[37]

After a round of buy-ups and mergers, a dozen publicly traded
companies now enroll nearly half of for-profit students. These companies have been Wall Street darlings—the highest-earning stocks of
any industry between 2000 and 2003, and two of the only successful IPOs in the dark months of 2008 and early 2009.[38] The largest publicly traded higher education company is the Apollo Group,
which operates the University of Phoenix and three other colleges.
In all, Apollo has 176 locations, plus many online programs, with a
total enrollment of 420,000 students in the United States, Puerto
Rico, and Canada, making it one of the largest university systems
in the world, and the largest single recipient of federal student aid.[39]

These institutions enroll proportionately more minorities, low-income students, and those who are first in their family to go to college. More than half of four-year students at for-profit colleges are financially independent (of their parents), compared to just 7 percent of students at four-year public colleges. The best for-profits are aggressively focused on innovating in the use of technology to create economies of scale and improve convenience. They are pursuing enrollment growth, which traditional colleges are not doing and which the president's attainment goals require. Jeff Conlon, the president of Kaplan Higher Education, says, "According to what the president says, we have to produce 63 million new graduates by 2025. At our current rate the United States is going to fall short of that by 16 million grads. The current system is fairly well maxed out. The schools like Kaplan will be, I believe, playing a key role in being able to solve the capacity issue."

The problem is that for-profit colleges aren't necessarily affordable. They may be cheaper to run, but they pass the entire cost of attending on to the student, so tuition is far higher on average than at public community colleges. More worrisome, some for-profits are keeping the worst excesses of the student-loan business alive even as Sallie Mae is being downgraded to junk status. As the credit crunch hit the student-loan sector in the fall of 2008, for-profits increasingly made private loans to their students themselves, putting them in the worrisome position of being both college and creditor. The Associated Press reported in August 2009 that one college, Westwood in Colorado, was hit with a class action lawsuit for misclassifying its loans. Thirty percent of Westwood's students take out loans at 18 percent interest, plus hefty fees. The concern was that the college was labeling the loans as consumer financing rather than student loans, which have different reporting requirements.[40]

Education Sector, Kevin Carey's think tank, found in 2009 that 43 percent of for-profit college students took out private loans in 2007–8, up from 15 percent in 2003–4. And the proportion of students at for-profit colleges who borrowed at least $40,000 nearly tripled to 30 percent in the same time frame. Bachelor's degree recipients at for-profit colleges have a $32,653 median debt, compared to $19,999 for all BAs.[41] So we're looking at a system that charges the typical middle-class student $11,000 a year for a bachelor's degree at a flagship public university, paid for with publicly subsidized loans at 6 percent a year, while the typical poor student pays $14,000 a year for an associate's degree at a nonselective technical school, financed with nonsubsidized loans at 18 percent a year.

In September 2009, the Government Accountability Office reported that students at for-profits are much more likely to default on student loans—23 percent default after four years compared to less than 10 percent of public university grads. The GAO found cases of for-profit colleges helping applicants get high school diplomas from diploma mills and cheating for them on tests designed to prove their ability to benefit from federal student aid. Also in September, the Department of Education announced it was forming new rulemaking committees to scrutinize colleges' marketing claims and pay-for-recruitment policies, which are illegal. This strikes fear into the heart of for-profits, because these areas have been the basis of past lawsuits and settlements, even for top brand University of Phoenix.

Carey, for one, doesn't want the for-profits put out of business. Instead, he wants greater attention paid to the excesses of the student-loan market. "For-profits have a legitimate role to play in meeting the rising demand for higher education—they're the only institutions that have both the willingness and ability to scale," he says. "But as for-profits grab a bigger share of the market, the government should crack down on misleading advertising and move more aggressively to cut colleges with high loan-default rates out of the federal financial aid system. Default rates are where the rubber meets the road. . . . If students can't pay back their loans, then by definition they are not getting sufficient value for their money."

Colleges as they're currently set up are under all kinds of perverse pressure to raise prices and increase spending, because of the way they're funded and run. In order to stop the cost spiral, the federal and state government should short-circuit some of these bad incentives and replace them with good ones. And students should vote with their feet, supporting colleges that do things differently.

Cost cutting in public higher education, it should be clear, is a moral imperative. State and federal subsidies helped create the tuition monster, and state and federal governments can combat it if they work in partnership with institutional leaders—not with across-the-board, feast-or-famine cuts, but with rational changes that focus on incentives for affordability and productivity. Families and students have a role to play as well. They need to become more informed consumers who aren't afraid to ask tough questions about the value of their degree.

1. Align institutional, state, and federal incentives

The University of Maryland is one state system that's completely changed its relationship to state government, leaving cost shifting behind. "We observed that there was a boom and bust cycle," Chancellor William Kirwan told me.

> In good times we got money from the state, in bad times we were the target of cuts. The cuts were often preceded by commentary that higher education is fat and happy, bloated. So the state board of regents, the thirteen college presidents and I needed to address the perception that we are inefficient and overfunded. We took on the issue in a transparent way: analyzing the extent to which we *were* overfunded, and targeting areas where we could become more efficient, including best practices from both the corporate world and nonprofits.

On the administrative side, Kirwan's committee consolidated backroom operations and purchasing, locking in everything from furniture to power at low bulk prices. On the academic side, they limited undergraduate majors to 120 credits—some had been creeping upward to 130 or 132. They required students to get 12 of those credits off campus, whether online, at another institution, through Advanced Placement exams, or in a study-abroad program. They're working with the National Center for Academic Transformation, described in chapter 4, to incorporate technology to lower instructional costs while improving outcomes. And they asked faculty to increase contact hours in teaching, advising, and research supervision by 10 percent.

The results have been hailed nationwide. "We've had a cumulative increase in state support of 32 percent," Kirwan says. "We

haven't raised tuition for four years. We've gone from the fifth highest public university tuition in the nation to the twentieth highest.
And we have a new compact with the state, a real sense of partnership." Kirwan says budget requests to the state have an entirely
different tone than in years past. They are working together with the
governor and state legislators to identify workforce shortage in areas
like biosciences and nursing. For every requested increase in funding, the universities agree to find 10 percent of the money through
further efficiencies. Even in the severe economic winter of 2008–9,
cuts to the UM system were just 3 percent, far less than the double-
digit cuts seen around the county. "I don't know the answer to why
more campuses haven't done this," says Kirwan. "I think that, generally speaking, change is hard. This has required a massive communication effort with faculty and staff and the state. We don't all hold
hands and sing 'Kumbaya,' but this approach has been very helpful
for the system. We're in a stronger place today because of it."

The right institutional and state leadership can clearly do a lot.
There's also a major opportunity for meaningful reform on the
federal level. The Department of Education should become a central
clearinghouse to help colleges avail themselves of the latest cost-
cutting interventions such as those described in the second half of
this book, with the public mandate of swiftly bringing tuition down
to 1970s-equivalent levels: a sum that students can pay with part-
time jobs and reasonable amounts of low-interest government loans.

Bob Shireman in the Department of Education has some interesting proposals for linking funding to affordability. "We have asked
Congress to distribute loans to schools on the basis of a formula: you
get more loan money if you provide more need-based grant aid and
if your tuition is below average for the sector, and if you have higher
completion rates for Pell Grant recipients." They're also trying to
combat the cartel effect with increased transparency. Starting in
2011, the Department of Education will publish an annual "shame
list" of the most expensive 5 percent of institutions in each of nine
categories—public and private, large and small. Schools will have to
publicly account for the reasons their tuition is so high. "Calculators
give people a better sense of what people would likely pay to go to
a particular school," after financial aid is factored in, Shireman says.
"These transparency efforts are promoting better consumer practice

that might help to drive improvements around tuition." It is then up to students and parents to be smart shoppers.

The federal government should take another look at student loans too. Because lending is correlated with tuition increases, the Department of Education should make it a goal to rein in the overall amount of student loans and better educate students on the differences between private and federal loans. Restoring bankruptcy protection for student loans, especially private loans, is important too. Requiring lenders to assume more risk will naturally restrict the supply of student loans. Students also need to know the rule of thumb that they shouldn't borrow more than their likely starting salary on graduation. Student loans have become a necessary part of the financing picture, but they shouldn't be the majority of it.

2. Obsess over efficiency

Keeping in mind that institutions have different goals, everything should be on the table for institutions committed to educational quality and lowering costs. The second half of this book will deal extensively with savings related to the use of newer technologies, but operational innovation is just as important. Here are three examples.

The European Union is currently engaged in the Bologna Process, with the aim of improving the efficiency and effectiveness of their higher-education systems. They are looking at cutting time-to-degree from five or more years down to four or even three. That's an instant 20 to 25 percent cost savings. Ball State University in Muncie, Indiana, began offering three-year bachelor's programs in 2005, now in over thirty majors, while the University of Houston—Victoria in Texas and Hartwick College in New York, both private schools, started offering three-year programs in the fall of 2008.

Southern New Hampshire University started something called the Advantage Program, which allows students to complete their first two years of core general education requirements at six different satellite locations. Classes are held from 8:30 a.m. to 12:30 p.m. five days a week with the same faculty and curricula as on the main campus. "My inspirational analogy was low-cost airlines," says the entertainingly candid president, Paul LeBlanc. "At the end of the day, Southwest delivers exactly the same core experience as a full-price airline: getting you from point A to point B with your bags intact."

The Advantage Program costs nearly 60 percent less than the regular tuition.

Brigham Young University—Idaho is a fascinating case. It's a private, religious, four-year liberal arts college that serves the increasingly diverse global population of Mormons: nearly half of their students are ethnic and racial minorities and nearly a quarter are on the Grant Scholarship, which targets low-income students who are the first in their families to go to college. They charged just $1,400 a semester in 2008–9. Not only that, the college is posting a 6 percent annual decline in costs, in real dollars. In fact, in 2009, they got permission from their trustees to increase enrollment from 22,000 to 30,000 without spending any more money. How do they do it?

A few ways. The most important is in who they hire. They look for PhD faculty with professional experience and a passion for teaching, and they make them teach a lot. The campus is fully occupied year-round—students are admitted on a rolling basis for either the fall-spring, spring-summer, or summer-fall cohorts. That way they get a third more students onto campus without having any more facilities.

Twenty percent of credit hours are offered online, in courses that are created carefully to match BYU–Idaho's learning model of preparation, participation, and post-class reflection. The only research the college conducts is in teaching techniques; they relentlessly measure and publish all kinds of learning outcomes, from critical thinking skills to standardized test scores to student's perception of their own learning, to make sure that they're improving in teaching and that the online offerings are just as good as the in-person classes.

Most importantly, the faculty is asked to teach four credits per semester for three semesters. That's twelve classes per year compared to just two to four per year for professors at typical colleges. "We had to raise our faculty salary when we did this and pay them on a year-round calendar," says Clark Gilbert, the former associate vice president for academics. "But since we look for people whose identity—the reason they came here—is to teach, ironically we get more out of them, and they're better, and we save money at the same time. It's only because the current model is so broken in higher ed that those things can go together."

BYU–Idaho's religious mission makes it something of a unique case, helping foster the school's strong sense of community and commitment to changing education. Still, everyone in higher education can learn from the efforts of an institution that is offering quality academic baccalaureate programs at a low price to an underserved population, and that, above all, is willing to try things differently. "You've got a lot of bleeding hearts who are willing to do nothing but ask for more money and don't take any personal accountability" for waste in the higher-education sector, says Gilbert. "I've spent ten years of my life pulling inner city kids out of a flawed background. I don't think the way to do it is to say subsidize, and don't change, a flawed model. We're putting the burden on ourselves to come up with a better solution."

Students concerned about cost can pursue their own Bologna Process by planning their coursework, summer school, and online classes carefully to cut their overall time in college, a strategy I'll discuss further in the Resource Guide.

3. Restore the concept of "free"

Colleges don't have to charge tuition. Free tuition was a tradition at public colleges and universities from California to New York until the 1970s. The nation's service academies, like West Point and the Naval Academy, still have free tuition today. New technology makes free and open education more possible for everyone.

At the College of the Ozarks in Missouri, aka "Hard Work U," 95 percent of students graduate debt free; all must work fifteen hours a week to help pay for their tuition. The college is one of seven members of the "Work College Consortium," mostly small rural private schools, some religious and others more countercultural. They all make work part of the deal to get a degree either at very low cost or tuition-free. The others are Alice Lloyd and Berea in Kentucky, Blackburn in Illinois, Ecclesia in Arkansas, Sterling in Vermont, and Warren Wilson in North Carolina.

Robin Taffler is the director of the Work College Consortium. She's worked at public universities in Massachusetts and Kentucky, and she says the work colleges are different. "I have to say they're joyous campuses. That is one thing that really struck me," she says. "The students take a lot of ownership at these schools. They are tolerant, respectful, and they learn to depend on one another very early on." Students aren't just doing busywork; they lower campus operations costs by maintaining the grounds, running the library, admissions, and registrar's offices, answering the president's phones, and on some campuses, working the land. "They raise the meat, sell it, cook it, serve it in the cafeteria—it's a whole cycle."

The Cooper Union, a prestigious private-design college in New York, takes a different approach to free tuition. The college has supported itself over the years with prudent deployment of the prime Manhattan real estate resources bestowed upon it by founder Peter Cooper, an industrialist and autodidact who believed that education should be "free as water and air."

"I sometimes feel as much like a real estate developer as a college president," says president George Campbell. The college even collects rent on the Chrysler Building. Still, Cooper Union's not any richer than, say, Amherst, which charges $48,400 annually for tuition, room, and board. After years of running deficits, Cooper Union's endowment now stands at $608 million—dozens of colleges have bigger endowments. Campbell says their mission and dedication to free tuition forces them to be much more frugal than many colleges of comparable educational worth. "We don't have a gym, swimming pools, climbing walls, a student center, not even a major cafeteria. We do have a dormitory but it only houses the freshmen. We're all about academics here. We're not for students interested in the traditional college experience of the campus and all these kinds of amenities that I think in many ways have gotten out of hand and are driving the cost up." Apparently there are many students who are fine with that. As other private liberal arts colleges were considering folding, in 2008, applications to Cooper Union surged 70 percent, making it far more selective than Harvard.[42]

Free might not be the right price for every school, but it is important as one among many models to show that no college, and no student, has to be held hostage to the cost spiral.

part two
_____

HOW WE GET THERE

four

COMPUTER SCIENCE

William Bowen and William Baumol argued in their 1966 book, *Performing Arts: The Economic Dilemma,* that modernization, mechanization, and efficiency just plain escape certain areas of human endeavor. If you want a proper Beethoven string quartet, you can't cut the cellist, and you can't squeeze in more performances by playing the music faster. Just as there is no substitute for the concert hall experience, the writers argued, there was no substitute for being in the classroom with a professor. Higher education and health care as well as the arts are subject to a "cost disease."

Today, live performance is still vibrant and without rival. However, the music aficionado has opportunities that go far beyond what could have been imagined when Beethoven was composing or even when Baumol and Bowen were writing. My husband's grandparents go to the movie theater to watch a live high-definition broadcast of the Metropolitan Opera's *Tosca.* If I search for "Beethoven" on YouTube I can watch 63,000 videos, like the late Austrian conductor Herbert von Karajan conducting the full Seventh Symphony in A Major. Contemporary composers can record entire symphonies from their bedrooms. Musicians from around the world can collaborate and perform for an audience of millions without ever meeting each other. The marginal cost of distributing a copy of a musical recording around the world has dropped to pretty much zero.

The same is happening in education. Since 2001, a growing movement, from MIT, Stanford, and hundreds of other universities worldwide to insurgent bloggers and entrepreneurs barely out of school themselves, is looking to social media to transform higher education. They're releasing educational content for free to the world and enlisting computers as tutors. Google has scanned and digitized seven million books. Wikipedia users have created the world's largest encyclopedia. YouTube Edu and iTunes U have made video and audio lectures by the best professors in the country available for free.

The face-to-face learning experience, like the live concert experience, remains valuable as one item on an expanding menu. At its best, research is showing, hybrid learning beats both online-only and classroom-only approaches. Learners can take in and retain more content faster and more easily, form strong mentoring and teamwork relationships, grow into self-directed, creative problem solvers, and publish portfolios of meaningful work that help jobs find them. These innovations hold out the tantalizing possibility of beating the cost disease while meeting the world's demand for higher education.

As exhilarating as this future sounds for students, there is plenty of anxiety about the transition. "Thinking Big in a Crisis" was the title of one higher-education policy summit in Washington, D.C., in the summer of 2009, featuring representatives from the worlds of journalism and architecture sharing war stories about the scary impact of the Web on existing business models.[1] The title of the Open Education conference I attended in Vancouver later that summer was "Crossing the Chasm."[2] The pace of transformation is uneven. Existing institutions don't want to give up their authority, nor faculty their jobs. Even among gung-ho early adopters, there's a divide over basic issues: some see an economic opportunity, while others are eager to spread free education; some want the university to absorb the new information technologies, others see the digital age absorbing the university. This chapter is about new applications of technology within existing institutional structures. The next chapter flips to the concept of hacking education outside traditional institutions, through DIY learning, experiential and workplace-based programs.

As a print journalist, I'm all too aware that a cardinal way the Internet has disrupted traditional knowledge industries is through disaggregation or unbundling of services. In the case of a daily newspaper, for example, Craigslist replaced the classifieds, Yahoo! Finance the stock listings, ESPN.com the sports scores, bloggers the op-eds. Newspapers are making shaky attempts to profit from their remaining unique strengths in local and investigative reporting.

Higher education is not just an industry. Still, from students' point of view, colleges do provide a bundle of services. You crack a book or go to lecture and learn about the world; you go to labs, complete problem sets, and write papers, building a skill set; you form relationships with classmates and teachers and learn about yourself; and you get a diploma so the world can learn about you. Content, skills, socialization, and accreditation.

The Web and allied technologies can make each of these services more accessible, higher quality, and cheaper, even free to the student. Content, whether text, video, audio, or game-based, has progressed the farthest along that path. Interactive teaching algorithms can adapt to your learning style on the fly, allowing you to grasp concepts intuitively and at your own pace. The Internet hasn't just changed the way we consume information, though. It has also altered the way we interact. Social media can help students and teachers form learning communities. Reputation, assessment, and certification are held jealously as a monopoly by existing institutions, but new tools and models are knocking on that door too.

"If universities can't find the will to innovate and adapt to changes in the world around them," professor David Wiley of Brigham Young University has written, "universities will be irrelevant by 2020." Wiley doesn't immediately come off as a bomb thrower. He is a thirty-seven-year-old LDS church member with five kids. He has close-cropped gray hair, glasses, a West Virginia accent, and a boyish, disarming manner he deploys to his advantage in his role as a "Nostradamus" in the intellectual vanguard of the open-education movement. The challenge, he says, is not to bring technology into the classroom. The millennials, with their laptops and their Facebook, have already done that. The challenge is to capture the potential of that technology to both lower costs and improve learning for all.

Wiley has been working since the early days of the Internet with open educational content and tools. As a college junior, he was hired to be the first Webmaster of his small, resource-starved alma mater, Marshall University in West Virginia. "I was working on developing a Javascript calculator for a Web page when it occurred to me that this calculator, unlike a real one in our elementary schools, can be used by 100,000 people all at the same time. You can pay to produce online resources once and they can be used by an infinite number of people. That seemed to be somewhere between terribly fascinating and the kind of realization that it makes sense to spend the rest of your life working on." In 1998 Wiley came to Brigham Young for a PhD in instructional psychology and technology, which is where he first heard about open-source software programs like Linux that are produced collaboratively and shared freely. "I said hey, that's exactly what we need to do with educational materials. Let's call it 'open content.'"

Open content—aka open courseware, or open educational resources, or OER—can mean any use of the Web to share the fruits of faculty time, from curricula to lesson plans to texts to original research. As Wikipedia is to a conventional encyclopedia, open content is to a conventional textbook or lecture hall. Both open-source software and Creative Commons share intellectual DNA with open educational content. Creative Commons (CC) is a nonprofit set up in 2001 to create the intellectual and legal framework to share or remix creative work found online.[3]

Creators of photos, writings, or any intellectual property can use CC licensing to designate their work to be freely shareable for commercial or noncommercial use, with or without attribution or alterations, all without the expense and red tape of commercial copyright. For example, you can search the photo Web site Flickr for CC-licensed images and use them like stock photos, for free, to illustrate a blog post, as long as you live up to the requirements of the CC license, such as crediting the creator or linking back to the original photo on Flickr.

More than a technical innovation, CC has spread to millions of works in all media and become a focus of what thinkers like Harvard law professor Lawrence Lessig, author of the book *Remix*, term the "copyleft" movement.[4] "What happened was unexpected," says Ahrash Bissel, former director of CCLearn, the educational division of Creative Commons. "We tapped into this social dimension of people who are hungry to be able to stand up and say yes, I am part of this new and exciting universe of possibility around distributed collaboration and adaptation."

Those values—distributed collaboration and adaptation— are central to open education. The ball got rolling in 2001 with the OpenCourseWare project at MIT, funded by the Hewlett Foundation. If you go to http://ocw.mit.edu/ today, you can find the full syllabi, lecture notes, class exercises, tests, and some video and audio for every one of the 1,900 courses MIT offers, from physics to art history. By the end of 2009 some 63 million current students, aspiring students, alumni, professors, and armchair enthusiasts around the world had checked them out. "Education has a long, long history of a gift economy around knowledge," says Steve Carson, a director of MIT's project, explaining why the university devotes up to $15,000 per course in development costs from its own budget to put each course online to everyone for free. "That ethos underpins both open-source software and educational sharing." More than two hundred institutions in thirty-two countries have posted courses online at the OpenCourseWare Consortium under CC licensing.[5] Countries from Kenya to the Netherlands have started their own open courseware repositories.[6] China's Ministry of Education has been funding the release of university courses since 2003; over 10,000 of their courses are now available for free online, many including video.[7]

The sites iTunes U and Youtube.com/edu are two more places where free audio and video from dozens of top-tier universities, museums, archives, and other cultural institutions can be found. A parallel academic movement in research is open access, unlocking databases and opening up the process of peer review to promote worldwide collaboration. The Directory of Open Access Journals lists 4,417 scholarly and scientific journals that are peer-reviewed, quality controlled, and available in full text to anyone who is curious.[8]

These materials have been accumulating for several years now, but most colleges have yet to fully take advantage of them. Students spend $1,000 a year on textbooks, on average, and countless faculty hours go to preparing and updating course materials. Can universities realize the power of Wiley's insight about the Javascript calculator at scale, and use it to cut costs and raise the quality of their offerings?

Dr. Judy Baker is a key figure shaping the open-source educational future. It is a perfect day in May when I meet her on the campus of Foothill College in Los Altos Hills, California, not far from Silicon Valley, where she manages distance learning. The campus of Foothill, with its sister campus, De Anza College, one of the largest community colleges in the country with 44,000 students, is a series of round hills dotted with dandelions and Hobbit-like hexagonal wooden buildings.[9]

With blond eyelashes blinking behind thick, square glasses, Baker looks the part of a geek—a geek who's passionate about connecting community college professors with open courseware. "The traditional printed textbook, homogenized, vanilla version, is basically the Hummer of higher education," she says. "It's just not viable in this day and age." Professors and students are starving for cheaper, higher-quality content that is easily remixed and customized: updated texts, multimedia, lesson plans, curricula, test banks. Community colleges have the greatest need for open content, Baker says. They are teaching half of the nation's students with a third of the resources per student enjoyed by state universities. The typical instructor is a "freeway flyer," an adjunct who may be teaching at five different colleges, lugging around five different big, heavy textbooks that are written for conventional four-year colleges, which have longer semesters and more prepared students. They often use only a sliver of the texts, which on average cost a community college student half as much as his or her tuition.

Baker is the administrative supervisor of the Community College Consortium for Open Educational Resources.[10] Nearly one hundred colleges have signed on to share textbooks that can be downloaded, edited, and used for free. Faculty, she says, have to be led by the hand to the wellspring of resources. "The biggest resistance is intellectual property rights," she says. "Many faculty have a lifelong dream that they will write a textbook. The reality is, particularly in a community college, it's a tiny, tiny proportion of faculty who actually do that, and even fewer who actually make more than minimum wage from it," when you consider the time it takes. So she first asks professors to try out the resources, and experience the joy of "free" as users. Then she appeals to their vanity. "'Think about it,' I tell them. 'You've done all of this work and over the years, maybe a thousand students have seen these great learning materials you've created. If you open-license them, I guarantee you within six months, you'll have 100,000 page views.'" And thus a sharer, ripper, and remixer is born.

Baker is sly. She is patient. She has a much broader agenda than just free textbooks. She has a vision of the future of open education and she wants to share it with the world. "I view open educational resources as a catalyst for faculty to leverage all the possibilities that are now available with the Internet. Not many people would state that as the benefit—that's my personal view. But whether they view it that way or not, that is an outcome."

Open courseware is a tremendous step forward in the transformation of higher education. For the autodidact, it may be all he or she needs. Many open-education mavens invoked the idea of some isolated genius growing up in the slums of Bihar State or HeiBei Province in 2015 who gets hold of an old smartphone and uses it to teach herself string theory. (The "pocket school" is a project of Paul Kim, chief technology officer of Stanford University's School of Education, that, in fact, puts simple mobile devices running educational programs in the hands of children in indigenous Mexican migrant worker camps, Indian villages, and refugee camps in Rwanda).[11]

But education is more than just access to knowledge, and the possibilities Baker alludes to go far beyond content. "If you didn't need human interaction and someone to answer your questions, than the library would never have evolved into the university," Wiley says. "A sufficient infrastructure of freely available content is step one in a much longer endgame that transforms everything we know about higher education."

Wiley is pursuing several different strategies toward this endgame, both nonprofit and entrepreneurial. He's the "chief openness officer" of Flat World Knowledge, a for-profit company that offers originally produced, open-source textbooks. Students can read them for free online, download a PDF for a few dollars, or get a printed copy for $29.95, a fraction of what most textbooks cost. Open licensing means faculty and students are free to mark up, excerpt, or submit edits to the original creator. In its first school year, the fall of 2009, more than four hundred faculty adopted Flat World Knowledge textbooks, saving students and their parents an estimated $3 million compared to traditional textbooks.[12]

Wiley has also cofounded a free online public charter high school, the Open High School of Utah,[13] that makes use of open-source content and curricula. Home-schooled students can complete their entire high school degree there. And at BYU and Utah State, where he used to teach, he's opened five of his courses up to anyone on the Internet for free, donating extra time of his own to review their work, and offering non-BYU students a signed certificate in lieu of course credit.

This open-teaching idea has been spreading around the web. In 2008, Stephen Downes, who works for a government IT research agency in New Brunswick, Canada, and George Siemens at the University of Manitoba, taught the first "Massively Open Online Course" called "Connectivism and Connective Knowledge"[14] to 24 registered students at the University of Manitoba and more than 2,200 unregistered students from around the world. "We took the role of a teacher and tried to fragment it so students would play teachers to each other," says Siemens. "The best person to teach you something is someone who's just mastered it."

Educational technologists celebrate the role of peer groups in learning. John Seely Brown and Richard P. Adler, in their 2008 article "Minds on Fire: Open Education, the Web, and Learning 2.0," cite research by Richard J. Light at the Harvard Graduate School of Education, who found that students' ability to form and participate in small study groups influenced their success in college more than multiple other factors.[15]

Despite appearances, the humble pizza-and-study group isn't some minor activity; it's the kernel of the university. When knowledge was scarce, universities grew as communities of scholars clustered around the latest information technology: rare, expensive, handwritten books. The first Western university, the University of Bologna, was founded in 1088 by people who wanted to study the Byzantine-era Justinian legal code. The very word *universitas* doesn't mean campus, or class, or a particular body of knowledge; it refers originally to the guild, the group of people united in scholarship.[16] The word "college" too comes from the Latin *collegium*, related to "colleague," meaning "community," "society," "guild."[17] Now that knowledge is a free, abundant commodity, the communities that form around it are just as important to education as they ever were.

As Facebook founder Ethan Beard told a Macarthur-sponsored conference on digital media and learning in the spring of 2009, for education, "social media can be the bridge between the high-tech and the high-touch." The Facebook version of a graduate education is currently being piloted at the University of Southern California's Rossier School of Education.[18] Jeremy Johnson is the chief technology officer of a company called 2tor, founded by John Katzman, also founder of the Princeton Review. Johnson gave me a tour of USC's online master's program in teaching that shows how social media can replicate much of what happens in a classroom. As he manipulated the cursor on his computer screen in California, I watched from New York. The 2tor platform looks a lot like Facebook, and that's by design, says Johnson, who draws a distinction between his program and the two standard "learning management systems" in use at most colleges today, Blackboard and Moodle.[19] "Any learning management system can deliver content, deliver exams, and have people read articles, but what you haven't been able to do before is build relationships—which are at least as valuable as the actual course content that you go through." 2Tor uses commercially available programs like Gmail, Google Docs, a program called Kaltura for video hosting, and Adobe Connect, the program that we were using for our interview, which allows multiple people to look at the same computer desktop while they chat in text or voice.

When you log in to 2tor's system, little widgets pop up to let you know your next deadline, or what percentage of assignments in a class you have completed. In the MAT@USC "news feed," students can read assignments and post responses. Each student in the program, which debuted in fall 2009, is given a small, simple Flip camera to post videos—for example, one assignment is to conduct an interview with a school administrator. Students also film themselves in the classroom as student teachers, and professors review the clips as part of their evaluations. Besides the news feed, which can be accessed anytime, students use the platform as a virtual classroom to meet up with fellow students and professors online for classes, bull sessions, or office hours. On screen during a real-time meeting, you can view the professor's slide show as the lecture, and students' comments, go by in a stream of instant messages. Push a button and you can see eight of your fellow students and the professor as live video talking heads, Brady Bunch style.

USC's MAT program is innovative in terms of the students' experience, but not in terms of institutional structure. They still charge the same for the online programs as they do for the in-person ones, for example, avoiding the key question of whether technology can cut costs. In fact, the dean of the education school, Karen Gallagher, seemed a little defensive that I was even asking. "I don't know if I'd use that word—efficiency," she said. "We actually haven't sat down to do a one-on-one cost comparison. If you want a USC degree you have to pay USC tuition." It's a telling comment; a sentiment comparable to those of Provost Berliner at Hofstra mentioned in chapter 3, and an indication that some traditional universities may not want to recover from the cost disease.

Rather than layering new technologies as bells and whistles onto existing classes, or adding a free textbook to a traditional lecture course, courses need to be completely redesigned using information technology strategically in order to save significant money and improve outcomes at the same time. The Open Learning Initiative at Carnegie Mellon University in Pittsburgh is doing some of the best research anywhere on using technology to address both efficiency and effectiveness.[20] Candace Thille, the director, is a forcefully intelligent woman with a background in management consulting. She overflows with enthusiasm when I mention that I've heard about Baumol and his string quartet.

"The music industry has overcome Baumol's disease," she says. "But one of the mistakes that people in higher education make is that they assume the same technologies that fix Baumol's disease in music are the ones that fix it in higher ed. They misunderstand what the service is that higher ed is performing." It's not just about content delivery, Thille says. If it had been, open courseware efforts like MIT's would have solved the problem. Her working definition of education's central service is "changing the knowledge state of the learner"—in other words, dealing directly with the "skills" element of the bundle. And within those parameters, she's getting amazing results.

Like MIT and other members of the OpenCourseWare Consortium, the OLI Web site provides a set of free online courses. They have been used at about fifty institutions ranging from large publics to small privates and community colleges; thousands of independent learners have tried them too. They cover topics befitting one of the country's top science and engineering schools: statistics, economics, physics, static engineering, biology, chemistry, and logic. What makes these courses different is how they're designed. They use a tutoring technology that has been developed at Carnegie Mellon over the past fifteen years. The principle, which Thille calls "concept-specific immediate supported practice," or "scaffolding," is simple. In an engineering lesson, say, the program shows you how to sum vectors, then gives you a picture of three vectors and asks you to do it yourself. Answer correctly and move on at your own pace. If you miss it, the electronic tutor breaks the problem down into predetermined steps and gives you a series of broader and broader hints at each step, until you get the answer. It's what might happen in a classroom under ideal circumstances, with a teacher of infinite patience, undivided attention, and inexhaustible resources of examples and hints.

Since all this learning and assessment is taking place on a computer, the OLI can track exactly how and how well each student is learning each concept. This provides targeted feedback to the students themselves, to their teachers (who can glance at a digital dashboard and see that George is behind on quadratics and Melissa has mastered derivatives) and to the OLI researchers, who in turn perform higher level studies of best practices—looking at whether 3-D videos teach math faster than 2-D charts, or what order of concepts in physics leads students to mastery faster. "An instructor told me this course was her best experience in fifteen years of teaching," Thille says. "She told me: 'When I come into the classroom I know what they know and don't know, the students know I know, and we all know what we're trying to get them to know.'"

When compared to students in traditional lecture-section-paper classes, OLI students learn more, learn faster, and enjoy it a little bit more too. Their most spectacular results were with a Carnegie Mellon stats course that was a blend of online practice and in-person instruction. The course met twice a week for eight weeks, versus four times a week for fifteen weeks in a conventional course. The speedy students learned more and retained the information just as well a semester later, without spending any more time on their homework. Putting a foot on the gas to a large course taught in several sections could potentially save a university $200,000 a year or more, the OLI estimates.

Studies of online learning are still new, but evidence is encouraging. In the summer of 2009, the U.S. Department of Education published a meta-analysis taken from more than 1,000 comparative empirical studies.[21]

They found students who took classes online learned more and performed better on average than those who stuck to traditional face-to-face classes. Hybrid approaches worked best of all. The most effective techniques weren't the use of fancy multimedia like video, pop-up quizzes, or little animated penguins. Instead, online students benefited most in the cases where they were able to move at their own pace, prompted to spend more time on task, reflect on what they'd learned, and collaborate.

Thille is part of a task force for a Department of Education project called the National Educational Technology Plan, detailing the uses of technology for learning, teaching, assessment, and productivity. She also works as a scholar for another organization that applies these insights at scale, the National Center for Academic Transformation. Over the past decade, NCAT has worked with hundreds of public universities to redesign individual courses "to prove that it is possible to improve quality and reduce cost in higher education." Carol Twigg, NCAT's founder, had been working in education reform for several years when in 1998 she landed a $9-million grant from the Pew Charitable Trust.[22] "We had a pretty big carrot. Part of the design included $200,000 apiece for institutions that would step forward and agree to try this. The brief was: We want you to improve student learning, reduce cost, and use technology. Other than that it's a blank slate."

Universities in NCAT's Course Redesign program have come up with a wide range of solutions for courses in all disciplines, from psychology to Spanish to math. These course redesigns blend social media tools and software-based drills with peer-to-peer instruction, tutoring, and traditional classroom settings. They combine tools like the OLI's tutoring modules with in-person meetings structured like labs, seminars, office hours, or study groups. For example, the Universities of Alabama and Idaho, LSU, Ole Miss, the University of Missouri–St. Louis, Virginia Tech, and Wayne State all got rid of lectures in intro math classes. Instead, they introduced an "emporium model" using self-paced tutoring programs like MyMathLab, published by textbook company Pearson. Using the program, students spend their time solving problems and get instant feedback, hints, and examples. Students can work from home or in a computer lab staffed, often late into the night, by professors, grad students, and peer tutors who are available for help if they get stuck. At Alabama, a representative example, the percentage who passed the course went up from less than half to more than 70 percent for first-time freshmen; women and African-Americans made even larger average gains, and student satisfaction rates were at an all-time high.

Toni Farley, a computer science professor at Arizona State in Tempe, used NCAT's guidance to redesign an intro computer science course, Computer Literacy, which had traditionally been taught to 2,200 students a year in four large lecture sections per semester. The new course was split into two hybrid sections combining online with class time, and one fully online section, all coordinated by a single instructor. Undergraduate "learning assistants," who were computer science majors, related better to the students, and worked more cheaply, replaced grad student TAs. The focus shifted from the old lecture-memorization-test format to a larger number of hands-on projects and assignments. Students went online to solve problems and collaborate on projects using discussion boards and wikis. They got automated grading and feedback on quizzes and tests. Students who were stuck on a programming or debugging problem were directed to a wealth of resources, some created for the class and others out there on the wider Web: message boards, screencasts, video demonstrations, and interactive tutorials.

The outcomes were dramatic. The cost per student in the course dropped by 44 percent, mostly because about 80 percent of assessment was automated. Students learned much better: even though the course moved faster, covered more material, and was deemed harder by the panel of outside expert advisors that Farley convened, the percentage of students who passed with a C or better rose from a lame 26 percent to a strong majority—65 percent. And students enjoyed the course, rating it higher on their evaluations: "The class far exceeded my expectations," wrote one representative student. "I got a whole lot more out of it than I was expecting. I was actually interested in what we were learning when I originally thought I was going to be bored out of my mind."

Farley said the most difficult part of her redesign effort was faculty attitudes. "The reaction from faculty outside the redesign process was fairly negative. There was little belief that our goals could be achieved and that the redesign was being handled properly." However, since seeing how successful her course was, other faculty both within and outside ASU have approached her to hear more about how she did it.

The most recent round of NCAT course redesigns at public university campuses across the country cut costs an average of 39 percent—a few courses cut costs by up to 75 percent. Outcomes improved by almost any measure you choose: test scores, grades, information retention, student persistence, student satisfaction, and graduation rates. "The coin of the realm is faculty time," as Carson at MIT's OpenCourseWare puts it. An estimated three-quarters of the costs of colleges and universities are personnel costs, so cutting costs means saving faculty and administrative time wherever possible. When faculty can build on existing high-quality course material, rather than reproducing the work from scratch; when systems automate what can be automated—grading tests and quizzes, providing immediate, standardized feedback and practice; and when students can help teach each other as peers, there are significant savings to be had over a traditional, butts-in-seats classroom model.

Twigg has seen these kinds of results repeatedly. "I tell you what's sort of amusing to me: I'm regarded as this genius futuristic thinker for doing what I thought was sort of obvious—applying technology to education," she says. While the Department of Education, think tanks, newspapers, and magazines hail NCAT's accomplishments, Twigg can't disguise a hint of frustration at how long it's taking for the redesign model to catch on. "It's one of my personal pet peeves. I'm getting tired of people saying how wonderful I am—I want them to do something along these lines!"

Administrators and faculty at traditional institutions have put a lot of faith and effort into the string-quartet myth. If you happen to play the violin or own a concert hall, and your salary depends on ticket sales to live performances, it's easy to see why you'd be motivated to keep iPods out of the hands of your attendees—even if it doesn't serve the larger goal of music appreciation. Professors are far from obsolete, but it's clear their time and training is being extravagantly wasted drilling students on Spanish pronunciation, repeating ten-year-old lectures, or grading multiple-choice tests. Twigg says of traditional educators: "They really believe that the instructor and student, nose to nose, face to face is the way students learn, and they continue to believe it in spite of all evidence to the contrary. The attitude is, don't confuse me with the facts."

Some opposition, in the face of demonstrated results for technological innovations like that found by the OLI, the Department of Education, and NCAT, is fear of change and perhaps of loss of salary. There is snobbery at work: the vanguard of online programs are at colleges that offer only associate's degrees, at the bottom of the Carnegie hierarchy. Perhaps as a result, at traditional universities, digital offerings may be treated as an afterthought, a poor relation of what goes on in the classroom. The emphasis is on "distance," as in, This is a long way from real learning. Sarah Stern, a student at the University of Colorado, took an online class over the summer after her freshman year while living and interning in New York City. Her experience with Mass Communication 3 shows everything that can go wrong with online courses. "The professor recorded the lectures last semester, in-class, so while you're watching the PowerPoint and listening to his lectures, you're also listening to him go off on tangents, and students telling stories, and stuff that was a waste of time, basically," she says. The course had all of the limitations of the online format and none of the flexibility. From two time zones away, Stern found herself getting up early on Saturday mornings to take exams within a strict four-hour window. A couple of times, the Web site went down in the middle of test time, and there was nothing to do but send an e-mail and wait.

Stern felt cut off from other students and from the professor. "I know I could have e-mailed him, but it wasn't like when you're in class or office hours and you can say, 'Am I doing this right?' It was kind of bizarre that we never spoke." She was happy to be able to pick up the extra course credit while pursuing her future career goals, but her opinion of online classes did not improve with the experience. "It's harder to stay on task when you're not in a classroom and you just have to sit and listen to lectures for hours. I think 75 percent of my friends would not do well in an online class. Whenever I have friends who are like, 'Yeah, I think I'm just gonna take classes online next semester,' that was always like the keyword for, I'm pretty much dropping out."

Online classes like these are an example of what David Wiley at BYU calls the "polo parable." Think about playing polo with ponies on a field, versus water polo in a pool. "They're both called polo and at a high level they're both the same activity," he says. "But no person in their right mind would think you can take a playbook and run the same strategies as in the pool. The idea that you can take tried and true teaching methods from the classroom onto the Internet and see success boggles my mind."

So how do you change the rules for the more fluid, immersive environment of water polo? One of Wiley's recent open courses was an exploration of the contemporary field of educational technology itself. To unite form with content, he designed it as an online role-playing game, with students from Europe, Hawaii, and Utah divided into "guilds" (merchants, monks, artisans, and bards, each with a different focus and skill set) completing "quests." It was his attempt to adapt an example of a spontaneous learning community that's native to the Internet—the community of gamers, who haze newbies but also share skills and trade tricks.

If Wikipedia and YouTube represent one direction of innovation for online education, Facebook and Twitter another, Second Life and World of Warcraft are yet a third. So-called serious games are some of the flashiest applications of technology to teaching. Engage: Transforming Teaching Through Technology (T^4) is a project at the University of Wisconsin at Madison that supports the development of simple, purpose-built games in areas like economics, foreign languages, music theory, math, and science.[23] Appropriately for America's Dairyland, UW's Food Science department developed a game called "Got Ice Cream?" for Food Science 201 and 301. Students assumed the role of an inspector monitoring proper safety techniques, quality control, and ice cream making at the Babcock Hall Dairy Plant. Compared to a control group that reviewed the same information through PowerPoint slides, the game players seemed to learn a little better. And they were much more likely to enjoy the experience.

As Steven Johnson argued in his book *Everything Bad Is Good for You*, games have surprising cognitive benefits. At their best they are rich environments where players move at their own pace through levels that increase in difficulty, getting instant feedback on performance. And, of course, they're fun. Sarah Robbins, who goes by the handle "intellagirl," in the gaming world and the blogosphere, is a PhD candidate at Ball State University and expert at the use of Second Life in teaching.[24] "When I started playing Star Wars Galaxies I got intrigued with the way the game taught you to play," she says. "The scaffolding of skills and abilities along with a social community create a method of learning I hadn't seen before." "Scaffolding," also used by the Open Learning Initiative, is a term you hear often in educational discussions; it refers to any kind of teaching aid that works like the training wheels on a bike to help a student until she can master a concept on her own. Video games are built with levels and modes of increasing complexity (in Guitar Hero, that's Easy, Medium, Hard, and Expert) that naturally reward continued practice.

The power of gaming communities is even more intriguing. Players starting out in Grand Theft Auto, Star Wars Galaxies or World of Warcraft can easily draw on the accumulated expertise of thousands of others. They can consult written guides, follow someone else's saved game online step by step, or post a question in a discussion forum ("how do i get my alchemy skill level up?" "just travel around the world picking herbs . . . you need to go through every area of azeroth").[25] Although gamers famously like to flame n00bs (newbies), they also like to brag about their accomplishments and thus share their knowledge.

Robbins was among the first instructors to develop university courses in Second Life, the worlds' biggest online alternate universe, where the avatars of half a million people interact, building everything from airships to discotheques. Robbins has helped students build and run businesses in Second Life as part of an entrepreneurship class, or model different kinds of markets for an economics class, or practice French with native speakers. Hundreds of universities have some sort of presence in Second Life, and they've created virtual learning environments ranging from art galleries to dentists' offices to a virtual border control to train Border Services Officers at a Canadian community college.

Intellagirl's ideas about the future of teaching are totally sci-fi.

I'm really excited about augmented reality applications made possible by recent developments in mobile technologies. I can't wait to scan across campus with my iPhone camera and see contextual information about the people and places caught on camera. For example, if I'm taking a botany course I should be able to head out onto campus and pan my camera across trees and get information about the tree that relates directly to what I've learned about how a particular tree grows from my course. I'm excited about the contextual, social learning communities that may form anywhere, anytime.

In 1929 Edwin Link developed a replica cockpit complete with instrument panels, mounted on pneumatic lifts so it could roll and pitch a trainee around. The Air Force bought several of Link's flight simulators in 1934 to teach pilots to fly in the middle of a cloud when visibility is nil.[26]

Today, sophisticated simulations are increasingly being adopted to teach not only flying but combat, driving, dissection, surgery, and multiple other skills. Computer control also allows students to do real research virtually, remotely, and cheaply. For example, the Faulkes Telescope Project, sponsored by the Las Cumbres Observatory Global Telescope Network, allows students in the United Kingdom, Israel, and around the world to peek through two high-powered telescopes, one in Hawaii and the other in Australia, and record their own observations.[27] The project's Web site reports how students, under the guidance of professional astronomers, are using the Faulkes telescopes to make small but meaningful contributions to astronomy.

Recall that disruptive innovation in higher education means unbundling the various services that college provides. Open courseware addresses the need for content, and technologies like games and Facebook-style social networking platforms deal with socialization. Accreditation and assessment, the source of the "sheepskin effect" and the economic promise that drives so many people to college, is proving the toughest nut to crack. "Why is it that my kid can't take robotics at Carnegie Mellon, linear algebra at MIT, law at Stanford? And put 130 of those together and make it a degree?"

Wiley asks. Visionaries say this process, too, can be revolutionized by the right applications of technology.

Jim Groom works at the University of Mary Washington, a public liberal arts college in Virginia, developing open-source publishing platforms like blogs and wikis for free use by people at the college and throughout the state. The tools use existing free software like Drupal and Wordpress. UMW Blogs has 3,500 users out of a campus of 4,200.[28] Groom says self-publishing allows students to easily collaborate and build a portfolio of work that represents their qualifications and experience far better than a diploma can. For example, in a literature class taught by Pulitzer Prize–winning poet Claudia Emerson, students created online literary journals; in a history class, the students created a local history Web site documenting local landmarks. Elsewhere on the Web, teachers have assigned students to write Wikipedia entries or film YouTube videos as research projects. Millions of people can see and comment on the work of undergraduates, which can help when they're looking for jobs.

Seneca College is an eight-campus public polytechnic in Toronto—polytechnic meaning a baccalaureate-level institution that focuses on career prep, particularly in fields like computers and electronics. Since 2005, Seneca has partnered in a unique, ongoing open-education experiment with Mozilla, the nonprofit foundation that oversees the open-source development of Firefox, the number two Web browser by market share.[29] "Students spend one week in a boot camp teaching them how to operate in Mozilla," explains Mark Surman, executive director of the Mozilla Foundation. "Then they go out and work on a bug. The kids are learning and working on a real task with real code."

Evaluating students on team-based projects can be a challenge, and so can coaching them on how to participate without annoying other contributors with constant questions. But the payoff is tremendous. Students are learning the ins and outs of writing and debugging code, as well as key collaboration skills like communicating about their successes and failures. They also have the opportunity to be part of a team, to build expertise and relationships in the community of professionals and skilled amateurs writing real software for real users.

This kind of portfolio building, whether through class work or internships, is already viewed as a crucial supplement to a diploma. It could become an increasingly important component of higher education, because of the new possibilities for how people connect and learn about each other over the Internet. It's a bit of a mystery as to why millions of people devote their valuable time to writing a product review on Amazon, editing a Wikipedia entry, or fixing a bug in a free software program. One explanation is that we do it for the inherent satisfaction of being useful; another is to get positive feedback from other people, to enhance both our self-image and personal reputations. In his 2003 novel *Down and Out in the Magic Kingdom*, science-fiction writer, blogger, and copyleft activist Cory Doctorow described an entire economy that ran on "whuffie," a reputation-based currency.[30] As people move forward in their careers, and especially for certain kinds of careers, whuffie becomes more and more important and formal accreditation less so. What if there was a way for students to start building whuffie from their first class, freshman year? That's what participation in social media and open-source projects can do.

Another possibility to remake the sheepskin effect is for institutions to create competency-based assessments, separate from the other functions of education. Western Governor's University is a national innovator in assessment-based learning. "We said, let's create a university that actually measures learning," the jovial president, Bob Mendenhall, says. "We do not have credit hours, we do not have grades. We simply have a series of assessments that measure competencies, and then on that basis award the degree."

WGU was formed as a private nonprofit in the late 1990s, when the governors of nineteen Western states decided to take advantage of the newfangled Internet to expand educational access to rural students across the region. Today they have 12,000 online students in all fifty states. WGU sustains its programs entirely on tuition, and a modest tuition at that. In 2008, *Time* magazine called them "the best relatively cheap university you've never heard of."[31] They charged $2,890 in 2008–9 for each six-month term. Why they charge by time, not by credit, gets to the heart of what makes WGU different.

To determine what a graduate of one of their programs should know, WGU started from scratch, convening external councils of employers like Google, Oracle, and Tenet Healthcare, along with academic experts. "We asked employers, 'what is it the graduates you're hiring can't do that you wish they could?'" Mendenhall explains. "We've never had a silence after that question." Then they created assessments to measure each skill or content area that makes up a degree. Before taking each online course, you take a pre-assessment, and if you do well enough, you can skip to the real assessment and pass out of the course altogether. I tried the pre-assessment for teachers, a four-hour timed exam with multiple-choice and essay questions. Mendenhall recalls one student who had been self-employed in IT for fifteen years but never earned a degree; he passed all the required assessments and took home his BA in six months. But most students do take advantage of the courses, which are structured in a way that's also quite innovative.

Students work at their own pace through online course modules, combinations of prerecorded lectures, readings, projects, and quizzes. For every eighty students, there's a PhD faculty member, certified in the discipline, serving as a full-time mentor. "Our faculty are there to guide, direct, counsel, coach, encourage, motivate, keep on track, and that's their whole job," Mendenhall says jovially. "Our faculty are judged based on the retention rate, graduation rate, and success of the students they're responsible for, and that's how I'm judged too." This is a huge departure from most universities where professors are judged largely by the research they turn out, with their scores on student evaluations a distant second.

Faculty mentors at WGU are not responsible for grading; that would be a conflict of interest. Instead, multiple-choice tests, math problems, and the like are graded by computer, while essays and in-person evaluations are judged by a separate cadre of graders. This also saves the time of the highest-paid faculty. What WGU is doing is, again, using the Internet to unbundle the various functions of teaching: the "sage on the stage" conveyor of information, the cheerleader and helpmate, and the evaluator. "We really don't teach or instruct," says Dr. Linda Gunn, a student mentor and regional coordinator. "We guide them to learning resources and supplemental information to help them gain their competencies."

This isn't just a more efficient use of teachers' time. It's a better experience for both teacher and student. Think of Judy Baker's "freeway flyer" adjunct, teaching five hundred students a semester at five different colleges, and responsible for the whole shebang: designing the courses, lecturing, administering tests, grading quizzes and papers. No matter how conscientious he may be, it can be tough to find any extra energy or time for students. "I have one colleague who's a wonderful teacher," says Wick Sloane, who teaches at Bunker Hill Community College. "She had one student burst into tears and another got angry because she couldn't stay and help them with a question, but she had to get in her car and rush off to adjunct at another campus."

WGU students get a personal advocate whose number-one priority is their success. "I was not looking for a career change," when she found WGU, says Dr. Gunn, who bubbles over with warmth. "Being able to provide education to people who would not normally have access and to help them achieve their goal and lifelong dream of earning a degree—it captivated me and I fell in love! This is more than a job to me."

WGU surveys both graduates and their employers to find out if they are lacking in any content areas or competencies so they can continue to fine-tune their programs. They certify teachers and nurses in all fifty states—they partner with schools and with hospitals so students can get hands-on experience. Their program worked for Tarra Patrick, who got her degree in education in January 2009. "I was always the kind of person who was bored in school because I would finish the work too quickly," she says. Patrick met her husband at the Army's language academy, where she graduated as a Chinese linguist; stationed overseas with her husband, she had taken a few university courses, and trained as a sign-language interpreter, but nothing stuck. On a sojourn back in the United States she got a position she loved as a long-term math substitute at her kids' school. "At the seven-week mark the principal pulled me in and said, 'you're the best teacher I've got in the building but you don't have any paper [certifications], so I can't have you teach.' I was absolutely devastated, in tears. I said, never again will someone tell me I can't have a job because I don't have the qualifications," she says. In her late thirties, "I knew that I didn't have another start-and-stop in me. It was coming close to my husband's retirement and if I was going to do it we needed to look for something a little bit different." Patrick completed her degree while stationed in the UK and raising her daughters. Within a month of graduating from WGU she found a new teaching position back in the states. "My experience at WGU has made me more aware of how many settings there are out there for people to be successful."

This open-mindedness is likely to spread as people get more familiar with what online institutions can do. I asked Abhijit Marathe, another WGU graduate, whether he'd be happy if his children followed in his footsteps and studied at an online, nonselective college like WGU. He surprised me. "To be frank, I would leave it to them, but I don't mind if they go and get the online degree, because ultimately what's important is getting the knowledge. How they get it, whether they go to a brick-and-mortar school, is immaterial."

Whether hybrid classes, social networks, tutoring programs, games, or open content, technology provides speed skates for students and teachers, not crutches. To save money and improve learning, educational technology has to be well-designed and carefully implemented. The roles of professors will shift, and new jobs will be created in place of the old. "Technology can't make a bad teacher into a good teacher," says Robbins, the Second Life fan. "Students who don't want to learn won't suddenly become great students when you put a gadget in their hands. Learning to teach with technology is less about 'how does it work' and much more about 'why should I use it.'"

The reasons are legion. Increasingly, this is going to be considered part of good teaching practice. Rather than dust off the same old mimeographed course packets year after year, professors these days have no excuse for not bellying up to the buffet of brand-new, free course materials and activities, or logging on to the wealth of wikis and portals to find and share best practices. Administrations and governments that profess to be interested in broadening access to affordable, quality education should be beating a path to the door of OLI, NCAT, and open-courseware discovery sites like CCLearn's OpenEd.

This is not to say that the shift to Web-enabled education has no tradeoffs. Psychology studies have shown in multiple contexts that human beings get all kinds of benefits in motivation, creativity, and productivity from being physically around other living, breathing humans. Sheer physical proximity is an important determiner of who becomes friends and forms romantic connections, whether among college students in a dorm or residents in a nursing home. Faculty members whose offices are no more than thirty yards apart are far more likely to coauthor a paper, even if they are in different disciplines. Computer programmers who were stuck together in a single "war room" to complete a project produced twice as much code as peers separated in individual offices. Stock and bond traders who work in a room together are more successful in trading than those who sit alone at their computers.[32] Over time, technology may get better at replicating the effects of proximity. There have been early studies investigating whether microblogging services like Twitter, immersive 3-D environments like Second Life, or real-time videoconferencing can provide people with some of the same benefits, like ambient social cues and motivation, that they get from actually being with collaborators in the workplace, or teachers and fellow students in the classroom.[33]

In the meantime, these experiments have to figure out a way to survive. The recent recession brought new urgency to the issue of how efforts like the OpenCourseWare Consortium and the Community College Consortium for Open Educational Resources can keep going long enough to be widely adopted. In September 2009, the Utah State University OpenCourseWare project became the first large open-content project to shut down because it ran out of money.[34]

Free content, it turns out, isn't exactly free: there are costs associated with producing materials for the Web, server and bandwidth expenses, not to mention the hands-on work of people like Baker. Open content promises to improve on traditional course materials while saving money at the same time, yet until they actually start to replace traditional materials, colleges won't realize significant savings. In an era of harsh budget cuts, individual institutions may find it difficult to justify investments that create "positive externalities," benefiting the community at large. (It's the opposite sort of market failure as with global warming, where the negative externalities of carbon emissions aren't paid for by polluters.)

The OER movement has to date been supported, to an astonishing extent, by one foundation: Hewlett, established by one of the founders of Hewlett-Packard. In the past ten years they made $78 million worth of open-courseware grants to projects at MIT, Rice, Carnegie Mellon, Stanford, Tufts, and Berkeley, and in Europe, Africa, and China.[35]

"The advent of the Web brings the ability to disseminate high-quality materials at almost no cost, leveling the playing field," says Cathy Casserly, who in her role at Hewlett shared in responsibility for making many of these grants. "We're changing the culture of how we think about knowledge and how it should be shared and who are the owners of knowledge. That was the vision of Bill Hewlett." The irony is, just as the higher-education community at large is starting to catch on to the possibilities inherent in online educational content, many of these grants are drying up. Casserly moved to the Carnegie Foundation for the Advancement of Teaching, where she helps OER projects calculate and define their value so that they will be supported, long-term, by institutions. "This is a movement but it's really just in its infant stages. . . . We need to figure out the models for this stuff. If it were easy it wouldn't be such a fun challenge."

MIT's open-courseware project has pointed one way ahead by documenting benefits for recruitment and improving the reputation of its faculty and programs. One professor's posted course, for example, sparked a collaboration with the Italian space program. Wiley suggests that open-educational initiatives should use open content as a teaser or loss leader to attract students toward online courses for credit—the "click to enroll" option.

Public support of open content could be crucial. Governor Schwarzenegger has called for digital textbooks to be adopted in schools across California.[36] Senator Dick Durbin, with the input of Wiley and others in the OER movement, has introduced The Open College Textbook Act of 2009,[37] a law that would mandate all educational materials, including curricula and textbooks, created through federal grants to be released under open license, and award special competitive grants specifically for the creation of open textbooks.

In the summer of 2009, the Obama administration announced $500 million in federal funds to create the "Online Skills Laboratory," inviting colleges, publishers, and other institutions to create free and open-source online courses, primarily at the community college level, with an emphasis on vocational topics.[38]

And Judy Baker's former boss at Foothill–De Anza Community College District, Martha Kanter, who spearheaded the Community College Consortium for Open Educational Resources, has been appointed as the federal undersecretary of education, the first person with a community college background to ascend to such a high post. She told me "using technology to bring down the cost of books" was a good example of the policies she would pursue to close America's college achievement gap: "Can we interest faculty across the country at all levels to use the new technologies in ways that will help increase the capacity of Americans to get into college and get through?"

Over its long history, and because of the weight of that history, higher education has been uncommonly resistant to innovation in teaching practices. It's clear we're just beginning to glimpse the full potential of what technology can do to transform education. From this position at the top of the first hill, it's not clear yet which innovations will become mainstays, the chalkboards, textbooks, and diplomas of the future, and which will be marginal applications or mere flashes in the pan. At this point, however, the hybrid, NCAT-style course-redesign models seem most compelling. Not only do they show some of the best learning results, but they're in keeping with the multifaceted history of the university, and they offer the reassurance of familiarity—a scaffolding, if you will, for the transition to new modes of teaching. In a more radical mode of reinvention, the WGU model of breaking up the functions of teaching, and focusing on assessments and competencies, also has the potential to be tremendously influential.

In the end, the goal is not to decide on the one best model. The ideal education is different for each individual, encompassing both scholastic and empirical knowledge, taking place over a lifetime in multiple modes, with time spent out in the field, working one-on-one with teachers and mentors, batting ideas back and forth with peers, and immersed in solo research and concentrated creative problem solving.

At the OpenEd conference in Vancouver in August 2009 I experienced hypercaffeinated, disaggregated, hybrid learning in real time. Hundreds of techies had traveled from New Zealand, South Africa,

Brazil, the Caribbean, the UK, and across the United States and Canada just to be in the same room with their Twitter followers and blogroll buddies. During each presentation, the presenter with slides up in front was speaking to the room, and people were raising their hands and asking questions—the centuries-old lecture model, with the slight update of PowerPoint. At the same time, a few hundred people around the world were following a live video stream, and they were contributing and commenting in a live stream via Twitter in an ongoing conversation with people in the room. Yes, this kind of multichannel chatter divides your attention, but the overall effect was a kind of dazzlingly enhanced cognitive reality.

At one point, I Twittered a compelling quote from the presentation I was watching on historical precursors to open education, by Norm Friesen, who holds the chair in e-learning practices at Thompson Rivers University in British Columbia.[39] The woman next to me saw my tweet pop up on her screen, looked over at me, and winked. The quote was from Paolo Freire, the Brazilian radical educator and author of *Pedagogy of the Oppressed*. In the 1960s he invested in slide projectors to teach reading to peasants using evocative pictures; later, in the 1990s, as the secretary of education for Sao Paulo, he established the Central Laboratory for Educational Informatics, and added televisions, tape recorders, and microcomputers to his arsenal for empowering the poor through knowledge.[40] The quote that struck me? "The answer does not lie in the rejection of the machine, but rather in the humanization of man."[41]

five

INDEPENDENT STUDY

Educational futurists fall into at least three guilds, to borrow the term from David Wiley's open online class. The ones in the last chapter—the artisans, let's say—write statistical reports and testify before Congress. They seek applications of technology within colleges to lower cost, increase access, and improve learning. Now for the monks and the merchants. The monks write blog posts packed with old movie clips and argue late into the night in pubs after conference sessions. They want to liberate knowledge and scholarship from the university altogether. Then there are the merchants, who wear ties and drink Coke Zero with venture capitalists. They see the need for change within the academy as an opportunity for profit.

The monk's world starts with a toaster.

Well, not quite a toaster. What Thomas Thwaites exhibited at London's Royal College of Art in the summer of 2009 was a couple of leafblowers, a suitcase full of chunks of iron ore, and a microwave, with which he had managed to smelt a piece of pure iron "about the size of a ten-pence coin." The Toaster Project was a solo attempt to fabricate, from raw natural materials, the same Chinese-made appliance that sells in British stores for £3.99 ($6.60).[1] Thwaites took his cue from sci-fi humorist Douglas Adams, who in his novel *Mostly Harmless* wrote of the average modern human, "Left to his own devices, he couldn't make a toaster."[2]

In his artist's statement, Thwaites wrote, "It's about scale, the total inter-reliance of people and societies, the triviality of some (anti) globalisation discourse, what we have to lose, and DIY." To translate: The chain of industrial processes, transportation miles, and person-hours that snakes behind even the simplest object is invisible even to the best-educated among us. Living within this invisible matrix is profoundly alienating. We ignore the cost to the environment and the fate of the people around the world who serve as cheap labor to make our cheap products. DIY is one possible response.

Not explicitly educational, the Toaster Project nevertheless illustrates two basic strategies important to DIY education. The first is to seek out the vividness of direct experience, to encounter the world, and, if possible, to make yourself useful. Henry David Thoreau argued for a Toaster Project approach to education. Students, he wrote,

> should not *play* life, or *study* it merely, while the community supports them at this expensive game, but earnestly *live* it from beginning to end.... Which would have advanced the most at the end of a month,—the boy who had made his own jackknife from the ore which he had dug and smelted, reading as much as would be necessary for this,—or the boy who had attended the lecture on metallurgy at the Institute in the mean while, and had received a ... penknife from his father? Which would be more likely to cut his fingers?[3]

The second strategy is to share information with a community. I found out about the Toaster Project on Google Reader, a free application. Every day when I'm surfing the Internet reading news and blogs, I can click a button and share what I'm reading on Reader, Facebook, or Twitter with several thousand of my friends and contacts, who also share their links with me. The Toaster Project is highly shareable; Thwaites put a lot of information online, including step-by-step videos. If I wanted to, I could probably draw on these resources and use my microwave to smelt iron too.

The monks contend that community- and practice-based learning can transcend the limitations of existing educational institutions. Jim Groom ("The great Reverend @jimgroom, Groom and Doom, Groom Fills The Room," as he was announced, via Twitter, at the 2009 Open Education conference in Vancouver) is a chain-smoker with glasses and an ever-present five-days' growth of beard. He has the discursive, occasionally irascible manner of a longtime graduate student. Groom's day job, as described in the last chapter, is educational technologist at the University of Mary Washington in Fredericksburg, Virginia. His secret identity is open-education blogodaemon and coiner of the term "edupunk."

"Edupunk is about the utter irresponsibility and lethargy of educational institutions, and the means by which they are financially cannibalizing their own mission," is the opening salvo of his first e-mail to me.

> Higher education has become a given for most high school students in our culture, and the fact that they have to pay out the nose has become a kind of unquestioned necessity to secure a job. But as we are increasingly seeing with big media, newspapers, and the like—traditional modes of information distribution are being circumvented, and higher education is just as vulnerable in this new landscape. . . . There remains a general refusal to acknowledge the implications of how easy it is to publish, share, teach, and even apprentice one another outside of the traditional logic of institutions.

What edupunk—DIY education, if you will—promises is an evolution from expensive institutions to expansive networks; it aims to fulfill the promise of universal education, but only by leaving the university behind. Educational futurist John Seely Brown talks about "open participatory learning ecosystems."[4] Alec Couros at the University of Sasketchewan calls my blend of news sources and contacts on Google Reader, Facebook, Twitter, blogs, and e-mail a "personal learning network."[5]

He draws a diagram that looks like a dandelion head. You, the learner, are at the center. The seeds are people, texts, courses, Web sites, blogs—any knowledge resource. George Siemens and Stephen Downes, who collaborated in offering the Massively Open Online Course, call their theory of learning in the digital age "connectivism."

Learning networks in previous decades were insular groups formed around academic journals, learned societies, and professional conferences. Today, galaxies of students, academics, professionals, and amateurs are using blogs, wikis, presentation tools like Slideshare, YouTube videos, and e-mail lists to collaborate, pursue, and present knowledge in any discipline. All are supported by, yet independent of, universities, other cultural and government institutions, and private companies, not to mention hours of volunteered time by enthusiasts. Just now I picked a topic out of thin air—Tuvan throat singing. In hardly more time than it takes me to type the words, I find YouTube videos, personal blogs, ethnomusicology papers on Google Scholar. A few more keystrokes and I've opened up a dialogue by sending an e-mail to Ted Levin at Dartmouth, who, I find, the *Washington Post* called the world's foremost expert on the subject.[6] In my e-mail, I ask him how often he responds to queries that he receives out of the blue. Just hours later I got an incredibly generous response in which Levin said, in part,

> Yes, a lot of people e-mail me with questions about Tuvan throat singing, and yes, I respond to each and every inquiry. But I don't respond equally. The depth of the response is commensurate with the thoughtfulness of the inquiry. . . . Since I'm committed to this kind of knowledge transmission, I believe it's my duty to share what I know with any serious seeker or researcher who comes along, whatever the portal by which he or she reaches me.[7]

Ideas travel faster over informal, digitally connected networks than when they are siloed inside academic departments. Such networks are especially useful in emerging, cross-disciplinary frontiers of research, where there are no established departments. In fact, the open-education movement is itself a primary example of this kind of learning network.

"Given the abundance of information and given the connective and social opportunities around technology, perhaps the teacher's role is one of multiple nodes amid an overall network," says Siemens. "The world has become more and more complex. As a student you need to create your own learning network that will allow you to make sense of the abundance of information. It's a process of wayfinding, social sensemaking." Like Hansel and Gretel leaving trails of crumbs through the woods, or like bees doing waggle dances to point one another to the nectar, "Students need to be able to connect, provide continual feedback to each other, and form sensemaking social systems."

To understand where the edupunks are really coming from, you have to go back to a radical Austrian priest in 1960s Latin America. Ivan Illich was a polyglot who taught reading and writing to Mexican peasants by centering the lessons on vital political ideas. In the 1971 book *Deschooling Society*, he focused on the problems of education's endlessly rising costs and the constant disappointment of the hope that it would promote democracy and self-determination. Compulsory schools, he said, with the power of the state behind them, alienate students from their own curiosity and ability by "teaching the need to be taught." Illich saw firsthand how schools made self-reliant rural people into "backward" illiterates, unable to participate fully in society without depending on state-funded instruction.

Today, developing countries from Senegal to Bangladesh have the same college enrollment rates that the rich world had a few generations back. There is an international arms race to funnel the majority of the population through at least thirteen years of schooling. Recall Meyer's critique of university education as a "cargo cult," with whole nations uncritically celebrating the idea that more is always better. The standard reformist responses to the demand for more higher education, presented throughout this book, involve expanding the reach of traditional educational institutions, whether by providing ever more money and resources, or more radically by improving productivity and efficiency through new technologies— but always with administrators, in collaboration with governments, defining learning objectives authoritatively for students.

Illich rejected all of this. "Our options are clear enough," he wrote. "Either we continue to believe that institutionalized learning is a product which justifies unlimited investment, or we rediscover that legislation and planning and investment, if they have any place in formal education, should be used mostly to tear down the barriers that impede opportunities for learning, which can only be a personal activity."[8]

"Deschooling," in his world, means replacing formal schools with a technologically enabled, largely self-directed, free, and open exchange of information. "We need research," he wrote, "on the possible use of technology to create institutions which serve personal, creative, and autonomous interaction and the emergence of values which cannot be substantially controlled by technocrats."[9]

People, he argues, should be trusted to decide what, when, and how they want to learn. The government or Thorstein Veblen's "technocrats" shouldn't decide for them.

The scheme Illich suggests to accomplish this, in chapter 6 of *Deschooling Society*, is a remarkably prescient description of a proto-Internet. He wants governments to support the exchange of cassette tapes and library books, in the mail, by subscription. He pictures learners placing classified ads in the newspaper to find study partners for languages, or to discuss a particular book. "The operation of a peer-matching network would be simple. The user would identify himself by name and address and describe the activity for which he sought a peer. A computer would send him back the names and addresses of all those who had inserted the same description."[10]

Illich's strongest point is this: It's a mistake to identify social welfare fully with the institutions that are meant to provide it. Institutions seek to grow and pursue their own ends, which are not identical with the ends of those they are intended to serve. More prisons doesn't mean more justice, and more schools doesn't mean more wisdom.

The university may be too identified with rationality and modernity, progress and justice, to spontaneously wither away. Nor, on most days, would we wish it to. However, maybe a form of genetic engineering is possible. The Internet-enabled "personal learning network" could be the prototype of a lightweight institution that is more open and available to more people, that doesn't take up more than its share of resources, especially money, and that interferes as little as possible with individual freedom.

Whether or not you buy the strong version of Illich's argument, it's hard to deny that the Internet changes the possibilities for how each of us can learn. In April 2009, a twenty-eight-year-old British naval engineer delivered his son at home using YouTube videos as an ad hoc birth coach. He got the idea because he had already used YouTube to learn to play guitar and solve a Rubik's Cube.[11] Alec Couros showed me a YouTube video of a nine-year-old boy trying to start a fire by whirling one piece of wood against another, a contraption called a bowdrill. He or his parent tagged the video "help with bowdrill," reaching out to the network for coaching. Sure enough, people offer suggestions in the comment section—"your spindle is too long," "apply more pressure," and so on. Thoreau would be proud.[12]

Is this kind of traipsing and trolling around really learning? Is it valuable? Can it change the course of people's lives the way we expect a university degree to do? Edupunks argue yes. In recent years, digital philosophers have become fascinated by the potential of a humanized use of technology to liberate people from all kinds of bureaucratic institutions that have defined modern life for more than a century. Books like David Weinberger's *Everything is Miscellaneous*, Yochai Benkler's *The Wealth of Networks,* and Clay Shirky's *Here Comes Everybody: The Power of Organizing without Organizations* suggest that the unique architecture of the Internet allows us to navigate ideas and accomplish tasks collectively without the restrictions of disciplines or hierarchies.

Much as Illich looked to the wisdom of rural communities in Puerto Rico and Cuernavaca, Mexico, the edupunks today draw on anthropology for alternatives to formal schooling. "Most people acquire most of their knowledge outside school," wrote Illich. In 1991, Jean Lave and Etienne Wenger published a classic study called *Situated Learning,* describing the kind of learning that takes place outside schools.[13] They studied midwives in the Yucatán, tailors in West Africa, and even urban addicts in recovery, and showed how each of these groups allows people to come in, watch, find mentors, and learn by doing. Wenger and Lave coined the term "communities of practice" to describe these groups.[14] Such communities are defined by shared engagement in a task, and shared understanding of goals and means to reach them. In the classic progression of a community of practice, an apprentice presents herself to the community and takes on simple beginning tasks at the elbow of an expert. Everyone is participating in real-world tasks, not academic exercises, so the learners' actions have consequences right away. This stage is known as "legitimate peripheral participation." As she progresses, she continuously reinforces her learning by teaching others as well. In a community of practice, it is understood that you are just as likely to learn from the mistakes of fellow beginners, or from people with just slightly more experience, as from wizened elders. Virtual communities of practice are thriving on the Internet, among bloggers, gamers, designers, and programmers. These groups have little choice but to teach each other—information technology has been changing so fast for the past few decades that traditional schools and curricula can't keep up.

There are many new attempts to consciously foster independent learning communities or communities of practice around free and open resources, in effect recreating the university in its embryonic medieval form. In the spring of 2009 I went to an edupunk panel featuring Groom, Campbell, and others at South By Southwest Interactive, the geeky brother of the Austin music and film conference. I was electrified when a long-haired, gap-toothed Englishman stood up and announced he had founded an online exchange "based on chapter 6 of *Deschooling Society*."

"I discovered Illich by chance through my own reading," Dougald Hine told me later, over Skype, "and become really enthusiastic about how you could organize a bunch of areas of services the government traditionally supplies to give people more control over them." The Internet, he says, shows us how.

> There was just something in the air that it was possible to put these ideas in practice in a new way, because people had the Internet and were using it to organize important parts of their lives. A lot of institutions and professional hierarchies, for all their good intentions, have a self-perpetuating dynamic which isn't particularly to do with the interests of those they are serving, whether client or patient or student. There isn't necessarily a reason for having these institutions, and technology makes that more obvious.

Hine is a founder of The School of Everything, a grandly named site functioning more or less like Illich's classifieds exchange. Learners can find teachers, paid or unpaid, or study partners on any topic they want. In the average week, about three hundred people make a connection. A lot of them are on typical hobbyist subjects: music, yoga, foreign languages. There are also university professors whose intense enthusiasm for their subjects is not shared by their bleary-eyed 8:00 a.m. lecture attendees, so they sign up to chat about philosophy or physics with people who want learning for its own sake. Similar, but commercial, sites in the United States are Teachstreet and Edufire; the latter provides a platform for real-time online video tutoring. And there's also the "classes" section of Craigslist in hundreds of cities.

The School of Everything conjures less a university department than a community bulletin board in an off-campus coffee shop, and that's by design. Hine argues that seemingly marginal or trivial areas of study—beekeeping or Malayalam or even the proverbial basketweaving—could emerge as vital under changing environmental and political circumstances. "There's a biodiversity of skills and learning which can be threatened by a focus on the priorities of today's employment market, as judged by government and educational institutions," he says. "The things that survive as hobbies may turn out to be important in ten or twenty years' time." For example, the Transition Town movement prepares communities for a post-fossil-fuel world by developing local economies and coming together to learn skills like composting, conflict resolution, and bicycle repair. They are using the School of Everything as one channel for their ideas. In the end, says Hine, the community of learners is even more important than what's studied. "Illich also saw that technology in itself was not necessarily a positive thing," he says. "It was only to the extent that it enabled people to have more convivial relationships, better ways of relating to each other, that it was beneficial."

Neeru Paharia is trying out a different combination of open educational resources with Internet communities to arrive at both free and open higher education. Paharia, the daughter of two Indian-born Silicon Valley engineers, brims over with infectious enthusiasm for a smorgasbord of creative projects. In 2002, she was a McKinsey consultant working on an animated philosophical film in her spare time, but she didn't know how to get the rights to any background music. She found her way to Creative Commons and became one of its first three employees, which seeded her interest in open education. So she started AcaWiki, a crowd-sourced compilation of summaries of academic papers that would be available for free, while the papers themselves are still behind a paywall.[15] In 2005, she moved on to a PhD program in behavioral economics at Harvard Business School. She would see the ads for colleges on the Boston T and wondered about a way to use social networking technologies to make open-educational content more accessible and affordable.

At a conference in Croatia in 2008, Paharia met Jan Philipp Schmidt, a German computer scientist running an open-courseware project at a university in Capetown, South Africa. Together with a Canadian and an Australian, they started the Peer2Peer University, an online social network for learners, with a grant from the Hewlett Foundation. "Open courseware is hard for the self-learner," she says. "We're thinking about all the other things that a university does for you: it provides you a clear path from A to B, a social infrastructure of teachers and other students, and accreditation so you actually get credit for what you do. So the question becomes: is there a way of hacking something like this together?" In the spring of 2009 Peer2Peer U launched its first ten pilot courses, on offbeat topics like creative-nonfiction writing, behavioral economics, data visualization, and open education itself. The idea was to test the waters in areas that had already attracted communities of self-motivated learners online. Would-be students can use the site to convene and schedule classes, meet online, and tutor each other; a volunteer facilitator will move each course along. Accreditation for the courses, however, remains elusive.

The University of the People is another use of open-educational resources, one that's been officially recognized by the United Nations. Shai Reshef, an Israeli entrepreneur with a shaved pate and calm blue eyes, decided to commit his fortune—made when he sold a for-profit educational-services firm to Kaplan in 2005—to opening an online-only, open-source university. The nonprofit, which also has yet to receive accreditation, is offering bachelor's degrees in business and computer science using open texts. In the fall of 2009 it enrolled its first class of 300 students from 100 countries. Students discuss the material in online forums with other students from all over the world and with volunteer faculty—those who have signed up to teach so far are professors, retirees, graduate students, and professionals in their fields. Reshef has seeded the organization with $1 million of his own money. He calculates that the school can become self-sustaining at a scale of 15,000 students. They charge minimal fees on a sliding scale, based on the student's country of origin, from $15 to $100 per credit—adding up to $4,000, maximum, for a full four-year degree program. "There are hundreds of millions of people around the world unable to afford higher education," he says. "We are offering them an alternative."

DIY academia doesn't have to partake of advanced technology. The edupunk spirit is alive wherever people create alternatives to higher education's cartel. Julia Fierro is a soft-voiced brunet, the daughter of an Italian immigrant. She graduated from the prestigious Iowa Writer's Workshop in 2000 and found herself teaching an honors creative writing class at Hofstra University, the private university on Long Island mentioned in chapter 3. "I was working the equivalent of full time and getting paid $10,000," Fierro says. One day, she mentioned in class that she wasn't a fan of James Joyce's *Ulysses*. "I was trying to open up their perspective and say there's more than just the literary canon. This one girl in class went and told the James Joyce scholar that I told her not to read James Joyce, and I got called into the chair's office." Fierro had neither a living wage, nor academic freedom, nor the ability to concentrate on what was most important to her, which was sharing her love of craft with other writers. But this is where her story departs from that of thousands of adjuncts around the country. Fierro went home and put an ad on Craigslist for a writers' workshop: $175 per person for eight weeks of meeting around her kitchen table. Since 2002, the Sackett Street Writers' Workshop has had over 850 students. Fierro estimates about half are older working professionals who see creative writing as an avocation, while the other half are younger and want to pursue it as a life path. For the latter, she created a class that helps people prepare applications for MFA programs; she also does private one-on-one manuscript reviews. Alumni of her program have found agents, published novels, nonfiction books, and short story collections, won awards and competitions. Taking an eight-week workshop costs about a tenth as much as the cheapest MFA program. Fierro is Sackett Street's only full-time employee; she nets about $40,000 to $50,000 a year, both teaching and running the program. She has eight other faculty, who also teach out of their homes, and earn as much or more from teaching a Sackett Street workshop as they would as adjuncts at a New York City university. The operation has almost no overhead: a few hundred dollars a year for web hosting and online ads. Workshop leaders are responsible for supplying tea and cookies. "My whole life I've just been like, 'Oh shit! How can I get paid to talk about books?'" Fierro says, and now she's found a way.

The experiential communities-of-practice model can reach nontraditional academic populations in a way that's also very edupunk. Dennis Littky is a psychologist who's worked in experimental education for over forty years. He runs fifty Big Picture charter high schools around the country with support from the Gates Foundation. They enroll low-income and minority students and graduate them at rates that are several times higher than surrounding high schools—"We do 95 percent in Detroit!" he marvels. Michael Tucker, of *LA Law* fame, played him in a 1991 TV movie about his firing and reinstatement from a New Hampshire high school because of his unorthodox practices.

"Over the last five years I started being kind of pissed off at colleges' inability to really educate these first-generation kids," Littky says, referring to those who are first in their families to go to college. "Something like 11 percent graduate. The hilarity is, when kids drop out of high school people blame the high school. When they drop out of college they blame the high school or the kid. What about the college? Do you take any responsibility?" He often found himself cosigning student loans for students who were navigating the system without the support networks middle-class kids enjoy. Their academic careers fell apart at the slightest bureaucratic snag. In the fall of 2009, Littky decided to try something completely different. He took eight of his graduates, low-income kids of color from around the country, moved them into a townhouse in Providence, Rhode Island, and created College Unbound.

College Unbound is designed as a three-year experiential learning community centered on an internship tailored as much as possible to each student's passion. In three years, the students will earn a bachelor's degree certified by nearby Roger Williams College. "I believe in engagement: life to text rather than text to life," says Littky. "It's not just about being online or offline, it's about finding the connection." Alex Villagomez grew up in Sacramento and graduated from one of Littsky's Big Picture schools, as did his older brother. A lack of money kept them both off the full-time college track. Villagomez was taking community college classes part-time and working at his old high school when he heard about College Unbound. Today Villagomez, nineteen, is the first in his family to go to college. Except he's not really going to college. His days are spent interning at a green architecture firm, his nights learning sign language, ballroom dancing, or discussing world issues with his seven roommates, and Saturday morning taking a graduate-level seminar. Monday and Friday mornings the eight College Unbound students meet in an intensive seminar that crunches three general-ed requirements at a time into one, with lots of writing. "Most of the world sees intelligence as students memorizing facts that don't necessarily add practical application to their lives and regurgitating them later in life," Villagomez says. "I believe intelligence is something much greater than that. It has a lot more to do with adaptability to an environment."

Littky puts a lot of faith in his students, and a lot of other resources as well—buying their work wardrobes, for example. Still, he's confident that this approach can scale, and crack the code for providing high-quality higher education to populations that have been resistant to other approaches. The cost doesn't have to be outrageous. Small class sizes are offset by decreased class time and the shortened time to degree. The keys are the involvement of employers in the outside community as mentors, and the community of students supporting each other. The University of Cincinnati has piloted a program called the Gen-1 Theme House with the idea that a structured first year in a learning community can help first-generation students succeed.[16]

Like Public Allies in chapter 3, College Unbound is workplace centered, but the small size of the learning community and the seminars put an emphasis on liberal arts values, not to mention providing the still-powerful imprimatur of the bachelor's degree. "My dream is to have thirty College Unbounds at various colleges—a school within each school," Littky says. "The president of Southern New Hampshire University," the college with the two-year Advantage Program and other innovations, "calls me and says, 'we're losing our freshmen, first-generation students. If I can have two of your College Unbounds here on my campus, if that catches on, maybe it can influence the whole college.'" Villagomez believes that something like College Unbound could work for a lot of the kids from his neighborhood back home. "Dropout rates happen because students see school at this pointless thing, because they don't understand the practical application, because it's not taught ... [We're] actively pursuing what we want to do and learning because we enjoy it."

The edupunks reassure me that pure learning and research, in the best humanistic tradition, can flourish outside traditional institutions and be more available to more people in more places. At the same time, whatever their antiestablishment rhetoric, the edupunks still have academic pedigrees, and for the most part, the academy signs their paychecks. Jim Groom has a PhD from the City University of New York in early American literature. Terri Bays, director of the 200-member Open Courseware Consortium, is a medievalist at Notre Dame. Brian Lamb, who organized the Open Education conference in Vancouver in August 2009, has an MA in English and teaches at the University of British Columbia. Stephen Downes, who publishes the online newsletter Online Learning Daily and taught the "Massively Open Online Course" through the University of Manitoba, has an MA in philosophy.

The future of higher education is happening on two sides of a coin. One face—the monks' world—is free and open education. Free is an attractive ideal, but free and sustainable is an elusive combination. These efforts are ultimately still dependent on the kindness of philanthropists, volunteers, and legislators. The other face—the merchants' vision—is the expansion of education as a privatized commodity provided by for-profit companies. Some open-educational innovators, like Wiley with Flat World Knowledge, are turning to the private sector to sustain innovations. Meanwhile, in investor circles from New York to Silicon Valley, the idea of education as a rich field ripe for disruption is gaining more currency than it's ever had.

In March 2009, Union Square Ventures, a New York City venture-capital firm that was an early investor in Twitter, held a daylong gathering called "Hacking Education." It became a top-trending topic on Twitter for the day, with thousands following Internet intellectuals like Jeff Jarvis, Danah Boyd, and Steven Johnson musing about the future of education and the role of technology. "One of the things the Internet is doing is siphoning power away from existing institutions," Union Square Ventures partner Albert Wenger told me later.

And so, I was thinking, what are areas of society that have ingrained institutions whose basis of existence was an old way of disseminating information? And obviously education is a primary example of that. . . . So, we call this "hacking education" because we tend to believe that this kind of dramatic, radical innovation comes from the outside. It comes from people who are not going to try and make things work inside the existing system, they're going to create a hack that completely bypasses the existing system.

Wenger's firm is looking for investments in technology companies that target learners directly.

At the end of May 2009 Berkery Noyes, a Silicon Valley venture-capital firm, held what was billed as the first-ever Venture Capital in Education summit. The Schwab Center at Stanford, a new complex of stucco buildings with barnlike exposed rafters, held about 200 people, representatives from VC firms like Sequoia Capital, companies like Google, NGOs like the Bill & Melinda Gates and George Lucas foundations, and a host of start-ups. The mood, in the depths of the recession, was a little bit like a party with too many boys; investors were described as "voracious" while startups played coy. VC and private-equity firms knew they were looking at a huge opportunity but they didn't know quite how to reach it. The economics of education, bound as it is by state legislatures and federal regulations, can be walled off to newcomers. Bill Hughes, the director of business development for Pearson, not only the largest textbook publisher but the largest English-language publisher, period, summed up the moment this way: "We have a strange paradox of an industry that hasn't really changed before, now erupting with all kinds of change. If we look at education as part of the world and the U.S. economy it ranks second only behind health care, yet we haven't had any real changes and not loads of investment." Peter Campbell of private-equity firm Generation Partners said, "A theme you hear from the president is that in the next twelve years we have to retake our primacy as the most educated nation on earth. As an investor, that's the kind of trend you want to align yourself with. . . . Yet technology has not arrived in education as it has in other sectors. Making things better, faster, cheaper? We're in the early days on that."

Knewton was one name people at the Stanford conference kept mentioning. Jose Ferreira, the founder/CEO, is a restless mind with a background in banking and Democratic politics. He worked with test-prep giant Kaplan and was famously dubbed "the Antichrist" by the guys who make the SATs after the tricks he ferreted out forced them to rewrite entire sections of the test. "The Internet disrupts any industry whose core product can be reduced to ones and zeros," he told me—news, music, movies. "It is blindingly obvious to me that it will happen with education. But here's the thing—education as an industry is bigger than all these other industries combined. It is the biggest virgin forest out there. As excited as people get about Google and search, or Microsoft and software, those industries are a fraction of the size of education."

Knewton's programmers are building what Ferreira calls an "adaptive learning engine." Not unlike the Open Learning Initiative programs, it is supposed to break down any bit of educational content—text, graphs, video, audio—tag it, and relate it to every-thing else in the system. The platform serves up constant quizzes to assess how a learner is doing, and keeps track of whether he got a particular concept more quickly using video, a comic strip, a short verbal description, or some combination of the above. "You get the exact content that's perfect for you every single day by concept. And the system learns—self-optimizing with incredible speed." Knewton is starting with test prep, the area Ferreira knows best, but eventu-ally he wants to offer his platform for use to power any kind of educational content, universities to elementary, proprietary or open-source. The more material and the more learners using the system, the more it can learn about how people learn.

Whether or not Ferreira has the perfect approach, he's far from alone in seeing the opportunity. There are educational tech start-ups that focus on test prep (Grockit, Knewton, Smart.fm), "learn-ing management systems" (Blackboard and Moodle are the giants here; 2tor, which built the system used by USC's Rossier School of Education described in chapter 4, is an intriguing alternative), flash-card-type memorization (Smart.fm, Quizlet), and course content. As a twenty-three-year-old Yale graduate, Richard Ludlow raised $6 million in venture capital for Academic Earth, a for-profit Web site that is trying to be the Hulu of video lectures. "My idea was to first, aggregate this huge critical mass of content disconnected over various sites; second, apply best practices in user-interface design and Web standards to do what Hulu has done [but] for educational content, and the third step—building an educational ecosystem around the content. Just showing the videos is one thing, but building the right interactive tools and the right commenting system will really create something of value." The Hulu comparison is a striking one. Among the cultural industries that have fallen under the spell of the Internet, the transformation has happened unevenly: newspapers before television, music before books. Hulu.com, just a few months after its launch in the spring of 2008, was widely considered to be the first Web site to really prove the concept that mass-broadcast television viewing can and will shift online. It did that by being attractive, well-designed, and easy to use, and by having a viable ad-based model. "We're talking about revenue sharing with a lot of universities," says Ludlow. "Most of this content is licensed noncommercial, but grant money to this movement is running out. With endowments dropping universities have to be selective about what they're funding. We're trying to find a way to make this sustainable by generating revenue and making sure it's in sync with the university's brand."

Some edupreneurs come from traditional universities but are pushed out by the drive of invention. That's the case with Dr. Stacey Simmons, who works in the center for computation and technology at Louisiana State University. Her start-up, Omnicademy, is a patent-pending method for professors to syndicate their courses to other colleges live over the Web, using a combination of video lectures and a social network environment. This could be a way for students to do as Wiley suggested—take a physics course at MIT and a robotics course at Carnegie Mellon, and have it all certified as transfer credits within their home university. Omniacademy started beta-testing in the spring of 2010. "I proposed this as a business plan: a start-up that would come out of LSU," she says. "The intellectual property office at LSU said, 'This is a little big for us—why don't you just go ahead?' So that's what I've been doing the last two years, writing the software, and I mortgaged my house to do it. Of course, now that we're almost ready, LSU is very interested!"

Startups like 2tor, Omniacademy, and Academic Earth depend,

more or less, on the established university system for their profit models. They are dwarfed by the growth of for-profit universities, which offer students a direct alternative to existing colleges—albeit one that itself ultimately relies on federal tuition subsidies. In chapter 3, I discussed the for-profits from a financial point of view, but it's also worth taking a look at what they mean for educational innovation and even for open education.

For-profit colleges have led the way in innovations like self-paced, all-online programs, assessment-based learning, and student-focused customer service. They have the advantage of focusing exclusively on learning. They are free from the slightest hint of snobbery. John Holt, in his radical 1976 critique *Instead of Education*, speaks approvingly of the Berlitz language school, which judges itself by how well it serves everyone who wants to study, not by how much it discriminates in choosing students. He calls schools like these "schools for do-ers, which help people explore the world as they choose."[17]

Dave Clinefelter, the provost of Kaplan University, would agree. Kaplan U has grown out of the test-prep company in just seven years to enroll 68,000 students in associate's, bachelor's and master's degree programs on seventy campuses and online. "Traditional universities look at yardsticks like how many students you denied entry to, what your peers think of you, and where your faculty published," he says. "We don't care about any of that. We care what our students learn and whether they get a job in their field. We want to be the best university in the world and we want to be able to prove it to people."

Michael Clifford never went to college. The son of a legendary Jewish bandleader who played with Tony Bennett at the Fairmont Hotel, he was a trumpet player "strung out on sex, drugs, and rock and roll," when he met Bill Bright, founder of Campus Crusade for Christ, and started a new life as a born-again Christian and successful tech investor. Thirteen years ago, Bright, then dying of cancer, gave him a life-changing piece of advice. "He knew I loved business and did a lot of charity work; he told me education is the one business where you can help people live better lives and make a lot of money for your investors." Today, Clifford chairs Significant Federation, a private-equity firm that is a principal investor in a half dozen higher-education companies, including the most successful IPO in 2008 (Grand Canyon University) and one of the most successful in 2009

(Bridgepoint Education). The colleges have almost 100,000 students, 90 percent online, and he has close to $100 million in capital.

Clifford's strategy is to take over the accreditation of a struggling bricks-and-mortar institution—in some cases just days away from running out of cash. "We're a SWAT team," he says. "We love fixing schools." Full-time, PhD professors and seasoned administrators run the home campus as a "learning lab," developing and testing curricula and texts for the much larger online programs. The college maintains all the identity trappings of a traditional university—sports, dance line, pep band, community service, and in Grand Canyon's case, a Christian mission. Clifford, whose personal charitable efforts include a soup kitchen and housing for 600 ex-gang members in LA, says that Grand Canyon online students who have never set foot on a campus like to log onto the Web site and check on the standings of a basketball team, or watch the live stream of Sunday chapel—just like the "subway alumni" who listened in to Notre Dame's football team on the radio in the 1920s. "What I'm proposing is that we are not only the future, but where I think the thing is going personally, we're going to see more public-private partnerships," he says. "I don't even use the term for-profit anymore. I say schools are market-driven or publicly funded. Everyone has to put his guns away and focus on providing the best experience for the student. Market-driven colleges can learn a lot from traditionals, and traditionals have a tremendous amount to learn from market-driven best practices." Market-driven, technically, only goes so far as a classification, since these schools are still dependent on federal student aid for the largest proportion of their revenues. However, people who have worked on both sides of the line tell me that for-profit colleges—operating under pressure to meet independent accreditation standards, federal and state regulatory burdens, pay taxes, satisfy the customer, and turn a profit too—of necessity pay far more attention to both outcomes and cost than your average nonprofit serving a similar population of students.

The prospect of a landscape dominated by explicitly market-driven universities and edupreneurs can seem distasteful—a travesty of the dream of free and open education, encroaching ever further on the ideal of education as a public good. I've had this reaction myself. Quite aside from its past ethical and financial lapses, the for-profit model, for the most part, doesn't support original research in disciplines that have no immediate commercial payoff. A for-profit Stanford is hard to imagine.

Still, it's worth remembering that businesslike thinking is both a necessary and venerable part of the educational ecosystem. Even monks have to eat. If they choose to live by the begging bowl, then the community has to figure out whether and how to support them. Everyone who understands the threat to the university as it currently exists is struggling to come up with new economic models to support teaching and research, whether through taxes, philanthropy, tuition, or most likely, some combination of these.

The architects of Education 2.0 have high hopes for the strength of openness, which sometimes shade into technological determinism. Yes, technology has managed to disrupt every other knowledge industry: newspapers, record companies, and publishers. But the old models for industries have often been wrecked before new ones can take their place, and the disruption itself creates winners and losers.

Will tools like open courseware and social networking actually equal free education? Both free as in speech and free as in beer, as the old open-source adage goes? And will these new changes doom universities to "irrelevance," as Wiley has written?

I tend to believe that there is no free lunch. Still, technology can create real efficiencies. And, crucially, new distribution methods can allow the cost of educational content and teaching to be distributed more equitably by students' ability to pay, from free to thousands of dollars. Today, Linear Algebra at MIT is available live, in person, and for credit to a few hundred enrolled students per semester who pay a base price of $50,000 a year. Through OpenCourseWare, hundreds of millions of people can experience the course recorded, not for credit, for free. A setup like Stacey Simmons' Omniacademy could allow for a middle option: a video version of the course supplemented with a set number of hours of live teaching support, either delivered remotely by an MIT grad student, or live and in person from a local instructor, for a charge somewhere between zero and several thousand dollars, with credit awarded by your local institution. The existence of such an option—call it MIT on Demand—might even enhance the MIT brand, as OpenCourseWare already has.

A company called Straighterline already offers an important

version of this idea: accredited online college courses for $399 per course, which includes ten hours of one-on-one tutoring. But the course credit is granted by just four small, unknown, community and for-profit colleges. This approach is half a step away from really blowing things up. It would just take a few more prestigious institutions getting on board to change the way people feel about online, on-demand education.

I'm still electrified by that quote from Freire—it's not the tools that are the most exciting thing about the transformation of higher education, it's "the humanization of man," especially the prospect of putting human beings in charge of their own learning. To the edupunks, the transformation of education through the use of the "read-write Web" is as much a cultural revolution as it is a technical improvement in knowledge delivery. David Wiley, a practicing member of the Church of Latter Day Saints, compares this period to the Reformation, when the advent of the printing press put the Lord's word into the hands of the people without the mediation of the church—a fascinating allusion given Meyer's idea of the university as the cathedral of rationality.

Gardner Campbell, an open-education figure who was responsible for hiring Jim Groom at the University of Mary Washington and currently teaches at Baylor University, does Wiley one better. He's argued in presentations that on the scale of disruptive technologies, the Internet is more than the printing press, it's the alphabet. "It's a new way of thinking. It's a meta-tool."

— six —

COMMENCEMENT

I have visited the university of the future.

Its classroom is a van bumping over dirt roads in Baja California, Mexico. The curriculum includes technology, economic and social development, anthropology, sociology, pedagogical techniques, and leadership and teamwork skills. Noah, a nineteen-year-old Princeton sophomore, is on his laptop in the front seat doing some last-minute debugging of an interactive storytelling software program—giving a new meaning to "mobile development," he joked—while Ricardo, a master's student at Stanford, is translating the program's directions into Spanish.

We spend the next two days meeting with indigenous Mixtec and Zapotec children at migrant farm workers' camps with haphazard access to doctors and schools. I watch kids as young as six pick up palmtop devices and tiny netbook computers made in China and programmed in India and Argentina, and within a few minutes, helping each other, with almost no directions, they're playing games that teach math skills, and writing and illustrating their own original stories.

Paul Kim, the chief technology officer of Stanford University's School of Education, has user-tested this "Pocket School" idea in Rwanda, Uganda, Kenya, and India over the past three years. His passion is to connect people around the world, from all backgrounds and circumstances, and empower them to teach themselves using appropriate technology that is designed and redesigned by an informal network of students and volunteers to be responsive to their needs. "Why does education need to be so structured? What are we so afraid of?" he asks, his penetrating questions always softened with a warm smile. "The more you expect from a kid, the smarter they're going to get."

Over the course of a few days, I witness him applying this approach not only to the children in the campos but to the students in the van. Noah, a self-taught programmer who plans to major in politics, is learning on an as-needed basis, with immediate feedback from his users (the children) and collaborating with students from other institutions. His "personal learning network" includes the world at large—when he has a question about a finer point of Flash or ActionScript 3, he simply Googles the key words, he says, "to see how someone else solved it before me." The BA he earns at Princeton will be valuable, but equally important to the course of his life will be the experiences he takes with him, not to mention the portfolio of socially engaged educational software programs and games he is creating.

Everyone explores, virtually and actually. Everyone contributes something unique. Everyone learns. This is the essence of the DIY U idea. It takes us back to the basics—the universitas (guild) and the collegium (community). People everywhere will have a greater ability to create their own learning communities and experiences within and outside institutions. This is happening now and will inevitably happen even more in the future. But how transformative will it be? Can the growth of these technologies and practices truly address the major challenges of cost, quality, and access? And if so, which of them are most valuable and most worth celebrating, supporting, and expanding?

Here's what I know for sure:

1. The promise of free or marginal-cost open-source content, techno-hybridization, unbundling of educational functions, and learner-centered educational experiences and paths is too powerful to ignore. These changes are inevitable. They are happening now. Innovative private colleges like Southern New Hampshire and for-profits like Grand Canyon, upstarts like BYU–Idaho and Western Governor's University, and community colleges like Foothill-De Anza represent the future.

2. However, these changes will not automatically become pervasive. Many existing institutions, especially those with the greatest reserves of wealth and reputation, will manage to remain outwardly, physically the same for decades, and to charge ever-higher tuition, even as enrollment shifts more and more toward the for-profits and community colleges and other places that adopt these changes.

3. In order to short-circuit the cost spiral, and provide access to appropriate education and training for people of all backgrounds, there is much hard work to be done in the way schools are funded and accreditation and transfer policies are set. College leaders need to have the will to change, as Chancellor Kirwan did at the University of Maryland, recognizing the central importance of efficiencies and changing the relationship between universities and their funders. Political leaders need to legislate change, as Senator Dick Durbin is by calling for open textbooks, and Bob Shireman by proposing to link funding for student loans to a college's proportion of Pell-eligible students. Above all, learners and their families need to recognize that alternatives to the status quo exist and demand change.

4. The one thing that can change dramatically and relatively swiftly is the public perception of where the true value and quality of higher education lies. It's no longer about the automatic four-year degree for all. Institutions can't rely any more on history, reputation, exclusivity, and cost; we now have the ability to peer inside the classroom as professors are lecturing and see students' assignments published to the world. So we have both the ability and the obligation to look at demonstrated results.

Both learners and providers need to get comfortable with identifying meaningful objectives—and meeting them. For individuals, the true value of education has to be intrinsic, not extrinsic. It can't be just about gaming the system, gaining the imprimatur of some exclusive external organization. The point of those one year, two years, four years, or ten years after high school is to help you figure out what you want to do, and to give you the ideas, skills, and connections you need both to do it, and to prove that you can do it. Period. For institutions, likewise, being allergic to talk of productivity and efficiency won't do anymore. Parents and families are going to vote with their dollars, and better options are only a click away.

The Reformation didn't destroy the Catholic Church, and the DIY educational revolution won't eradicate verdant hillside colonial colleges, nor strip-mall trade schools. DIY U examples will multiply, though. Most likely, in bits and pieces, fits and starts, traditional universities and colleges will be influenced by them to be more open and democratic, to better serve their communities and students. Along the way, we'll encounter rough spots, growing pains, unintended and unforeseen consequences—but the alternative is to be satisfied with mediocrity, and insufficient supplies of it at that.

Certainly, when only one-fifth of the relevant population worldwide is enrolled in existing higher-education institutions, there is a whole lot of greenfield space to cultivate variations. "We have what I call a law of thirds in this country," Peter Smith, who has spent a distinguished career in higher education and now works for the for-profit Kaplan University, told me.

> About one-third don't graduate high school in ten years. The second third—actually more like 40 percent of the total—get a little college. And the third third gets an associate's degree or more. This has been pretty flat for the past thirty years. When you juxtapose that against the workforce needs of the country, we're several million down now and we'll be 7 to 8 million down within a few years. And in this global economy, we've got—let's take China as an obvious example. As soon as they become as productive as we are they will swamp the economy with qualified workers. We have to do better than "sort of" educating one-third plus a few to an associates' degree level. We don't need incrementalism—we need new models.[1]

Brian Lamb, an educational technologist at the University of British Columbia, sketches out for me one potential vision: "For universities, here's the nightmare scenario. Imagine Google enters a partnership with the two or three top educational publishers, builds on the existing open-educational resources already released, uses the reach of Google to coordinate discussion and peer-based networks and develops a series of tests that they also certify. What then?"

Judy Baker at Foothill-De Anza both has an idea of what a new model will look like, and is in a position to help it happen.

> The way I see it, higher education, ten, twenty years from now is going to look very different. It won't be the brick and mortar and the semester and a course in this and a course in that. It's going to be more outcomes based and skill based, project based. You don't have to take these sixty courses or whatever it is to be a journalist. Someone will identify your gaps and then you address the gaps, in whatever way is possible. And that may mean taking an online course from New Zealand, being in a discussion forum with people in Canada, an internship in Mexico with Habitat for Humanity. You just need to get the knowledge and skills whatever way you can and then test out or present a portfolio. And when you add it all up, a few years later, you actually are ready to be a good journalist.

The science of evolution teaches that new dominant species emerge when environments shift, and that small changes can have greatly amplified effects over time. Even more fascinating than predicting which of these higher-education models might ascend within ten or twenty years, and which are the dinosaurs, is the potential of DIY U practices to release great stores of what Paul Kim calls the world's last renewable resource: human creativity.

The whole project of formal education has been based on the idea of society transmitting its ideas, values, and technologies from one generation to the next, and from dominant civilizations and cultures to "backward" or "primitive" ones. In the modern era we added the task of making and incorporating new discoveries into the curriculum year after year. As our society got more complex, we developed bigger and bigger institutions to teach more and more people more and more things.

Well, now the world is changing too fast, and the need is growing too much, for institutions to keep up. Scientists say we have less than ten years to reinvent how we get energy, how we get around, and how we make things if we don't want our civilization to collapse from the effects of global warming. And to do that, we as a species also have to find better ways of communicating, making decisions, and understanding and weighing each others' needs.

No one person knows how to do this; it requires a new synthesis of the wisdom of the ancients and cutting-edge discoveries. Our best hope is to get better at empowering individuals to find answers for themselves. In other words, forget about giving the guy a fish, or teaching him how to fish, either. Teach him how to teach himself, and he'll always be able to acquire the skills he needs to find food, skills you haven't even thought of yet for things you didn't know you could eat. Fishing itself, it happens, is a great example of this. Today, 90 percent of fish species are over-exploited. Fish farming is people's fastest-growing source of food and will probably remain so through 2025, says James S. Diana of the University of Michigan at Ann Arbor. The world needs people who can figure out new ways to repair the oceans and to find or grow renewable sources of food.[2]

The lucky thing is that we humans are hard-wired to learn and discover. Jaak Panskepp, a neuroscientist at Washington State University, studies emotional systems in mammals. In the sniffing and outstretched neck of a rat combing a maze for food, he sees a universal mammalian urge, as basic as rage or fear. Writes Emily Yoffe in *Slate*:

> It is an emotional state Panksepp tried many names for: *curiosity, interest, foraging, anticipation, craving, expectancy.* He finally settled on *seeking.* Panksepp has spent decades mapping the emotional systems of the brain he believes are shared by all mammals, and he says, "Seeking is the grand-daddy of the systems." . . . For humans, this desire to search is not just about fulfilling our *physical* needs. Panksepp says that humans can get just as excited about abstract rewards as tangible ones. He says that when we get thrilled about

the world of ideas, about making intellectual connections, about divining meaning, it is the seeking circuits that are firing.[3]

This ongoing search—the heartbeat of DIY U—is crucial to our evolution and our survival.

seven

RESOURCE GUIDE

for a Do–It–Yourself Education

A listing of Web sites of the organizations mentioned in this chapter or elsewhere in the book can be found at the end of this resource guide, beginning on page 163.

The system and institutions of higher education need to change, will change, and already are changing. It will take some time before the official college guides are updated, and the conventional wisdom catches up with reality. In the meantime, this resource guide is offered to help anyone navigate the system as it stands today.

Most people want to discover what they want, and then go after it. They don't want to drown in debt or feel like failures for not following a particular prescribed path. At different times in your life, your goals may include satisfying curiosity, having a laugh, landing a job offer, finding a mentor, acting as a leader, plugging into a professional network, developing your values and views, building a portfolio of work, speaking a new language, or stumbling on that one blazing experience that provides insight and perspective for a lifetime.

The so-called traditional path—graduating from high school at eighteen, going straight to college and living on campus, graduating at twenty-two and going straight into the workforce with a college-appropriate job—describes the experience of just 10 percent of people today. If you belong to the other 90 percent, whether you're sixteen or sixty-one, here's how to take the first steps down your own personal learning path.

Luckily for me, when I was finishing this book I met a young woman who perfectly illustrates the beauty of walking your own path. Molly Crabapple, twenty-six, has a Goth style—long black hair, dresses, and exotic eye makeup—that complements her swoopy, swirly, Victorian illustrations. She's her own personal creation, down to her name: an accomplished artist who has published a graphic novel, *Scarlett Takes Manhattan*, exhibited her work around the country and the world, has more than 4,000 followers on Twitter, and has her own "DIY empire"—Dr. Sketchy's Anti-Art School. This is a regular gathering of artists who come to a bar to spend the evening drawing a live model, who might be a burlesque dancer, fire performer, or other downtown celebrity. Dr. Sketchy's has almost one hundred chapters around the world, in Bogota, Helsinki, Paris, and Kansas, each of which pays her and her cofounders a small fee. Not bad for a self-described art school dropout.

The way I look at it, a complete personal learning plan ought to have four parts: finding a goal and the credentials or skills needed, formal study, experiential education, and building a personal learning network. Crabapple was kind enough to serve as my model and explain how she did each part her own way.

Let's say you want to be a professional, not an artist like Crabapple. Even if four years of college, three years of professional school, a state licensing exam, and other standard steps to success are part of your plan, the basic sequence that she followed still holds true. You won't succeed in any prescribed path until you first look within yourself to identify your own goals. As many nonpracticing lawyers can attest, don't put the cart before the horse by seeking formal education before you know what you want to do. Employers increasingly require experiential education, such as internships. As for personal learning networks, this is a new way of thinking about an old truth: relationships are crucial to your success in any field.

1. The goal and the credentials or skills needed

You may have a childhood dream to pursue or you may have to start from a blank page and do some inner research to find out what direction to head off in. "I've been drawing since I was a little girl," says Crabapple. "My mother worked as an illustrator for most of her professional career, so I never had the idea that art wasn't something you could make a living at. I started thinking about art as a career in high school, and discovering I could turn a buck from it in college made up my mind."

Whatever you choose, make sure you know the formal requirements. Your chosen career may require a four-year degree, a specialized certificate, an apprenticeship, or just a lucky break. Crabapple knew that a bachelor's degree was nice to have, but not a requirement for her chosen line of work.

"Since the field I work in is pretty much all freelance, you're never asked about a degree or lack thereof. There are definitely schools—I'm thinking Art Center in California—that can give you a great education and scads of professional connections, but even in that case, it's the experience that's more important than the degree."

In order to be successful in any educational program, the first subject you have to study is yourself. Treat it like any project: get a new notebook, a file folder, or if you have access to a computer, start a file labeled "About Me." Then start making a list or drawing a map of things that interest you or represent you. Just for fun, you might want to try sketching it using markers, cutting pictures out of magazines that appeal to you and making a dream collage, or downloading free mind-mapping software like **FreeMind**.

What are your interests and talents? Do you like to work alone or be surrounded by people? Stay home in your pajamas or travel the world? Do you like being around animals, younger people, or older people? Do you like gardening, cars, video games? Consider taking a few personality tests—the Meyers-Briggs test is probably the best known. You can find them online for free at the **Jung Career Indicator**, **Career Explorer**, or the **Personality Test Center**.

Think about how you learn best, not only your favorite subjects in school but the settings where your informal learning skills shine. Don't just look at your grades and SAT scores. Are you good at remembering lines from movies or song lyrics? Have a great sense of direction? Like to cook and make up recipes? Need to get up frequently and stretch when you're studying? Can you beat Rock Band? Like to talk over the plots of TV shows with friends? These are all clues to different learning styles. You can take quizzes for these too, like **Peterson's Education Planner** and **Learning Styles Online**.

Other people can be a huge help in this quest. Is there a teacher, coach, pastor, guidance counselor, or a relative or family friend you trust? Don't ask them directly what you should do for a living, because odds are they'll just advise you to go into their own line of work or what they always dreamed of doing. Instead, ask for honest, constructive feedback about yourself, your strengths and weaknesses, what makes you stand out. Marshall Goldsmith, a successful executive coach, leads the heads of big companies who want to grow and learn and get better at what they do go through something called a 360-degree review. This means they ask for feedback from everyone they know: coworkers, employees, friends, and family. If one or two people point something out about you, it's easy to dismiss it as just their opinion. If lots of people do, it's more likely to be the truth. Going through your own mini-360-degree review will give you the kind of information you need to make a solid decision about what to do next.

Reading biographies of or interviews with people you admire is a great idea. A book I devoured was *The New New Journalism* by Robert S. Boynton, which consists of profiles of my favorite nonfiction writers like Joan Didion and Jon Krakauer. It had all the details on how they got where they are and how they do their work day to day. A personal learning plan can be much easier to see in retrospect, when you can understand how a chance encounter, a bold decision, or hours and years of diligent practice led to an opportunity.

Once you've gotten some insight about yourself, you'll want to apply that knowledge to an initial career direction. You could try the extreme sports method taken by two young men, Sean Aiken and Daniel Seddiqui. Each had graduated college without having any idea what he wanted to do for a career. So they took off on major road trips, Aiken trying out fifty-two jobs in fifty-two weeks, and Seddiqui pulling off a job in every state. You can read about their journeys from lobster fisherman to Bourbon Street bartender at oneweekjob.com (Aiken) and livingthemap.com (Seddiqui). "Shortly after graduating from college, I made a promise to myself," Aiken wrote. "I will not settle for a career that I am not truly passionate about." (If you have no budget for travel, check out the local version of this at Aimee Davison's blog One Hundred Jobs, where she's taking on 100 ultra-short-term gigs for $100 each).

If you don't want to go the *On the Road* route to self-discovery, you can try some shortcuts.

- The military gives a special test called the **Armed Services Vocational Aptitude Battery** (ASVAB), available online, that correlates skills in various academic areas to specific careers. (Be aware that getting in touch with them may lead military recruiters to take an interest in you.)
- The Bureau of Labor Statistics' **Occupational Outlook Handbook** has comprehensive information on every career under the sun: average salaries, projected growth in number of openings, required education. They also have a Web site geared for high school students that asks the simple question of "What Do You Like?" to point users in the direction of information on careers that might be interesting.
- The **Career Key** offers a Career Key Test that helps pinpoint suitable careers, college majors, and training programs and also includes a What Your Test Scores Mean booklet; it takes about fifteen minutes and costs $9.95 (it can be purchased together with "What Job is Best for Me," a 2009 e-book, for $14.50).
- *US News & World Report* yearly profiles the thirty "best" careers based on strong outlooks and job satisfaction. Their Web site also includes questions that can help you find the best location for you to work, as well as lists such as "Overrated Careers," "Ahead-of-the-Curve Careers," "Best-Kept-Secret Careers," and even "The 7 Best Jobs for Facebook Addicts."
- Don't overlook skilled trades. The site **Career Voyages**, sponsored by a federal initiative, can connect you with a registered apprenticeship in a trade from autos to nanotech.
- The Department of Labor has a newly redesigned **Office of Apprenticeship** Web site as well. Even in the depth of the 2009 recession, the *New York Times* reported, employers were going begging for welders, critical care nurses, electrical linemen, and respiratory therapists. [1]
- There's a great 2009 book called *Blue Collar and Proud of It* (Deerfield Beach, Fla.: Health Communications, Inc.) written by Joe LaMacchia, a successful landscaper in Newton, Massachusetts, who skipped college, and Bridget

Samburg. The book's a complete guide to finding fulfilling noncollege careers from trucker to solar panel installer. There's lots of good information and personal stories on the Web site at bluecollarandproudofit.com.

- **Studentjobs.gov** can help you find a job opportunity within the federal government.
- **The Vault** Web site has information about various companies, industries, and professions, as well as sample resumes and cover letters. Basic membership, free of charge, allows one to receive industry newsletters and job alerts, to apply to jobs online, and to download the four most popular Vault career guides.
- *What Color Is Your Parachute? For Teens* by Carol Christen is another book packed with career resources.

In my experience, most people who feel adrift haven't done enough research. They pick something because their family or friends do it, they see something on TV, or they happen to hear that there are a lot of jobs in a particular field. If you take the time to do a little research you'll be well ahead of the pack. It doesn't mean making a final decision for the rest of your life. The Bureau of Labor Statistics has found that most people hold an average of 9.6 jobs between the ages of eighteen and thirty-two. What matters is that you are setting out to pursue a goal and building skills that you can take with you from job to job.

Engaging in a little self-examination will make it more likely that you pick the right educational path. If your desired job direction requires an apprenticeship, an audition, a specialized certificate, or an associate's degree, you may not need to head straight off to a bachelor's degree. If your friends and family, or your own gut, are telling you that you don't seem happy, focused, or at your best in a traditional academic setting, going straight to college might be the wrong thing to do. Talk to your parents about how to structure a year or two off so you can try out some of your interests and discover new ones.

Paul Shaffer, the bandleader for the *Late Show* with David Letterman, says in his 2009 memoir *We'll Be Here the Rest of Our Lives* that he asked his parents if he could take a year off before college to try out the music thing. The rest was history.[2]

2. Formal study, open education, and self-learning

Most people need to pursue some kind of formal study after high school to achieve their career goals. Your choices will be informed by cost, test scores, location, and other circumstances. Your course of study should ideally be a blend of technology-assisted learning with traditional classroom time. Don't forget to take advantage of free and open resources.

Crabapple attended the Fashion Institute of Technology, but left short of a degree partly because of money and partly because she was restless to get out and start working. She also took night courses in French and Arabic at the New School, a college in New York that has always been geared to adult learners. "I've had some ferociously good teachers, including professor Sal Catalano in college, who practically beat anatomy into his students with a stick. I've also had unspeakably lazy professors who put on movies and fell asleep."

For the first time in history, the Internet allows everyone to access much of the same content that's available at Ivy League colleges, and beyond, for free. This wasn't true even five years ago. The experiences available to the independent learner are limited only by time and interest. Have you ever looked up an entry on Wikipedia or gone to lyricsonline.com to get the words to a favorite song? Then you've used online learning resources. There is no excuse for signing up to major in some field and then realizing you hate it, when every topic is free for you to explore in open courseware. Even if you're definitely headed for a traditional college, open courseware is an essential way to discover new interests and to develop self-learning skills like reading carefully, asking for help when you need it, and deliberate practice.[3] You can also use free and open courseware to bone up on basic subjects like English and math so that when you do get to college, you can place out of "developmental" courses and spend your money on credits that are actually transferable and build towards a degree.

What skills and knowledge will you really need, in work or in life? It's a complicated question. Robert Lerman, a professor of social policy and economics at American University and a fellow at the Urban Institute, wrote a paper on a novel way of finding out—by actually asking people what skills they used every day. The Survey of Workplace Skills, Technology, and Management Practices

(STAMP), called up over 2,000 workers, white- and blue-collar, between October 2004 and January 2006. They found that less than 15 percent of all workers ever have to write anything more than five pages long, and less than a quarter use any math past fractions. Even for the "highest-skilled" workers, when asked what education was required to do their job, the average answer was between two and four years of college.

On the other hand, the vast majority of workers reported having to use skills that aren't normally taught in high school or college. Three out of four workers say they have to teach or train people. Sixty percent said they need to deal with people who are hostile or upset. About half say they have to manage people. In survey after survey of employers, Lerman writes, they rate nonacademic and noncognitive skills as important or more important than test scores or grades in hiring; these skills can also predict your earning. They include self-esteem, whether you take responsibility for your actions, empathy, and goal setting.

Here's a short list of topics that I think are more universally useful—and possibly more interesting—than anything in the core liberal arts curriculum.

  • *Metacognition or thinking about thinking.* Tools from psychology and spiritual traditions around the world can help you become a more informed observer of your own mind, moods, and thinking processes. What makes you calm or agitated? Can you soothe yourself? Can you accurately identify and express your own emotions?

    In an age where information is a commodity, more and more of our education needs to be about learning how to learn, and focusing on what's important. In 1799 the American Philosophical Society offered a prize for the best plan of an American system of education. Benjamin Rush, a prominent Philadelphia physician, suggested getting rid of Greek and Latin. He wanted to set up special schools instead "for teaching the art of forgetting." Techniques like meditation and yoga can help clear your mind so you can focus on what you want to learn or accomplish and block out the rest.

- *How to write a budget and manage money*. Avoiding debt, saving, investing for the future, and managing spending are key life skills that have gotten more complicated in the last generation. Until they are taught in all high schools, you need to teach yourself. Sign up for a free online service like **Mint.com** to track your spending for you. Go to **annualcreditreport.com** and get a free credit report, then use it as a guide to start paying down your debt a dollar or two at a time, starting with the highest-interest debt first. Find the savings account with the best possible return on bankrate.com and start putting away a dime of every dollar.

- *How to improve your relationships*. Nothing is more important to happiness than the quality of relationships with family, romantic partners, and friends. Yet you can graduate from the best colleges—and many people do—without knowing the first insights from psychology, sociology, or religion about how to relate to people.

- *Physical fitness and health*. Health is right up there with love in determining people's happiness. Every American adult needs an exercise routine to help relieve stress and stay healthy, but most of us don't learn a lifelong, sustainable exercise practice in school.

- *Home economics*. Cooking and baking, basic nutrition, laundry and housecleaning, gardening, simple home and auto repairs. Mastering these skills will save you money, improve your quality of life, be good for your health, and they might even help you get along with the people you share a kitchen with. Moreover, they're being enthusiastically revived and shared by people around the world as a return to a simpler, more satisfying way of life, and preparation for a future where it will become increasingly important to use energy and materials more efficiently.

- *How to understand and interact with digital technologies*. Everyone needs to know basic programming concepts and the use of social media from blogging to smartphones. Rapid technological change is a permanent fixture in our society. Ongoing adaptability is the name of the game.

Once you have some questions in mind, from the subjects above or some of your own, it's time to get online and explore the world of open-educational resources.

- If you've never seen a **TED Talk**, now is a good time to start. TED (for Technology, Entertainment, Design) has a small but excellent collection of short video lectures by scientists, authors, artists, political figures, and more. They can give you clues about fields you might want to study, like behavioral economics or biophysics.
- **OpenEd**, by Creative Commons, is one of the most comprehensive search tools out there for discovering educational resources on the Web.
- **The OpenCourseWare Consortium, Connexions, Community College Consortium for Open Educational Resources**, and **Wikiversity** are each a vast universe of open educational content organized into short units or full-length courses.
- **The Open University in the United Kingdom** is one of the world's largest and oldest distance-learning institutions, serving mainly students from the UK and Europe. They also maintain a Web site called **OpenLearn** that has freely available courseware pared with discussion forums, so you can connect with other students who are making their way through the same material.
- As profiled earlier in the book, **MIT** has the original open-courseware site.
- Yale also has a good collection of open material, **Open Yale Courses**. For example, you can view economist Robert Shiller lecturing on financial markets.
- **CosmoLearning** is "designed to work as a free home-school," providing a well-organized selection of videos, courses, documentaries, books, quizzes, lecture notes, and more.
- **SpacedEd** is a Web site that offers free and low-cost short courses based on research developed by a professor at Harvard Medical School. Many medical and general interest topics are covered.

- The **Open Learning Initiative** from Carnegie Mellon also has a small selection of free courses that have been proven to work well in topics like physics and math. It includes a section for self-learners.
- **Bon Education** maintains a list of open education resources from around the world.
- **Academic Earth**, founded by Yale graduate Richard Ludlow, is like an academic Hulu. It collects and rates videos of lectures from colleges like Yale, MIT, Harvard, Stanford, UC Berkeley, and Princeton. It was named one of *Time* magazine's best Web sites of 2009.
- **YouTubeEDU**, a YouTube subsite, brings together videos and channels from dozens of colleges and universities. The site **iTunes U** does the same, and also includes video and audio material from cultural institutions like the Metropolitan Museum.
- **The Internet Archive** is a nonprofit digital library of Internet sites and other cultural artifacts—video, audio, texts, and live music. On the homepage, last I checked, were photographs of the San Francisco Bay Bridge and an image of the original manuscript of the Gettysburg Address.
- **Europeana** is a digital library with 4.6 million items from libraries, archives, museums and other institutions across Europe. Read Charles Darwin's letters or listen to Pavarotti singing Verdi.

This is just the beginning—new resources are coming online all the time.

Anyone can take advantage of open-educational resources informally, on the fly, and for background or to supplement for-credit courses. If you're really excited about these resources, have interests that reach beyond conventional academic programs, and are comfortable working on your own, you might be an autodidact— someone who's able to accomplish significant learning and research independently. For inspiration and more resources, check out blogs by Pippa Buchanan (**Fighting Tiger**) and Lisa Chamberlin (**Open Ph.D.—An Experiment in Higher Learning**). Buchanan is an

Australian living in Berlin and Chamberlin is a veteran educator and blogger in the United States. Both have launched projects to assemble alternative graduate degrees on their own, for free, using open educational resources. *The Teenage Liberation Handbook: How to Quit School and Get a Real Life and Education* by Grace Llewellyn (Eugene, Ore.: Lowry House, 1991) is a classic guide for anyone who wants to pursue an independent learning program.

Most people, though, learn best within some kind of community. If you'd like to find a teacher or a class—or start one of your own—check out **Unclasses** or **Peer2Peer University**, "an online community of open study groups for short university-level courses." Both are free. **Teachstreet** and the **School of Everything** have both free and pay classes, in topics ranging from music to permaculture. If you want live video tutoring, check out **eduFire** or **Knewton**. **Grockit** offers test prep that works like an online game.

Educational technologists including David Wiley at Brigham Young University, Alec Couros at the University of Regina, Sasketchewan, and George Siemens and Stephen Downes at the University of Manitoba regularly offer courses that are available to anyone on the Web. Check out Professor Wiley's **OpenContent** site for an open course finder, a wiki, and much more.

Maybe you're looking for an informal open-learning experience that is more face-to-face. Although you can view plenty of free videos on chainsaw maintenance at **Wikieducator**, that seems like something you'd want to practice in the real world with someone who's more experienced.

Luckily, in cities around the country, people are gathering to learn and teach each other cooking, gardening, fabricating, building, sewing, bike repair, electronics, furniture-making and lots of other hands-on skills, for free. Search Google **"skill share"** and your home town to find events or organizations in your area. As the Boston, Massachusetts, Skillshare Web site explains: "We believe everyone can teach and learn something." Similarly, **3rd Ward** in Brooklyn, New York, is "a member-based design store for creative professionals" offering "interdisciplinary courses in visual art, technology, fabrication and craft" and in Portland, Oregon, there's a **Free School** "dedicated to social change through free education and community building." *Make* magazine, *ReadyMade* magazine, and

Etsy, the marketplace for handcrafts, are all centers for this kind of activity, listing events in cities around the country to help you build a business out of your craft.

Let's say you've thoroughly checked out the world of open resources, but you still need a degree to accomplish your goals. Here's how to find a college that can prepare you for the future. For best results, go beyond the *US News and World Report* rankings to find a college. The jobs Web site **Payscale** did a detailed "Best Colleges" survey that lists the median salary as reported by actual graduates of each college. Among state universities, University of California–Berkeley and University of Virginia are tops for median salaries of their graduates. They also list some of the most popular schools by job, and the most popular jobs by school. Since 2000, the National Survey of Student Engagement has been sent to randomly selected first-year and senior students at participating colleges. The questions address five categories: how challenging the academics are, how active and collaborative their learning process is, how much interaction there is between faculty and students, whether they have opportunities for valuable learning experiences outside the classroom, and how supportive the campus learning environment is. Many of the results are held in secret by institutions. Since 2007, four hundred colleges have released their scores publicly on *USA Today*'s Web site.

Once you've narrowed down your search, read those glossy brochures critically. A twenty-first-century university should publish lots of information about how their students are performing in the real world—surveys like the **Collegiate Learning Assessment** and the **National Survey of Student Engagement**, demographics, graduation rates, job placement rates, and salaries. The main advantage of a traditional college over open education and distance learning is face time with peers and faculty, so the college should advertise plenty of both. Ask what kinds of transfer credit they accept, how they foster internships and work experience, and how many students travel or volunteer. Check out the college's career center Web site and see if it looks alive.

Check out student blogs and see if they're interesting and well-written. Can't find any? Not a great sign.

E-mail a faculty member in a field you're interested in—faculty e-mail addresses are listed on the college Web site—with a question about the program. If they write you back promptly, this should give you a clue about how engaged faculty are with students.

Red flags include colleges that talk up their physical plant, such as their gym, stadium, or food courts. Follow the geranium rule: on a campus visit or in photos, if you see lots of fancy landscaping and construction signs, this is a sign that the college may be focusing more on fund-raising and perks than on the quality of the student experience. This is also a sign that tuition bills may be headed up in the near future.

Speaking of which, if money is a serious issue in your college search, you can check whether the college is raising tuition less than the national average of 7 percent a year for public colleges and 3 percent for privates. You can find and compare tuition numbers at Peterson's or the National Center for Education Statistics' **College Navigator**. Peterson's gives students' average graduating debt, and the College Navigator gives your expected costs over two years.

Soon the Department of Education will begin maintaining its own list of the most and least affordable colleges. The College Navigator also allows you to search colleges by enrollment and whether they offer "extended learning options" like online learning, weekend classes, or life experience credits, which can all shorten your time to degree and thus save money.

Kaileen Crane dropped out of high school at sixteen, got her GED, and spent a few years working at convenience stores and Dunkin' Donuts. "I always knew I wanted to go to college, but I didn't want to waste my money," she said. "I've seen a lot of people do that—sign up and realize they didn't want to do it. It doesn't go well. They weren't ready to take on the responsibilities, they had other things they wanted to be doing. . . . They wind up thousands of dollars in debt. Last Christmas my dad brought it up again that I should be going to school and I agreed, it was about time." At twenty-one, Crane is in her second year at Southern New Hampshire University's Advantage Program. This is the private nonprofit university in New Hampshire, mentioned in chapter 3, that started a stripped-down two-year program for students to cover their general-education requirements, earn an associate's degree, and transfer to SNHU or another college to complete the bachelor's degree. The program is taught by SNHU faculty and runs at a streamlined four hours a day, four days a week, allowing her to work at a convenience store to support herself. The cost is $10,000 a year, a 60 percent discount from SNHU's traditional program. Crane plans to finish her bachelor's at SNHU and become an English teacher. "I like explaining things, I like telling people what to do, and I really love the English language and the way it's used," she says. "People look at me funny if I start a conversation about some word. Maybe I can help them enjoy language as much as I do."

There are three parts to Crane's story that make her likely to be successful. The first, and most important, is that she understood herself. She didn't waste time and money going to college until she felt ready. Taking that time made her extra motivated to succeed. "I always wanted to go to school," she says. "But after spending some time on my own and seeing other people who supported themselves without an education, just the prospect of supporting myself on an $8 an hour salary for the rest of my life was enough to get me in gear. It's not a very pleasant way to live." Second, she found a program that was affordable, with a clear path to a degree. And finally, she's picking a career that she finds intrinsically interesting, and, as a nice bonus, is in a field with solid growth.

If I were looking for a college today, I would want to see one that talks about how it incorporates technology to give you more options and allow you to spend your time in class interacting with the teacher and not just taking notes on a lecture. The **National Center for Academic Transformation** Web site lists dozens of public institutions that have gone through the Course Redesign program to improve learning outcomes and cut costs, including the University of Tennessee, Louisiana State University, the University of Alabama, Florida Gulf Coast University, and Ohio State University. Carnegie Mellon, which hosts the **Open Learning Initiative**, Rice University, which hosts **Connexions**, the University of Wisconsin, which hosts **Engage**, and the Foothill–De Anza Community College System are all places where people are thinking creatively about teaching and learning. So are Brigham Young University and BYU–Idaho, for those who happen to be comfortable with a Mormon lifestyle. The entire University of Maryland system is incorporating systemwide innovations, including more distance learning, that are drawing attention nationwide.

Interested in an online degree? Programs such as **Western Governors University** seem to work best for people who are organized and motivated and who already have specific career goals and strong support systems such as friends and family outside of class. "Western Governors University is not for you if you don't understand how to self-motivate," says Tarra Patrick, who earned her teaching degree remotely at the age of thirty-nine. "I think it's really popular for people like me because we're the people that fell through the cracks who are smart; our report cards read 'does not apply themselves,' 'not living up to their potential.' We probably got a lot of 'talks too much,' because we were bored. We want to learn and move on."

College Choices for Adults is a great resource launched in the fall of 2009 with support from the Lumina Foundation. It has the best information on online, competency-based, and other distance-education programs. It's easy to compare colleges by measures of student engagement, student demographics, and results of alumni surveys. The **Education Degree Source** Web site, **eLearners.com**, and **Online Education Database** are all commercial online education databases that can help you find online colleges and programs and also have rankings of online colleges like Western Governor's.

If you're coming to a degree program after a lot of work experience, **Excelsior College**, in Albany, New York, is a national innovator in methods of evaluation, assessment, and accreditation for nontraditional learning experiences. In addition to their own courses, they offer several other ways for working adults to earn credit: fifty-one examinations in a variety of subjects, extensive experience with accepting local and international transfer credits, and a portfolio assessment program where students have the opportunity to write a résumé, document, and package their life experiences, whether in work, volunteering, or travel, for college-level course credit. Excelsior even has a course that teaches students how to create and submit such a portfolio.

Colleges That Change Lives: 40 Schools That Will Change the Way You Think About Colleges by Loren Pope (New York: Penguin, 1996) is a much-praised book that highlights some of the nation's best small liberal arts colleges.

The **California Institute of Integral Studies** deserves a special mention for its unique bachelor's degree completion program for adults who have already had the equivalent of two years of college. It's an interdisciplinary degree that happens in small groups for a valuable liberal arts experience.

Curtis Bonk's book *The World Is Open* (San Francisco: Jossey-Bass, 2009) is a massive exploration of the field of online learning with the premise that "with the emergence of the Web, anyone can now learn anything from anyone else at any time" and with lots of information about institutions that represent the cutting edge of digital learning.

If you have a specific professional interest, do some research to see if there's a targeted program for it before you head off to a conventional liberal arts college. Specialized programs tend to be better integrated with the working world. For example, **Animation Mentor** is a unique, eighteen-month, non-accredited online training program started by professional animators at Pixar and other top companies. Students who want to learn the art of animation must buy their own computer and software as well as pay $18,000 tuition. In return, they train in an environment that's as real-world as possible, with weekly live Web conferences with mentors who currently work in the industry, and graduate with a professional-quality demo reel. One year after graduation, 78 percent are working in the field. Imageworks, the digital division of Sony Pictures, sponsors the **Imageworks Professional Academic Excellence** program as a partnership with a dozen schools, including Carnegie Mellon, Stanford, and Pratt Institute School of Art & Design. Maybe you have a dream company that you want to work for, like Google, Disney, Zipcar, or Zappos. Try calling their human resources department, asking what education you need to work there and what colleges they recommend. The answer might surprise you.

There are some new job areas that are vocational in the old sense of a calling, so alternative educational structures have arisen naturally. This includes holistic health fields like yoga, naturopathy, reiki, massage, acupuncture, and nutrition. The **Yoga Alliance** offers teacher certification and support services nationwide.[4] The **Institute for Integrative Nutrition** in New York City trains people to become holistic health advisors. With schools that are not traditionally accredited, you'll want to make extra sure that you do your homework. Talk to graduates—not just the ones who the program handpicks as spokespeople.

Special note: How to cut education costs.

If money is a concern, and for most people it is, there are several key strategies you can use to limit the cost of a degree.

First, consider carefully if you really need a bachelor's degree, or if your goal requires a certificate, apprenticeship, or experience in the field. These include the trades, of course.

As Molly Crabapple's experience shows, it also includes most of the performing and fine arts—acting, dance, painting, etc. You might be better off spending time auditioning and studying in specialized programs than paying for a bachelor's degree. The same goes for the hospitality industry and culinary school—try working in restaurants or hotels first to see if this is really the life for you before you pursue a degree that can cost as much as a liberal arts college.

When you're applying to colleges, filling out the FAFSA, the **Free Application for Federal Student Aid**, is a must. The sooner you fill it out and submit it, the more aid your school may have available for you. The Obama administration has proposed simplifying the application. You can find information on filling it out from the Department of Education's "Completing the FAFSA" Web site, whether or not you have help from parents. A tax preparation office like H&R Block may be able to give you some quick help for a reasonable fee. (You can fill out the FAFSA for free through the Department of Education's site.)

Once you are in school, earn your degree faster by taking extra classes online, in the summer, or at night. Make sure you work with an academic advisor to choose classes that will transfer and that will definitely lead to a degree.

Combine credits from different institutions, perhaps combining online credits with on-campus credits, or classes at a community college with others taken at a more expensive college. Again, you'll need the help of an academic advisor to ensure that your credits will transfer.

Apply to colleges that charge less—or no—tuition up front, such as Deep Springs College, Cooper Union, some community colleges, or those in the Work Colleges Consortium. Or apply to very expensive schools. If you have good grades and test scores and demonstrated financial need, a private college with a big endowment is likely to offer a more generous package of grants and loans than a public university.

Search for scholarships, but don't pay any money to do it. Use a tool like **Fastweb** or the **College Board's** scholarship finder.

Finally, on student loans: The reality is that most students take out loans to pay for college. Borrowing can be the lesser of two evils, for example, when the alternative is working so many hours that you have no time to concentrate on schoolwork; most experts say that more than 20 hours is tough for full-time students. Loans should not be an onerous burden, though. A good rule of thumb is that your entire debt upon graduation should not be more than your expected salary one year out of college. For engineering or computer science grads, that may be $65,000. For liberal arts grads, it's more like $35,000. The same rule holds true for graduate school.

If you make the decision to borrow, you'll want to max out your eligibility for federal direct student loans, since they give you the best terms for repayment. Currently they are available for up to $5,500 for the first year of school, $6,500 for the second year, and $7,500 after that. **FinAid** is a great comprehensive Web site about student loans and other financial aid questions. **IBR Info** is a nonprofit source of information about the new federal-loan repayment and forgiveness programs. *Public-service loan forgiveness* allows people to cancel their remaining loan debt after ten years of eligible work and loan payments if they work in eligible jobs; are employed by any nonprofit, tax-exempt 501(c)(3) organization or by a federal, state, local, or tribal government (this includes the military and public schools and colleges); or are serving in a full-time AmeriCorps or Peace Corps position. *Income-based repayment* allows anyone to limit her monthly loan payments according to her income, so they don't become too burdensome. Both of these, unfortunately, work only for federal student loans under the direct loan program, not for private loans or parents' PLUS loans. If you have federal student loans with a lender, you may be able to consolidate the loans into the direct loan program to become eligible for these programs.

3. Make sure that experience is part of your education

These days, work finds you, and learning can happen wherever you are. The Internet allows you to publish a portfolio of skills and accomplishments acquired through jobs, internships, travel, volunteering, and participation in online and real-world communities. This process takes place before, during, and after school, and ideally, for the rest of your life.

In Crabapple's case, she "filled up sketchbooks. Begged friends to model for me. Read biographies of artists I admired and tried to absorb their influences. Copied paintings. Vastly abused the New York City Public Library." Crabapple also learned a copious amount from traveling. She graduated high school early and left for Paris, where she worked at the legendary bookstore Shakespeare and Company. She sketched her way through Portugal, Spain, Morocco, Turkey, and Turkish Kurdistan, where she was thrown in jail for sketching a mosque on the Syrian border.

I never took a class in journalism. Yale University offered only one journalism class the whole time I was there and I had another seminar that met at the same time that I needed to take to graduate. Although I worked on my writing and research skills as a literature major, I learned most of my job-specific skills through experience. As an undergrad, I edited my student newsmagazine. We did everything that needed to be done, from selling ads to laying out pages to writing and editing. Most of the people I worked with on the magazine are still in the journalism business. I also did four internships, the first one for free at a now-defunct start-up arts magazine in New Orleans the summer I was fifteen, the second at now-defunct women's magazine *McCall's* for $6.40 an hour, the third at *More* magazine for women over forty, which paid $11 an hour, and the last my senior year of college at the *Village Voice*, which paid whenever I managed to publish something.

Travel was also an important part of my education. A year after graduating, while freelancing, I was looking for some way to cross over from writing book reviews and soft feature stories into real news. So I got a small grant from a Jewish organization and flew off to Israel for the summer. I wound up writing two stories for the *Village Voice*, one about Palestinian juveniles in Israeli military prisons, and the other about a group of homeless people who were protesting by living in a tent city in the richest square in Tel Aviv. The second one appeared on the cover, showing the *Village Voice* editors that I was ready to write about serious news and politics. Within a year I had started contributing to the "Generation Debt" series.

College alone, even the so-called "best" colleges, can't prepare anyone to get a good job or lead a good life. It's a process, and it's different for everyone—that's why it's called a personal learning path. Don't let setbacks along the way discourage you. Any experience can become part of your education.

Colleen Kirby is the second of five kids. She grew up in St. Louis and graduated from a Catholic girls' high school. Neither of her parents finished college; they run a successful restaurant, and they didn't offer her much in the way of guidance or encouragement on her educational path. "My parents, I wouldn't say they dropped the ball, but they didn't really seem to get the whole financial aid system," she says. "They weren't asking me what do we need to do, they didn't sit down and fill in the forms for me. I was a decent student but when I didn't think they were going to pay for me to go to college I definitely let things slide." Kirby's parents' laissez-faire attitude extended to actually failing to sign the promissory note for her student loans, which meant she had to drop out of the local commuter college after her freshman year, swallow her pride, and transfer to community college.

"I started working full time at Target, which was my high school job, and spent two and a half years at the community college. When all my friends graduated with their four-year degree, I was getting my two-year degree," she says. Eventually, Kirby returned to the commuter college and finished her BA after another two years, working full time all the while. "I had already figured out how to manage my time well. I was definitely more mature."

Kirby's story has a happy ending. She found an "awesome" job on her college's career center Web site, working as an asset manager at a local equity fund company, where she still works two and a half years later. "It actually helped me in interviewing. People were impressed that I had such a strong work history. When I interviewed for this job my boss and the other woman both had a nontraditional education background. They were like, 'Oh, that's cool, you've shown you can do two things at once and be successful.'" Kirby wishes that her parents had been more supportive and engaged with the application and financial aid process. "It's not fair," she says, but she didn't let it stop her. "You have to keep moving toward your goal."

Beyond work, if travel or service piques your interest, there's more out there than just the **Peace Corps** (that program, which turns fifty in 2011, is expanding its ranks; however, it is highly selective and requires a college degree). **Volunteers for Peace** offers placement in over 3,000 volunteer projects in more than 100 countries throughout Europe, Asia, Africa, and the Americas. **Global Citizen Year** is a new program that offers recent high school graduates a scholarship-funded "gap year" focusing on international development work. **Students Abroad** is the state department's new Web site (launched in conjunction with their March 2008 public affairs campaign) to provide resources for college students who hope to travel internationally, including safety tips, travel alerts, the locations of embassies, and how to apply for passports and visas. **STA Travel** helps young people plan trips and organize to study, work, or volunteer abroad. **WorldTeach** volunteers can spend a summer or a year teaching in a developing country. **Transitionsabroad.com** is a magazine aimed especially at expats that connects you to all types of opportunities. There's a whole galaxy of blogs and Web sites out there dedicated to "lifestyle design," by adventurous young people who are finding ways to travel and work around the world. For $1,000 a month you could be living in style on a tropical island and working remotely. One inspiration for the lifestyle-design track is the book *The 4-Hour Workweek* (New York: Crown Publishers, 2007) and blog by Tim Ferris.

If you're excited about service and volunteering, whether in your local community or abroad, you're in luck. On April 20, 2009, the late senator Edward Kennedy, in his last Senate appearance, presided over the signing of the Edward Kennedy Serve America Act, which expands federally funded national service from 75,000 to 250,000 slots by 2017. **Americorps** is a great place to get started looking for opportunities. So is **Idealist.org,** which lists thousands of jobs and tens of thousands of volunteer slots. **Public Allies** places young people in positions with nonprofits in their own communities. You don't have to have gone to college to participate in their program. Colleen Kinder's *Delaying the Real World* (New York: Running Press, 2005) is a great guide to getting started with your travel or service adventure. The book is targeted especially for recent college grads, but can work at any age.

4. Keep expanding your personal learning network

A personal learning network is your ultimate educational resource. It's the universe of people, texts, books, Web sites, blogs, any and all knowledge resources and relationships that help situate you in a community of practitioners.

"I really kept my eyes open," when she was first building her network, says Crabapple. "Took my idols out to lunch and picked their brains. New York has one of the largest creative communities in the world, and I checked out bulletin boards, trolled Craigslist, and spoke to anyone and everyone I could to tap into it." Today, she's an avid user of Facebook, Twitter, and her own Web site and blog, and even gives talks on digital marketing and branding.

Paul Shinn is a successful software engineer who completed only one year of college at Worcester Polytechnic Institute. "Most of my knowledge has come from personal research, books, and blogs," he says. He credits his success to a combination of hard work, good luck, self-teaching, and smart networking—getting ahead by helping your friends. His experiences are applicable to people in almost any field, at any level of education.

Shinn is constantly concerned with keeping up his skills. "Almost all of my knowledge and ability has been self-taught and developed alone," he says. "I've done plenty of personal research, writing plenty of test programs and exploratory work. These have helped me to grasp new technical material ahead of my peers." Open-educational resources as described above are one of many ways to build your personal learning network.

Equally important to keeping up with technical knowledge, he says, is helping people in his community of practitioners. "Career-wise, my friends are the catalyst for my success. I've worked mostly at places where either my friends could arrange an in-person inter-view, or my reputation preceded me between employers," he says.

"I've volunteered my time and efforts in the past to help develop software or fix bugs for various parties. . . . These have helped me build a reputation. Helping other people with soft-ware development issues, while employed or not, goes a long way. A friend who can specifically name a roadblock that was cleared with an outsider's help has a lot of power to recommend that person and to get them in the door." Software engineers have the ability to pitch in on open-source projects or Web sites like **Stack Overflow** where programmers share and help each other resolve issues. Volunteering your services to help others is a great way to get your foot in the door, whether your interest is catering, jour-nalism, theater, gardening, or architecture. Shinn says another good tip is to create a public portfolio of work. "Having a body of work readily available for inspection makes it easier for employers to vet a candidate, saving valuable time before a phone or in-person interview."

Justine Lackey is a self-taught bookkeeper with her own success-ful business. She has taken some college classes, but not adding up to an associate's degree. "I moved to New York City at nineteen and squeaked out a living waitressing and doing all sorts of side gigs: focus groups, coat-check girl at the occasional loft party, office temp work. . . . Basically if it was legal and it paid, I did it," she explains.

> Around 1995–96 I was working for a nightmare PR firm, in a job that was totally awful. It was so bad that I left my resignation letter on the boss's desk while he was at lunch, and I left the office before he returned. I went downstairs, called up an artist friend, from a pay phone no less, in tears because I was broke and now jobless. She invited me down to her place for a glass of wine. At the time she was a very successful graphic artist and also did photo retouching. We went from a glass of wine, to me sorting her paperwork. The next week I began working for her doing administra-tive work and accounting. Luckily I had the tiniest bit of experience using the QuickBooks program from one of my temp gigs. I started learning bookkeeping simply, just

using the tutorial in QuickBooks. Because I didn't have money to buy them, I began reading business and accounting books in Barnes and Noble (because frankly B&N is a LOT more interesting when it comes to people watching than the library). A few weeks into my gig this artist recommended me to a friend who also needed accounting help. And thus I began to weave my web through introductions, and referrals, and at times some shameless self-promotion.

Lackey has a word of advice that is helpful for people no matter what line of work they're in. "At first acquiring this new skill was a combination of trial and error, but perhaps more important was fearlessness," she says. "If someone asked me if I could do something, even if I had no experience with that particular accounting concept, I would say yes. Then, I would go and find out the information I needed using the Internet, or books, or the appropriate tax agency. Late at night I would toy with the QuickBooks program until I got it to cooperate or I figured out the function that I needed."

Like Crabapple and Shinn, Lackey talks about the importance of relationships with clients and professional mentors. "I developed strong relationships with several accountants who took me under their wing. This was extremely useful because I could use them as sounding boards when I came up against complex accounting problems, or needed clarification regarding tax law and classifying particular debits or credits. Having a good pool of accountants also helped me get new clients because I became their 'go-to girl' to whom they consistently referred others." Today Lackey has her own business, works four days a week, and even has an assistant.

Good relationships, the ability to teach yourself, and fearlessness are traits that will take you farther in life and in your career than any degree. In fact, without them, the fanciest degree will be useless.

If you're looking for ways to expand your personal network, check out **Koda**, one attempt to create a job engine that works more like a social network. The site is fun to use and lets you create a profile that has more personality and depth than a résumé on a site like Monster, but is more professional than your Facebook profile. (Keep in mind, when having fun on the Web, that any information that shows up on a Google, Facebook, or Myspace search is fair game to a potential employer. Make sure you control your privacy settings and are careful about what you post online.)

On Koda, the companies that want to reach out to young grads create their own profiles. "As a junior in college, you may have no idea that marketing positions exist in law firms, for example," says cofounder and CEO Jeff Bergen. "When we started two years ago, at that time I didn't know you don't have to take your accounting degree and go to the big four accounting firms. There's so much more out there than the Fortune 500 companies. We wanted to make it more needle and less haystack." Koda has started to partner with colleges to enhance their offerings.

Another fascinating example of a "whuffie" or reputation-based job network is **Behance**. Behance allows all kinds of creative workers such as photographers, graphic designers, and illustrators to upload multimedia portfolios. These can be seen, commented on, and voted up or down by the creative community—portfolios that get more votes get promoted on the site and become easier to find. Top companies like Saatchi & Saatchi, JWT, R/GA, Crispin, Ogilvy Nike, Apple, Facebook, Zappos, Target, and Netflix have all actively recruited from the site. Interestingly, the site has a family connection to the history of higher education. Scott Belsky, who founded the site in 2007 at age twenty-eight, graduated from Harvard Business School and worked at investment banking giant Goldman Sachs; he also happens to be the grandson of test prep king Stanley Kaplan. "My grandfather started the test-prep industry out of a desire to make college admissions more of a meritocracy—because, back in the day, the SAT was the only way the underprivileged could gain admission to top colleges," Belsky says. "I admire my grandfather's intention, and I see a parallel need in the creative community."[5]

CBcampus.com (aka Career Rookie) is a division of Career Builder dedicated to helping college students find internships, part-time jobs, and careers after graduation, by helping you build and post your resume, allowing you to subscribe to job alerts and giving you skills quizzes to work through.

Brazen Careerist is another social/career network aimed especially at Generation Y.

Being part of the first generation of students who craft their own personal learning paths as a matter of course, not happenstance, will be challenging. There's lots of resistance to overcome, both internal and external.

For first-generation students like Colleen Kirby, the challenge may be that families aren't much help. For older students like Tarra Patrick, the challenge may be dealing with lost time, regrets, or a checkered educational path. And for middle-class teenagers, the hardest part of forging your own personal learning path may be dealing with parental anxiety about admission to the "right" school. I've had a number of parents tell me that as much as they truly believe the educational landscape is changing, it's hard for them to sanction their own kids being part of that change. "To some degree I lack the courage of my convictions. . . . I'm developing very strong convictions that the existing system is fundamentally and probably irreparably broken, but I would not yet take my kids out of their school," Albert Wenger at Union Square Ventures said. "It's one thing to experiment by investing money in start-ups or reading books, and it's another to experiment with your own children." And my own editor at *Fast Company* magazine, Bob Safian, wrote in an editor's note to a piece that I published on educational technology, "Someone has to be progressive and pioneer a new way. But I'm not going to take that risk with my son's future. If he gets into Harvard— or some other college—I'll spend the money to send him."

However, even parents' attitudes may be changing with the generations. Meagan Francis is a freelance writer and a mother of five in her early thirties who wrote an essay in the online parents' magazine *Babble* in July 2009 that was picked up by the *Chicago Sun-Times*, the *Toronto Star*, and Yahoo!, drawing hundreds of comments. Her topic? "I'm not paying for my kids' college."

"There are many different paths to career success—the problem is you have to be a little bit of an out-of-the-box thinker," she told me. "There's lots of people who get some college, some training, and go on to have successful careers. Besides, it's not like if you don't finish college by the time you're twenty-one you'll never finish. There's this push to get all eighteen-year-olds straight to college and start by the time they're twenty-two in the job market. I think a lot of kids aren't there yet in their brains." Francis speaks from experience. She herself went to a state college at eighteen, and ended up dropping out after three semesters. She went back later, after marrying and becoming a mom, and dropped out again when she started making money as a freelance writer. Francis says that based on the people who commented on her column, the conventional wisdom is already changing. "I would say 70 percent of people who respond are like, yes, good for you! That's fantastic! That's what I'm going to do too!" Another 20 percent were more cautiously supportive, while just 10 percent objected to the idea of encouraging their kids to take other paths.

Parents, peers, and teachers may be helpful and supportive, or they may stand in your way. No matter where you find yourself, the key is realizing you have more options for shaping your own education than almost anyone has ever had at any point in history. The future is up to you.

WEB SITES MENTIONED IN DIY U

2tor. www.2tor.com

3rd Ward (Brooklyn, New York). www.3rdward.com

The 4-Hour Workweek (Tim Ferris). www.fourhourworkweek.com

Academic Earth. www.academicearth.org

AcaWiki. http://acawiki.org/Home

Advantage Program (Southern New Hampshire University). www.snhu.edu/7212.asp

Aiken, Sean, "One Week Job" blog. www.oneweekjob.com

Alice Lloyd College ("work college"). www.alc.edu

Americorps. www.americorps.gov

Animation Mentor. www.animationmentor.com

Armed Services Vocational Aptitude Battery (ASVAB). www.asvabprogram.com

Art Center College of Design (Pasadena, Calif.). www.artcenter.edu

Berea College ("work college"). www.berea.edu

Berlitz. www.berlitz.com

"Best Colleges, Best College Majors, Best College Degrees" (Payscale). www.payscale.com/best-colleges

"Best Colleges" and other lists (US News and World Report). www.usnews.com/sections/education/

Big Picture Learning (charter high schools). www.bigpicture.org

Blackboard. www.blackboard.com

Blackburn College ("work college"). www.blackburn.edu

Blue Collar and Proud of It. www.bluecollarandproudofit.com

Boston Skillshare. www.bostonskillshare.org

Brazen Careerist. www.brazencareerist.com

Bridgepoint Education. www.bridgepointeducation.com

BrighamYoung University. www.byu.edu

BrighamYoung University-Idaho. www.byui.edu

Buchanan, Pippa, "Fighting Tiger" blog. www.battlecat.net

Bureau of Labor Statistics, Occupational Outlook Handbook. www.bls.gov/OCO/

Bureau of Labor Statistics, "What Do You Like?" www.bls.gov/k12/

California Institute of Integral Studies. www.ciis.edu

"Career Advice and Guide for Job Searches" (US News and World Report). www
.usnews.com/money/careers/

Career Builder, CBcampus.com aka Career Rookie. www.careerrookie.com

Career Builder. www.careerbuilder.com

Career Explorer. www.careerexplorer.net/aptitude.asp

The Career Key. www.careerkey.org

Career Rookie aka CBcampus.com. www.careerrookie.com

Carnegie Mellon University, Open Learning Initiative. http://oli.web.cmu.edu/
openlearning/

CBcampus.com aka Career Rookie. www.careerrookie.com

Chamberlin, Lisa, "Open Ph.D.—An Experiment in Higher Learning" blog.
http://openphd.wordpress.com

College Board, "Scholarship Finder." http://apps.collegeboard.com/cbsearch_ss/
welcome.jsp

College Choices for Adults. www.collegechoicesforadults.org

College Navigator (National Center for Education Statistics). http://nces.ed.gov/
collegenavigator/

College of the Ozarks ("work college"). www.cofo.edu

College Unbound. www.collegeunbound.org

Collegiate Learning Assessment. www.collegiatelearningassessment.org

Community College Consortium for Open Educational Resources. www.oer
consortium.org

"Completing the FAFSA" (Department of Education). http://studentaid.ed.gov/
students/publications/completing_fafsa/index.html

Connexions. www.cnx.org

Consultants Bon Education. http://boneducation.com/edtech-resources/
open-education-resources

Cooper Union. www.cooper.edux

CosmoLearning. www.cosmolearning.com

Couros, Alec, Open Access Course: Social Media and Open Education.
http://educationaltechnology.ca/couros/1673

Craigslist. www.craigslist.org

"Cory Doctorow's Craphound.com" (Cory Doctorow's blog). www.craphound.com

Creative Commons, OpenEd. http://opened.creativecommons.org

Creative Commons. www.creativecommons.org

Davidson, Aimee, "One Hundred Jobs" blog. http://onehundredjobs.blogspot.com/

Deep Springs College. www.deepsprings.edu

Department of Education, "Completing the FAFSA." http://studentaid.ed.gov/
students/publications/completing_fafsa/index.html

Directory of Open Access Journals. www.doaj.org

Doctorow, Cory, "Cory Doctorow's Craphound.com" blog. www.craphound.com

Drupal. www. drupal.org

Dr. Sketchy's Anti-Art School. www.drsketchy.com

Ecclesia College ("work college"). www.ecollege.edu
Education Degree Source. www.educationdegreesource.com
eduFire. www.edufire.com
eLearners.com. www.elearners.com
Engage (University of Wisconsin). http://engage.wisc.edu/
Etsy. www.etsy.com
Europeana. www.europeana.eu
Excelsior College. www.excelsior.edu
Facebook. www.facebook.com
Fashion Institute of Technology (New York, New York). www.fitnyc.edu
Fastweb. http://edu.fastweb.com/v/o_registration/flow/step1
Ferris, Tim, *The 4-Hour Workweek*. www.fourhourworkweek.com
"Fighting Tiger" (Pippa Buchanan's blog). www.battlecat.net
FinAid. www.finaid.org
Flat World Knowledge. www.flatworldknowledge.com
Foothill–De Anza Community College District. www.fhda.edu
FreeMind. http://freemind.sourceforge.net
Free School (Portland, Oregon). http://portland.freeskool.org
Gen-1 Theme House (University of Cincinnati). www.uc.edu/cechpass/gen1/
Global Citizen Year. http://globalcitizenyear.org
Google Reader. www.google.com/reader/
Google Scholar. http://scholar.google.com/
Grand Canyon University. www.gcu.edu
Grockit. www.grockit.com
H&R Block. www.hrblock.com
IBR Info. www.ibrinfo.org
Idealist.org. www.idealist.org
Imageworks Professional Academic Excellence program. www.imageworks.com/
    jointheteam/academicresources.php
Indira Gandhi National Open University. www.ignou.ac.in
Institute for Integrative Nutrition. www.integrativenutrition.com
Internet Archive. www.archive.org
iTunes U. www.apple.com/education/mobile-learning/
The Jung Career Indicator. www.humanmetrics.com/vocation/JCI.asp
Kaltura. www.kaltura.com
Kaplan University. www.kaplanuniversity.com
Knewton. www.knewton.com
Koda. www.koda.us
Learning Styles Online. www.learning-styles-online.com/inventory/
"Living the Map" (Daniel Seddiqui's blog). www.livingthemap.com
Lumina Foundation. www.luminafoundation.org
Make magazine. www.makezine.com
MIT, OpenCourseWare. http://ocw.mit.edu
Monster. www.monster.com
Moodle. www.moodle.org
MyMathLab. www.mymathlab.com
National Center for Academic Transformation. www.thencat.org
National Center for Education Statistics' College Navigator. http://nces.ed.gov/
    collegenavigator/
National Survey of Student Engagement. http://nsse.iub.edu

National Survey of Student Engagement—interactive results and analysis at *USA Today*.
   www.usatoday.com/news/education/nsse.htm
The New School (New York, New York). www.newschool.edu
NPR (National Public Radio). www.npr.org
Occupational Outlook Handbook (Bureau of Labor Statistics). www.bls.gov/OCO/
OER Africa. www.oerafrica.org
Omnicademy. www.omnicademy.com
"One Hundred Jobs" (Aimee Davison's blog). http://onehundredjobs.blogspot.com/
"One Week Job" (Sean Aiken's blog). www.oneweekjob.com
Online Education Database. www.oedb.org
Online Learning Daily. www.downes.ca/news/OLDaily.htm
OpenContent. www.opencontent.org
OpenCourseWare (MIT). http://ocw.mit.edu
OpenCourseWare Consortium. www.ocwconsortium.org
OpenEd (Creative Commons). http://opened.creativecommons.org
Open High School of Utah. www.openhighschool.org
OpenLearn (Open University). http://openlearn.open.ac.uk
Open Learning Initiative (Carnegie Mellon University). http://oli.web.cmu.edu/
   openlearning/
"Open Ph.D." (Lisa Chamberlin's blog). http://openphd.wordpress.com
Open University, OpenLearn. http://openlearn.open.ac.uk
Open University of the Netherlands, Wikiwijs. www.opener.ou.nl
Open Yale Courses (Yale University). http://oyc.yale.edu
Payscale, "Best Colleges, Best College Majors, Best College Degrees." www.payscale
   .com/best-colleges
Peace Corps. www.peacecorps.gov
Peer2Peer University. www.p2pu.org
Personality Test Center. www.personalitytest.net
Peterson's Education Planner. www.educationplanner.org/education_planner/
   discovering_article.asp?sponsor=2859&articleName=Learning_Styles_Quiz
Peterson's. www.petersons.com
"Pocket School" project. www.stanford.edu/~phkim/project/consulting.html
Princeton Review. www.princetonreview.com
Public Allies. www.publicallies.org
Reader (Google). www.google.com/reader/
ReadyMade magazine. www.readymade.com
Sackett Street Writers' Workshop. www.sackettworkshop.com
Scholar (Google). http://scholar.google.com/
Scholarship Finder (College Board). http://apps.collegeboard.com/cbsearch_ss/
   welcome.jsp
School of Everything. www.schoolofeverything.com
Seddiqui, Daniel, "Living the Map" blog. www.livingthemap.com
Siemens, George and Stephen Downes, Connectivism and Connective Knowledge.
   http://ltc.umanitoba.ca/connectivism/
Skillshare (Boston, Massachusetts). www.bostonskillshare.org
Slideshare. www.slideshare.net
Smart.fm. www.smart.fm
South by Southwest Interactive. http://sxsw.com/interactive
Southern New Hampshire University, Advantage Program. www.snhu.edu/7212.asp
SpacedEd. www.spaceded.com

STA Travel. www.statravel.com

Stack Overflow. www.stackoverflow.com

Sterling College ("work college"). www.sterlingcollege.edu

Straighterline. www.straighterline.com

Studentjobs.gov. www.studentjobs.gov

Students Abroad. http://studentsabroad.state.gov

Teachstreet. www.teachstreet.com

The Toaster Project. www.thetoasterproject.org

Transforming Teaching Through Technology (T⁴). http://t4.jordan.k12.ut.us/t4

TED. www.ted.com

Transition Towns. www.transitiontowns.org

Transitions Abroad. www.transitionsabroad.com

Twitter. www.twitter.com

Unclasses. www.unclasses.org

University of Cincinnati, Gen-1 Theme House. www.uc.edu/cechpass/gen1/

University of Maryland. www.umd.edu

University of Phoenix. www.phoenix.edu

University of the People. www.uopeople.org

University of Wisconsin, Engage. http://engage.wisc.edu/

The Urban Assembly. www.urbanassembly.org

US News and World Report, "Career Advice and Guide for Job Searches."
   www.usnews.com/money/careers/

US News and World Report, "Education Center" (including "Best Colleges" and
   other lists). www.usnews.com/sections/education/

Vault. www.vault.com

Warren Wilson College ("work college"). www.warren-wilson.edu

Western Governors University. www.wgu.edu

"What Do You Like?" (Bureau of Labor Statistics). www.bls.gov/k12/

Wikieducator. www.wikieducator.org

Wikipedia. www.wikipedia.org

Wikiversity. http://en.wikiversity.org

Wikiwijs (Open University of the Netherlands). www.opener.ou.nl

Wiley, David, Introduction to Open Education. http://open.byu.edu/ipt692r-wiley/

Work Colleges Consortium. www.workcolleges.org

WorldTeach. www.worldteach.org

Yale University, Open Yale Courses. http://oyc.yale.edu

Yoga Alliance. www.yogaalliance.org

YouTube. www.youtube.com

YouTubeEDU. www.youtube.com/edu

NOTES

Introduction

1. "In 2003–04, some 69 percent of high school seniors expected to attain a bachelor's degree or higher (34 percent expected to attain a bachelor's as their highest degree, while 35 percent expected to continue to graduate or professional school). Another 18 percent expected some postsecondary education but less than a bachelor's degree." National Center for Education Statistics, *The Condition of Education 2006,* "Indicator 23."
2. H. G. Wells, *The Outline of History: Being a Plain History of Life and Mankind,* p. 1305.
3. Evan Schofer and John Meyer, "The World-Wide Expansion of Higher Education in the Twentieth Century," p. 5.
4. Philip G. Altbach et al., "Trends in Global Higher Education: Tracking an Academic Revolution," p. iv.
5. Ibid.
6. Ibid.
7. "Among reporting states in 2006, the averaged freshman graduation rate (AFGR) was 73.2 percent." National Center for Education Statistics, "High School Dropout and Completion Rates in the United States: 2007."
8. "Attainment Rates, Workers Aged 25–34, 2006: 10th among OECD countries for both Bachelor's and Sub-Bachelor's attainment. . . . The United States is also among the lowest ranking of OECD countries in the difference in attainment rates between the youngest and oldest workers." Arthur M. Hauptman and Young Kim, "Cost, Commitment, and Attainment in Higher Education: An International Comparison."
9. Barack Obama, "Remarks of President Barack Obama—Address to Joint Session of Congress."
10. "Among students who started at a 4-year college or university, 53 percent . . . had completed a bachelor's degree at the end of 5 years." National Center for Education Statistics, *Condition of Education 2004,* "Indicator 19."
11. Mark Kantrowitz, "Would Forgiving Student Loans Stimulate the Economy?"
12. Project on Student Debt, "Student Debt and the Class of 2008," p. 1.
13. American Institute of Economic Research, "The AIER Cost-of-Living Guide," p. 2.
14. I. Elaine Allen and Jeff Seaman, "Staying the Course: Online Education in the United States, 2008," p. 1.
15. William J. Hussar and Tabitha M. Bailey, "Projections of Education Statistics to 2018: Thirty-seventh Edition."
16. "Site Statistics," MIT Open CourseWare, 18 December 2009.
17. Clark Kerr, *The Uses of the University,* p .1
18. "Research has shown that only about 15 percent of higher education students still fit the traditional definition of young adults age 18 to 22 who live on campus and go to school full time." From Michael J. Offerman's blog "The Other 85 Percent" at www.theother85percent.com/about/.
19. Barbara Means, *Evaluation of Evidence-Based Practices in Online Learning: A Meta-Analysis and Review of Online Learning Studies.*
20. Kenneth Gray, *Other Ways to Win: Creating Alternatives for High School Graduates,* p. 3.

Chapter 1

1. Frederick Rudolph, *The American College and University: A History*, p. 21. Rudolph was class of 1942 at Williams College, another of the early "little colleges" (founded 1793). He later became a professor there. In the early 1960s, colleges were beginning a second huge expansion and becoming more self-conscious about their role as a formative influence on American society. Rudolph's 1962 bestseller *The American College and University: A History* looked back to the earlier period of transformation, and became a classic of the new academic study of higher education. It tells how the little colleges of the eighteenth century gave way to grand universities.

2. Ibid., p. 47. Harvard was founded in 1636, Yale 1701, Princeton 1746 (as the College of New Jersey), University of Pennsylvania 1749, Columbia 1754 (as King's College), Rutgers 1755 (as Queen's College), Brown 1764 (as the College of Rhode Island), Dartmouth 1769, and William and Mary 1776.

3. So stated a 1963 Harvard admissions brochure: "Obviously age does not guarantee excellence. It may produce simply smug somnolence and hardened arteries. But the University has grown with the country." John R. Thelin, *A History of American Higher Education*, p. xiii.

4. John V. Lombardi, "The Next Big Thing: Crisis and Transformation in American Higher Education."

5. Rudolph, *The American College and University*, p. 34.

6. Thelin, *History of American Higher Education*, p. 301.

7. Rudolph, *The American College and University*, p. 333.

8. Ibid., pp. 288, 65.

9. Thelin, *History of American Higher Education*, p. 20.

10. In 2008, Mark Bauerlein, an English professor at Emory, wrote the book *The Dumbest Generation: How the Digital Age Stupefies Young Americans and Jeopardizes Our Future (Or, Don't Trust Anyone Under 30)*. At least one member of the young generation feels the same way about him, apparently. On ratemyprofessors.com, one of his students has written, "The worst professor I have had at Emory, by far. If you don't mind giving up your dignity as a student for an easy grade, go for it. Irresponsible, self-absorbed, and generally oblivious. Strong bias against contemporary and non-Western literature."

11. Helene Wieruszowski, in *The Medieval University*, writes that the bowdlerizing of the classics was necessary to make them palatable to the Church: "By tying the philosophies of the pagans and infidels to the 'bandwagon' of theology, Aristotle and Averroes could be made acceptable to orthodox Christians" (p. 45).

12. Lowrie J. Daly, *The Medieval University: 1200–1400*, p. 8.

13. Book 2, chapter 1. Full text available at http://freespace.virgin.net/angus.graham/ Hugh.htm.

14. On August 21, 1855, the *New York Times* reported in arch, bemused tones on the "Commencement Exercises of Amherst College," where Emerson addressed the literary societies: "All were astonished. Those who were sure they understood him certainly were mistaken. Some he set furiously a-thinking, as runaway horses are apt to start off others, but what they thought they could not tell."

15. Christopher J. Lucas, *American Higher Education: A History*, p. 200.

16. Rudolph, *The American College and University*, p. 216.

17. Ibid. p. 69: "0.6 percent of 16–25 year olds in early 1800s . . . 1.75 percent over the next 50 years." David O. Levine, in *The American College and the Culture of Aspiration, 1915–1940*, writes (p. 132) that in the first decade of the twentieth century, only 2

percent of eighteen- to twenty-four-year-olds were in college. In 2008, that number hit 40 percent, an all-time high in the United States.

18. Rudolph, *The American College and University*, p. 197.

19. Ibid., pp. 252–54.

20. Ibid., p. 185: "On over 100 occasions pre-1789 the Gen'l Court of Mass appropriated funds for Harvard College, which clearly was not capable of taking care of itself."

21. Thelin writes that medical schools were the real pioneers in for-profit education; in the first half of the nineteenth century most of them were for-profit and actually sold tickets to lectures. Some medical colleges were just diploma mills with "no campus, no laboratories, no faculty, and no curriculum." *History of American Higher Education*, p. 54.

22. Rudolph, *The American College and University*, p. 263.

23. Harvard president Charles William Eliot (1834–1926) was a visionary and sweeping reformer. Not only did he drop Greek, but he also did away with compulsory chapel (1886) and the "Scale of Merit," which Harvard's Office of the President Web site describes as "a nitpicking … grading system," in favor of letter grades. The new elective system was known as "spontaneous diversity of choice," which sounds nice and modern. www.president.harvard.edu/history/21_eliot.php.

24. Rudolph, *The American College and University*, p. 406.

25. Thelin, *History of American Higher Education*, p. 75.

26. Ibid., p. 103.

27. Levine, *The American College and the Culture of Aspiration*, p. 55.

28. Rudolph, *The American College and University*, p. 50.

29. John Cook Bennett, an early Mormon leader claiming to have served an apprenticeship with his uncle as chancellor of the imaginary "Christian College," in 1832 got an Indiana state license to confer doctorates and other advanced degrees for fees ranging from $10 to $25 ($200 to $532 in 2008 dollars), even though no American university yet granted legitimate versions of those degrees. Thelin, *History of American Higher Education*, p. 56.

30. "The new faculty ethos was personified in Thorstein Veblen." Thelin, *History of American Higher Education*, p. 128.

31. Thorstein Veblen, *The Higher Learning In America: A Memorandum On the Conduct of Universities By Business Men*, p.191.

32. Thelin, *History of American Higher Education*, p. 214.

33. Levine, *The American College and the Culture of Aspiration*, p. 113.

34. The cover of the June 7, 1937, issue showed a photo of a bobby soxer's ankles—the timeless allure of the "co-ed." The phrase "American Dream" really wasn't so ancient; actually it was coined by historian James Truslow Adams in his 1931 book *The Epic of America*.

35. Levine, *The American College and the Culture of Aspiration*, p. 138.

36. Thelin, *History of American Higher Education*, p. 278.

37. Lyndon Johnson, "Remarks at Southwest Texas State College Upon Signing the Higher Education Act of 1965."

38. "The State Education Law provides a separate basis for funding SUNY community colleges, whose students are 83% white, and equivalent CUNY schools, which are over 70% non-white. In times of fiscal crisis, the predominantly non-white CUNY Community Colleges are required to compete with other city agencies for scarce resources while the overwhelmingly white SUNY community colleges have earmarked funds set aside for their support." Ronald B. McGuire, "The Struggle at CUNY: Open Admissions and Civil Rights."

39. Christopher Jencks, *The Academic Revolution*, chapter 11.

40. Thelin, *History of American Higher Education*, p. 299.

41. The October 25, 1948, issue was yet another with fetching co-eds on the cover, this time with pompoms, cheering on the UC Bears.

42. October 17, 1960.

43. Thelin, *History of American Higher Education*, p. 288.

44. The Carnegie Foundation revised the classifications in 2005 and made them much more complicated, replacing the single classification system with a set of multiple, parallel classifications. See http://classifications.carnegiefoundation.org/.

45. Nicholas Lehman, *The Big Test*, p. 132.

46. Levine, *The American College and the Culture of Aspiration*, p. 178.

47. According to a 2009 report by the National Center for Educational Statistics, "On Track to Complete? A Taxonomy of Beginning Community College Students and Their Outcomes 3 Years After Enrolling: 2003–04 Through 2006," roughly half of community college students either complete a credential or transfer to a four-year college six years after enrolling as full-time students. Nearly two-thirds of students who begin in a four-year institution finish their bachelor's degree six years later.

48. Savio, quoted in Mark Kurlansky's *1968: The Year That Rocked the World*, p.108.

49. "FBI Director J. Edgar Hoover saw Reagan's request for confidential information as a chance to finally quell the protests at Berkeley, which were sparking demonstrations at schools across the country," wrote Seth Rosenfeld, "Reagan, Hoover, and the UC Red Scare."

50. Jeffrey Kahn, "Ronald Reagan Launched Political Career Using the Berkeley Campus as a Target."

51. Dan Lips, "Reagan's ABCs."

52. "Not for a decade have politicians made a serious effort to address young people as voters, and in that time they've really put the screws to us, cutting student aid, standing by while education costs soar and more and more of us scrape by without health insurance or a permanent job. The response, from the 'Rock the Vote' generation, has been . . . nothing. Less voting, more apathy, and little in the way of protest beyond the occasional sit-in when student activity fees go up." Anya Kamenetz, "A Sleeping Class: Young Americans Fight for Every Cause But Their Own. Wake Up, Already." Youth voting did go up in 2004 and again in 2008, to near record levels, but the stereotypes of "a quiet generation" didn't stop.

53. In 2000 testimony before Congress, college affordability expert and executive director for policy analysis at the College Board Lawrence Gladieux cited a graph available at www.ed.gov/about/bdscomm/list/acsfa/edlite-figure9.html that shows the purchasing power of the maximum Pell Grant. (Most students got less than the maximum. The graph notes: "Until 1986 the Higher Education Act limited the Pell Grant award to no more than 50% of a student's cost of attendance. That limit was increased to 60% from 1986 to 1992, and thereafter it was removed altogether.")

54. National Center for Education Statistics, *The Condition of Education 2009*, "Indicator 21: Immediate Transition to College."

55. Claudia Goldin and Lawrence F. Katz, *The Race between Education and Technology: The Evolution of U.S. Educational Wage Differentials, 1890 to 2005*, p. 289.

56. "Between 1972 and 1980, the overall immediate enrollment rate was approximately 50 percent (see table A-21-1). The rate then increased, reaching 67 percent by 1997. The enrollment rate declined through 2001 to 62 percent before increasing again to 67 percent in 2007." National Center for Education Statistics, *The Condition of Education 2009*, "Indicator 21: Immediate Transition to College."

57. High school graduation rates are a matter of debate. The National Center for Education Statistics reports in *The Condition of Education 2009*, cited above, that in 2005–6, 73.2 percent of the 2002–3 freshman class graduated from high school with a regular diploma, based on self-reporting by forty-eight states. But an independent analysis of Department of Education data, "Diplomas Count 2009," by Education Week and the Editorial Projects in Education (EPE) Research Center, a nonprofit in Bethesda, Maryland, put the national graduation rate at 69.2 percent for the class of 2006, up from the 1996 nadir of 66 percent.

58. Hauptman and Kim, "Cost, Commitment, and Attainment in Higher Education."

59. The magic table is in the National Center for Education Statistics' *Digest of Education Statistics* "Table 192. College enrollment and enrollment rates of recent high school completers, by race/ethnicity: 1960 through 2006," http://nces.ed.gov/programs/digest/d07/tables/dt07_192.asp. It shows that in 1974, 47 percent of whites who had recently finished high school enrolled in college; the number for blacks and Hispanics was exactly the same, 47 percent. In 2005, 73 percent of whites enrolled in college, while only 56 percent of blacks and 54 percent of Hispanics did.

60. Finaid.org is one of the best resources on the Web for information on student loans. Based on the National Postsecondary Student Aid Study (NPSAS) conducted by the National Center for Education Statistics at the U.S. Department of Education, it reports that "The average student loan debt among graduating seniors was $23,186 (excluding PLUS Loans but including Stafford, Perkins, state, college and private loans)....The median cumulative debt among graduating Bachelor's degree recipients at 4-year undergraduate schools was $19,999 in 2007–08."

61. Rudolph, *The American College and University*, p. 177.

62. Thomas Jefferson, "Report of the Commissioner as Appointed to fix the site of the University of Virginia, &c August 4, 1818," from Gordon C. Lee, ed., *Crusade Against Ignorance: Thomas Jefferson on Education*, p.114.

63. Rudolph, *The American College and University*, p. 139.

64. Polls are notably unreliable on this matter; experts estimate that people claim to go to church twice as much as they really show up. www.christianitytoday.com/ct/2007/novemberweb-only/145-42.0.html.

Chapter 2

1. Becker writes in the introduction (p. xi) to the second edition that between the late 1950s and the 1970s "interest in the economics of education has mushroomed throughout the world."

2. Bureau of Labor Statistics, "Education and Income: More Learning Is Key to Higher Earnings."

3. State grants to students were another $8.5 billion. Sandy Baum et al., "Trends in Student Aid 2009."

4. Hauptman and Kim, "Cost, Commitment, and Attainment in Higher Education: An International Comparison."

5. Presidential remarks announcing the "American Graduation Initiative" in Warren, Michigan, 14 July 2009.

6. Goldin and Katz's 2008 study, *The Race between Education and Technology*, mentioned briefly in chapter 1, won accolades for its detailed exploration of the relationship between education and wages in America.

7. "The college wage premium shows a sharp decline from 1915 to 1950, jaggedness from 1950 to 1980, and a rapid increase after 1980. At century's end the premium to college graduation was about the same as at century's beginning." Ibid., p. 324.

8. Germany's education system is unique in the Western world, based on extensive apprenticeship and co-op programs established with the help of strong unions; they also historically have one of the lowest rates of youth unemployment in the Western world. Gary Martin. "A portrait of the youth labor market in 13 countries, 1980–2007," pp. 3–21.

9. Richard Rothstein, "Supply, Demand, Wages and Myth."

10. In 2000, according to an annual Labor Day report, "Executive Excess" by the Institute for Policy Studies and United for a Fair Economy, the average CEO made 525 times the average American worker; by 2008, with the recession dampening CEO bonuses and stock-option values, the difference was "just" 344 times.

11. Charles Miller, head of the Spellings Commission on the Future of Higher Education, has calculated his own, much lower, college premium based on six years to degree and other assumptions. "[P]roperly using the *present value* of the lifetime earnings, adjusted for the cost of going to college and the difference in the number of working years, and excluding those graduates with advanced degrees, calculated at the three percent discount rate used in the report," he wrote, "produces a *lifetime earnings differential of only $279,893* for a bachelor's degree versus a high school degree!" as quoted by Doug Lederman, "College Isn't Worth a Million Dollars."

12. U.S. Census Bureau, Current Population Survey, "March and Annual Social and Economic Supplement, 1996–2008."

13. Stephen Greenhouse, "As Plants Close, Teenagers Focus More on College."

14. According to the OECD's report *Education at a Glance 2008*, the United States spends 7 percent of GDP, or roughly $968 billion, on education at all levels.

15. David H. Autor et al., "Trends in U.S. Wage Inequality: Revising the Revisionists." In an interview with me, Autor said, "One of the striking facts about the U.S. labor market in the last fifteen years is the simultaneous growth of relatively high-skilled and low-skilled jobs."

16. Claudia Goldin and Larry Katz, "Why the United States Led in Education: Lessons from Secondary School Expansion, 1910 to 1940."

17. Jencks, *The Academic Revolution*, pp. 262, 198.

18. "Black students who graduated in the 1992–93 school year had an overall default rate that was over five times higher than white students and over nine times higher than Asian students." Erin Dillon, "Hidden Details: A Closer Look at Student Loan Default Rates."

19. Ron Haskins et al., *Promoting Economic Mobility by Increasing Postsecondary Education.*

20. Danette Gerald and Kati Haycock, "Engines of Inequality: Diminishing Equity in the Nation's Premier Public Universities."

21. Mark Blaug, *The Economics of Education and the Education of an Economist*, p. 91.

22. Ibid, p. 26.

23. John Holt, *Instead of Education*, p. 42.

24. Bill Mears, "Sotomayor Says She Was 'Perfect Affirmative Action Baby'."

25. The Legislative Analyst's Office of the state of California says it cost $47,102 per year in 2008–9 to house an inmate in state prison. The total state spending on higher education was $33 billion for 1.7 million students, or $19,447 per student. (www. lao.ca.gov). With additional cuts to higher education in progress, that budgetary bias in favor of prisons is only likely to grow.

26. Josh Keller, "At Transfer Time, Thousands of California Students Hit a Dead End."

27. Rudolph, *The American College and University*, p. 206.

28. Richard Vedder, *Going Broke by Degree: Why College Costs Too Much*, p. 196.

29. Students who are charged out-of-state or full-fare tuition and who are too affluent to qualify for a tuition discount may still take advantage of federally subsidized student loans, meaning they are taking a slice of the aid pie from students who need the money to get in the door of any college. The same dilemma arises in the dozen or so states that have guaranteed merit scholarships to the state universities for all high school graduates with a certain grade point average, such as Georgia's HOPE scholarship; studies have shown that this money goes disproportionately to students from the middle class and above.

30. The University of Miami offers what may be the nation's only graduate degree in enrollment management. "Enrollment is a 'cradle to grave' process that starts at the first point of student contact—the prospect—and continues to and through graduation. A campus-wide initiative to improve, stabilize or maintain a successful institution, enrollment management benefits not only the institution and its students, but also the faculty, staff and community." www6.miami.edu/UMH/CDA/UMH_Main/0,1770,3564-1,00.html.

31. Many of the questions are multipart: http://www.fafsaonline.com/. In June 2009, Education secretary Arne Duncan announced an initiative to simplify the form and allow applicants to plug in the answers to many questions using their tax returns.

32. Higher-education experts make a distinction between affordability—whether college is easily accommodated in a family budget, which is more of a middle-class concern—and access, the basic means to get in the door.

33. Gerald and Haycock, "Engines of Inequality."

34. Richard D. Kahlenberg, *The Remedy: Class, Race, and Affirmative Action*.

35. Jane V. Wellman, et al., "Trends in College Spending: Where Does the Money Come From? Where Does It Go?"

36. Ken Gray, in his 2006 book *Other Ways to Win: Creating Alternatives for High School Graduates*, and James Rosenbaum in the 2001 book *Beyond College for All: Career Paths for the Forgotten Half*, both argue this point persuasively: people need clearly marked options.

37. "Since 1993, MDRC has been conducting a rigorous evaluation of the Career Academy approach . . . one of the few studies of a high school reform initiative that uses the design of a randomized, controlled field trial. . . . Findings from the study provide compelling evidence that the Academies produced substantial and sustained improvements in the post-high school labor market outcomes of youth." MDRC, "Project Page: Career Academies," www.mdrc.org/project_29_1.html.

38. The Urban Assembly, www.urbanassembly.org.

39. Public Allies, www.publicallies.org.

40. Richard Rothstein, "How Can Colleges Help Graduates Pursue a Career?"

41. Edward Lazear, "Stimulus and the Jobless Recovery."

Chapter 3

1. Hofstra University, www.hofstra.edu/debate/.

2. *The Brian Lehrer Show*, www.wnyc.org/shows/bl/.

3. Mark Santora, "For the Last Presidential Debate, a Nation's Eyes Will Turn to Hofstra."

4. "Michelle Obama: Barack's Book Sales Paid off Our Student Loans."

5. Ruth Padawer, "Keeping Up with Being Kept."

6. *New York Daily News*, "Howard Stern in Virgin Territory."

7. Tamar Lewin, "Higher Education May Soon Be Unaffordable for Most Americans, Report Says."

8. National Center for Public Policy and Higher Education, "Measuring Up 2008."

9. Goldin and Katz, *The Race between Education and Technology*, p. 300.

10. "There are roughly 95 million youth living in the United States born between the years 1978 and 2000. . . . By contrast, there are only about 78 million Baby Boomers, the generation that rules the country today." Eric Greenberg and Karl Weber, *Generation We: How Millennial Youth Are Taking Over America and Changing Our World Forever*, p. 4.

11. William J. Baumol and William Bowen, *Performing Arts: The Economic Dilemma*.

12. Wellman et al., "Trends in College Spending."

13. John W. Curtis and Monica F. Jacobe, "Consequences: An Increasingly Contingent Faculty."

14. James M. Owston, "Survival of the Fittest? The Rebranding of West Virginia Higher Education" Owston also found a separate count of 785 colleges and universities that changed their names during the years from 1992 to 2001.

15. Melody Gordon, "Faculty Senate Prepares for Program Cuts."

16. Wes Rucker, "Neyland Stadium Renovations Cost University of Tennessee Plenty."

17. Even if the stadium construction costs are funded by alumni, a common practice, the university pays for the development officers who raise the money and allow it to be earmarked that way, and general-funds money will go to maintain the building. In times of economic hardship, some colleges have created special scholarship-only funds to ensure that alumni donations are directed toward access; other colleges have simply done away with their football teams.

18. Lisa Foderaro, "Well-Regarded Public Colleges Get a Surge of Bargain Hunters."

19. Rudolph, *The American College and University*, p. 198.

20. Hauptman and Kim, "Cost, Commitment, and Attainment in Higher Education," p. iv.

21. State subsidies hit a twenty-five-year low of $6,445 in constant dollars in 2005. State and local support is up since then, to $7,059 per student in 2008, but the share of total education funding that comes from *net* tuition—payments from students, minus grants to students—kept increasing, to 32 percent in 2008. State Higher Education Executive Officers, "State Higher Education Finance FY 2008."

22. Wellman et al., p.26.

23. From $2,000 to $2,300 per semester for full-time undergraduates.

24. For these figures and those in previous two paragraphs, Baum et al., "Trends in Student Aid 2009."

25. Edward L. Andrews, "My Personal Credit Crisis."

26. Ibid.

27. Anya Kamenetz, "The Profit Chase."

28. Jonathan D. Glater, "Marketing Code for Student Lenders." Sallie Mae and Nelnet staffed a few dozen call centers for colleges so that when a student called her financial aid office, she'd actually be speaking to the lender's employees. Others plied financial aid officers with cruises, vacations, and freebies, and set up schemes wherein colleges could profit directly by making loans. Sallie Mae, Citibank, and a lender called Education Finance Partners eventually paid nearly $7 million to settle the probe, which touched dozens of well-known universities like Columbia University, the University of Southern California, and the University of Texas at Austin.

29. Anya Kamenetz, "Student Loans: MyRichUncle Is Out of Cash."

30. Scott Jaschik, "Bucking the Tide on Private Loans."

31. Anya Kamenetz, "Johnny Comes Marching Home to Loans."

32. Deanne Loonin et al., "Paying the Price: The High Cost of Private Student Loans and the Dangers for Student Borrowers."

33. Student Loan Justice, http://studentloanjustice.org/New%20York.htm
34. Helen Lew, "Audit to Determine if Cohort Default Rates Provide Sufficient Information on Defaults in the Title IV Loan Programs."
35. Ibrinfo.org, a site maintained by the nonprofit, nonpartisan Project on Student Debt, gives full info on these programs. Student advocates have told me they're having trouble getting the Department of Education to sufficiently publicize or educate students about the program.
36. Libby Nelson, "Students at For-Profit Colleges Are Most Likely to Default on Loans, Report Says."
37. Jason DeParle, "Trade Schools Near Success as They Lobby for Survival."
38. Bridgepoint Education and Grand Canyon Education, discussed chapter 5.
39. Anya Kamenetz, "Universities Inc.."
40. Justin Pope, "For-Profit Colleges Boost Lending."
41. Dillon, "Hidden Details: A Closer Look at Student Loan Default Rates."
42. Lisa Foderaro, "Applications Surge at Cooper Union."

Chapter 4
1. Sponsored by Jobs for the Future, June 22, 2009; videos at http://makingopportun ityaffordable.org.
2. Open Ed annual conference, http://openedconference.org/.
3. Creative Commons, http://creativecommons.org/about/.
4. "There was a norm about ownership: nobody owned Wikipedia exclusively. The content of Wikipedia got created under a copyright license that guaranteed it was always free for anyone to copy, and that any modifications had to be free as well. This "copyleft" license—the brainchild of Richard Stallman—set the final founding norm for this extraordinary experiment in collaboration." Lawrence Lessig, *Remix: Making Art and Commerce Thrive in the Hybrid Economy*, p. 157.
5. OpenCourseWare Consortium, www.ocwconsortium.org.
6. OER Africa, www.oerafrica.org. Open University of the Netherlands has an OpenER project with the adorable name Wikiwijs (Wiki + wise) www.opener .ou.nl.
7. "The Chinese Ministry of Education has since 2003 been operating a national OCW program called China Quality OpenCourseWare. Chinese universities submit proposals, and can receive between $7,300 and $14,600 per course that is made freely available online." OpenEd 2009 presentation by Stian Håklev, MA candidate, Ontario Institute for Studies in Education, University of Toronto. http:// openedconference.org/archives/511.
8. Directory of Open Access Journals, www.doaj.org.
9. Foothill College, www.foothill.fhda.edu/index.php.
10. Community College Consortium for Open Educational Resources, http://oer consortium.org/.
11. Programmable Open Mobile Internet, www.stanford.edu/~phkim/project/consult ing.html.
12. "38,000 College Students to Save 3 Million Dollars in Fall 2009 Semester" (press release, Flatworld Knowledge, 20 August 2009), http://www.flatworldknowledge .com/sites/all/files/38000_students_save_3_mm_0.pdf.
13. Open High School of Utah, www.openhighschool.org.
14. Connectivism and Connective Knowledge, http://ltc.umanitoba.ca/connectivism/.
15. John Seely Brown and Richard P. Adler, "Minds on Fire: Open Education, the Web, and Learning 2.0."

16. From the Online Etymology Dictionary:"c.1300,'institution of higher learning,' also 'body of persons constituting a university,' from Anglo-Fr. université, O.Fr. universitei (13c.), from M.L. universitatem (nom. universitas), in L.L.'corporation, society,' from L., 'the whole, aggregate,' from universus 'whole, entire' (see universe). In the academic sense, a shortening of universitas magistrorum et scholarium 'community of masters and scholars;' superseded studium as the word for this." (www.etymonline.com, accessed 11 November 2009).

17. "The word 'college' was loosely used in the seventeenth century as signifying any company or collective body. Burton, in *Anatomy of Melancholy* (1621), says, 'They have whole colleges of Curtezans in their Towns and Cities.' Randolph, in *The Muse's Looking-Glass* (1638), calls play-houses 'colleges of transgression,' and speaks of 'Black-Friar's College.' Jonson, in *Staple of News*, says 'a canter's college is proposed.' Dryden even speaks of a 'college of bees' (*Flower and Leaf*), and Amory, in John Buncle, uses the same phrase more than half a century later. It becomes evident, then, that the words 'college' and 'collegiate' might be used without any thought of an organization founded for purposes of learning. (See Jonson: Epiccene, Ed. Henry, Aurelia, p. 138.)" Myra Reynolds, *The Learned Lady in England, 1650–1750*, p. 374, n. 8.

18. University of Southern California, Master of Arts in Teaching, http://mat.usc.edu/.

19. Blackboard, with its huge market share and its tendency toward tight control of systems and content, is the despised Microsoft of the educational technology community. "One thing that has stuck with me in my quest to bury BlackBoard [sic] over the last four years has been just how shamelessly BlackBoard's [sic] PR message is so hypocritical when looked [at] against their baseless legal aggression against their competitors," writes Jim Groom on his blog. http://bavatuesdays.com/blackboard-innovate-educate-litigate/.

20. Open Learning Initiative, http://oli.web.cmu.edu/openlearning/.

21. Barbara Means et al., *Evaluation of Evidence-Based Practices in Online Learning*.

22. National Center for Academic Transformation, www.thencat.org.

23. "Engage," http://engage.wisc.edu/.

24. Robbins blogs at http://ubernoggin.com/.

25. "The Unofficial Elder Scrolls Pages," http://forums.uesp.net/viewtopic.php ?f=5&t=14900.

26. Paul E. Ceruzzi, *Beyond the Limit: Flight Enters the Computer Age*, p. 168. Link's simulators were called "blue boxes" for the military paint color.

27. Faulkes Telescope Project, http://faulkes-telescope.com.

28. UMW Blogs, http://umwblogs.org.

29. Mozilla, www.mozilla.org.

30. Cory Doctorow, *Down and Out in the Magic Kingdom*.

31. Kathleen Kingsbury, "Go Western, Young Man."

32. Anya Kamenetz, "The Laws of Urban Energy."

33. "The role of information and communication technology for the next generation of work environments and office buildings will go beyond its use as mere productivity tools. Information technology will also play a major role as a medium and mediator for supporting informal communication and conveying social awareness and atmospheres in organizations." From a fascinating chapter by Norbert Streitz et al. about the creation of "social architectural spaces" using mobile devices and ambient displays, in O'Hara et al, eds., *Public and Situated Displays: Social and Interactional Aspects of Shared Display Technologies*, pp. 387–409.

34. Marc Parry, "Utah State U.'s OpenCourseWare Closes Because of Budget Woes."

35. $68 million in grants between 2002 and 2006 were reviewed in Daniel E. Atkins et al., "A Review of the Open Educational Resources (OER) Movement: Achievements, Challenges, and New Opportunities," Report to the William and Flora Hewlett Foundation, February 2007, http://www.oerderves.org/wp-content/uploads/2007/03/a-review-of-the-open-educational-resources-oer-movement_final.pdf. An additional $10 million were announced during 2008.

36. Michael B. Farrell, "Schwarzenegger's Push for Digital Textbooks."

37. S.1714 "Open College Textbook Act of 2009: A bill to authorize grants for the creation, update, or adaption of open textbooks, and for other purposes," http://thomas.loc.gov/cgi-bin/bdquery/z?d111:s.01714:.

38. "The American Graduation Initiative: Stronger American Skills through Community Colleges," The White House Office of the Press Secretary, 14 July 2009, www.whitehouse.gov/blog/Investing-in-Education-The-American-Graduation-Initiative/ (accessed 6 November 2009). The administration also makes a clear case for technology-assisted teaching: "Online educational software has the potential to help students learn more in less time than they would with traditional classroom instruction alone. Interactive software can tailor instruction to individual students like human tutors do, while simulations and multimedia software offer experiential learning. Online instruction can also be a powerful tool for extending learning opportunities to rural areas or working adults who need to fit their coursework around families and jobs."

39. Professor Friesen's blog and the full presentation can be found at http://learningspaces.org/n/node/25.

40. The sequel to Freire's famous *Pedagogy of the Oppressed* is *Pedagogy of the City* (1992) which recalls his years in Brazil's national government.

41. Paulo Freire, *Education for Critical Consciousness*, p. 31.

Chapter 5

1. Toaster Project, www.thetoasterproject.org.

2. Douglas Adams, *Mostly Harmless*, p. 118.

3. Henry David Thoreau, *Walden*, p. 82.

4. Brown and Adler, "Minds on Fire: Open Education, the Web, and Learning 2.0."

5. Couros introduced me to the term; properly crediting ideas is always tricky in the blogosphere, but on his blog he points to Stephen Downes, who in turn credits David Warlick, an educational consultant in North Carolina who blogs at 2 Cents Worth http://davidwarlick.com/2cents/ with the coinage. An earlier synonym is "personal learning environment."

6. David Brown, "Tuvan Throat-Singers Perform Feats of Harmonic Acrobatics," *Washington Post*, 15 January 1996, republished on Friends of Tuva Web site, www.fotuva.org/music/wash_post_96915.html (accessed 5 November 2009).

7. Here's Levin's full response: "Yes, a lot of people e-mail me with questions about Tuvan throat singing, and yes, I respond to each and every inquiry. But I don't respond equally. The depth of the response is commensurate with the thoughtfulness of the inquiry. To the (American) guy who e-mailed from Kiev to tell me he was researching an article on Siberian shamanism for *National Geographic* and asked if I could phone him and tell him something about how shamans in Tuva use throat singing, I e-mailed back a reference to my book, *Where Rivers and Mountains Sing: Sound, Music, and Nomadism in Tuva and Beyond*, and told him he was welcome to write me again if he still had questions after reading the book. I never heard back from him. But to the guy who wrote that he was about to leave for Tuva to spend a

year on a Fulbright and clearly knew a lot about throat singing already but wanted detailed information on singers, regional variations, etc., I wrote a long response, and we've since become good friends (six years later, he's still in Tuva—married to a local woman, fluent in Tuvan language, and managing a throat-singing ensemble that tours internationally). And to the guy who e-mailed that he was taking his PhD qualifying exams at Berkeley with the aim of writing a dissertation on Tuvan music and wondered if I'd agree to compose five questions on Tuvan music for his exam and work with his committee to evaluate his answers, I said yes, and then spent a few hours with him in a diner during a trip to California last spring to help him prepare for the exam.

My point: that 'research' via Internet can get you only as far as the doorstep in certain kinds of knowledge seeking, and that to go beyond that requires that you step off the Internet and into more personalized forms of knowledge transmission. Since I'm committed to this kind of knowledge transmission, I believe it's my duty to share what I know with any serious seeker or researcher who comes along, whatever the portal by which he or she reaches me."

8. Ivan Illich, *Deschooling Society*, p. 49. American educator Paul Goodman made a very similar argument a few years earlier in *Compulsory Mis-Education and the Community of Scholars*.

9. Illich, *Deschooling Society*, p. 2.

10. Ibid, p. 134.

11. Steven Morris, "Father Delivers Baby Son after Watching YouTube Childbirth Clips."

12. Uploaded on 21 February 2009; by the time this book went to press the video had been viewed more than 4,000 times and received nineteen comments with (more or less) helpful suggestions.

13. Jean Lave and Etienne Wenger, *Situated Learning: Legitimate Peripheral Participation*.

14. A community of practice doesn't have to be located all in the same place, or have a hard division between who's inside and outside. What matters is "participation in an activity system" (ibid., p. 98). This is a community of do-ers, as John Holt would call it.

15. "AcaWiki is like a 'Wikipedia for academic research' designed to increase the impact of scholars, students, and bloggers by enabling them to share summaries and discuss academic papers online." AcaWiki, http://acawiki.org/Home.

16. "The Gen-1 Theme House is an off-campus residence designed to provide its residents with a safe, orderly, and highly structured environment in which to live, learn, and work. The primary objective of the Gen-1 Theme House is to provide first-year, first-generation students with the support needed to make a successful transition from high school to college." Gen-1 Theme House @ Stratford Heights, University of Cincinnati, www.uc.edu/cechpass/gen1/ (accessed 11 November 2009).

17. Holt, *Instead of Education*, p. 18.

Chapter 6

1. Peter Smith is the former assistant director-general for education at the United Nations Educational, Scientific, and Cultural Organization (UNESCO), founder and former president of both California State University–Monterey Bay and the Community College of Vermont, as well as a former U.S. congressman and lieutenant governor for the state of Vermont. He now works for Kaplan Higher Education. He is the author of *The Quiet Crisis: How Higher Education Is Failing America* (San Francisco: Jossey-Bass, 2008).

2. ScienceDaily, "Aquaculture's Growth Seen as Continuing."
3. Emily Yoffe, "Seeking: How the Brain Hard-Wires Us to Love Google, Twitter, and Texting. And Why That's Dangerous."

Chapter 7

1. Louis Uchitelle, "Despite Recession, High Demand for Skilled Labor."
2. Shaffer did, after all, go to college, where he majored in sociology—which is a reminder that people are usually interested in a variety of things, so your studies and jobs don't have to be lined up too perfectly. Life is about more than the career path.
3. Florida State University psychologist K. Anders Ericsson, in landmark studies of experts, has coined the term "deliberate practice" to describe a key component of building expertise: "For example, the critical difference between expert musicians differing in the level of attained solo performance concerned the amounts of time they had spent in solitary practice during their music development, which totaled around 10,000 hours by age 20 for the best experts, around 5,000 hours for the least accomplished expert musicians and only 2,000 hours for serious amateur pianists. More generally, the accumulated amount of deliberate practice is closely related to the attained level of performance of many types of experts, such as musicians . . ., chessplayers . . . and athletes. . ." Ericsson, "Expert Performance and Deliberate Practice."
4. Interestingly, yoga trainers are organizing to resist state attempts to regulate them, which is one of the key steps to professionalization. "Yoga is the study of the self through direct experience," Suzanne Leitner-Wise, president of U.S. 1 Yoga Teacher Training, told the *Washington Post*. "You simply can't put regulations on that. It's just dumb." Maria Glod, "Va. Yoga Regulation a Stretch for Teachers."
5. Quote from an interview by Danielle Sacks, used with her permission.

BIBLIOGRAPHY

Adams, Douglas. *Mostly Harmless.* New York: Harmony Books, 1992.

Allen, I. Elaine, and Jeff Seaman. "Staying the Course: Online Education in the United States, 2008." Sloan Consortium, November 2008. www.sloan-c.org/publications/survey/staying_course.

Altbach, Philip G. et al., "Trends in Global Higher Education: Tracking an Academic Revolution." Report prepared for the UNESCO 2009 World Conference on Higher Education. 2009. http://www.unesco.org/en/wche2009/resources/global-reports/

American Institute of Economic Research. "The AIER Cost-of-Living Guide." January 2009. http://www.aier.org/bookstore/membership?page=shop.browse&category_id=25

Andrews, Edward L. "My Personal Credit Crisis." *New York Times Magazine.* 14 May 2009. www.nytimes.com/2009/05/17/magazine/17foreclosure-t.htm.

Arenson, Karen. "Columbia to Pay $1.1 Million to State Fund in Loan Scandal." *New York Times,* 1 June 2007. http://query.nytimes.com/gst/fullpage.html?res=9F02E7D91530F932A35755C0A9619C8B63.

Autor, David H., et al. "Trends in U.S. Wage Inequality: Revising the Revisionists." *The Review of Economics and Statistics* 90, no. 2 (2008): 300–23. http://econ-www.mit.edu/faculty/dautor/papers.

Baum, Sandy, et al. "Trends in Student Aid 2009." The College Board, 2009. www.trends-collegeboard.com/student_aid/.

———. "Trends in College Pricing 2009." The College Board, 2009. www.trends-collegeboard.com/college_pricing/.

Baumol, William J., and William Bowen. *Performing Arts: The Economic Dilemma.* New York: Twentieth Century Fund, 1966. http://openlibrary.org/b/OL7771246M/Performing_Arts_the_Economic_Dilemma.

Becker, Gary. *Human Capital: A Theoretical and Empirical Analysis with Special Reference to Education.* Chicago: University of Chicago Press, 1964.

Bird, Caroline. *The Case Against College.* New York: McKay, 1975.

Blaug, Mark. *The Economics of Education and the Education of an Economist.* New York: New York University Press, 1987.

Bolles, Richard Nelson, and Carol Christen. *What Color Is Your Parachute? For Teens.* Berkeley, Calif.: Ten Speed Press, 2009.

Bonk, Curtis J. *The World Is Open: How Web Technology Is Revolutionizing Education.* San Francisco: Jossey-Bass, 2009.

Bradwell, Peter. "The Edgeless University: Why Higher Education Must Embrace Technology." London: Demos Publications, 2009. www.demos.co.uk/publications/the-edgeless-university.

Brown, John Seely, and Richard P. Adler. "Minds on Fire: Open Education, the Web, and Learning 2.0," *Educause Review.* January/February 2008. www.educause.edu/EDUCAUSE+Review/EDUCAUSEReviewMagazineVolume43/MindsonFireOpenEducationtheLon/162420.

Bureau of Labor Statistics. "Education and Income: More Learning Is Key to Higher Earnings." *Occupational Outlook Quarterly.* Fall 2006. www.bls.gov/opub/ooq/2006/fall/oochart.pdf.

Curtis, John W., and Monica F. Jacobe. "Consequences: An Increasingly Contingent Faculty." American Association of University Professors, 2006. www.uff-fsu.org/art/AAUPContingentFaculty.pdf.

Daly, Lowrie J. *The Medieval University: 1200–1400.* New York: Sheed & Ward, 1961.

Davidson, Cathy N., and David Theo Goldberg. *The Future of Learning Institutions in a Digital Age.* Cambridge, Mass.: MIT Press, 2009. Also available online at http://mitpress.mit.edu/books/chapters/Future_of_Learning.pdf.

DeParle, Jason. "Trade Schools Near Success as They Lobby for Survival." *New York Times,* 25 March 1992. http://www.nytimes.com/1992/03/25/news/trade-schools-near-success-as-they-lobby-for-survival.html.

Dewey, John. *Democracy and Education.* Middlesex, England: The Echo Library, 2007.

Dillon, Erin. "Hidden Details: A Closer Look at Student Loan Default Rates." Education Sector. 23 October 2007. www.educationsector.org/analysis/analysis_show.htm?doc_id=559757.

Ericsson, K. Anders. "Expert Performance and Deliberate Practice." Available at www.psy.fsu.edu/faculty/ericsson/ericsson.exp.perf.html.

Farrell, Michael B. "Schwarzenegger's Push for Digital Textbooks," ABC News. 14 June 2009. http://abcnews.go.com/Technology/Economy/story?id=7827997&page=1.

Foderaro, Lisa. "Applications Surge at Cooper Union." *New York Times,* 8 February 2009. http://www.nytimes.com/2009/02/09/education/09cooper.html.

———. "Well-Regarded Public Colleges Get a Surge of Bargain Hunters." *New York Times.* 1 March 2009. http://www.nytimes.com/2009/03/02/nyregion/02suny.html.

Freire, Paulo. *Education for Critical Consciousness.* New York: Continuum, 1973.

———. *Pedagogy of the City.* New York: Continuum, 1992.

———. *Pedagogy of the Oppressed.* 30th anniv, ed. New York: Continuum, 2000.

Gardner, John W. *Excellence: Can We Be Equal and Excellent Too?* New York: W. W. Norton & Co, 1987.

Gerald, Danette, and Kati Haycock. "Engines of Inequality: Diminishing Equity in the Nation's Premier Public Universities." The Education Trust, 2006. http://president.asu.edu/node/91.

Glater, Jonathan D. "Marketing Code for Student Lenders." *New York Times.* 9 September 2008. www.nytimes.com/2008/09/10/business/10loan.html.

Glod, Maria. "Va. Yoga Regulation a Stretch for Teachers." *Washington Post.* 2 December 2009. www.washingtonpost.com/wp-dyn/content/article/2009/12/01/AR2009120103822.html

Goldin, Claudia, and Lawrence F. Katz. *The Race between Education and Technology: The Evolution of U.S. Educational Wage Differentials, 1890 to 2005.* Cambridge, Mass.: Belknap Press of Harvard University Press, 2008.

———. "Why the United States Led in Education: Lessons from Secondary School Expansion, 1910 to 1940." NBER Working Paper W6144. 1 August 1997. http://ideas.repec.org/p/nbr/nberwo/6144.html.

Goodman, Paul. *Compulsory Mis-Education and the Community of Scholars.* New York: Random House, 1964.

Gordon, Melody. "Faculty Senate Prepares for Program Cuts." *The Daily Beacon,* 25 February 2009. http://dailybeacon.utk.edu/showarticle.php?articleid=54733.

Gray, Kenneth *Other Ways to Win: Creating Alternatives for High School Graduates.* London: Corwin Press, 2006.

Greenberg, Eric, and Karl Weber. *Generation We: How Millennial Youth Are Taking Over America and Changing Our World Forever.* Emeryville, Calif.: Pachatusan, 2008.

Greenhouse, Stephen. "As Plants Close, Teenagers Focus More on College." *New York Times,* 25 June 2009. www.nytimes.com/2009/06/26/business/26grads.html.

Haskins, Ron, et al. *Promoting Economic Mobility by Increasing Postsecondary Education.* Washington, D.C.: Pew Charitable Trusts Economic Mobility Project, 2009. www.urban.org/publications/1001280.html.

Hauptman, Arthur M., and Young Kim. "Cost, Commitment, and Attainment in Higher Education: An International Comparison." Jobs for the Future (May 2009). www.jff .org/publications/education/cost-commitment-and-attainment-higher-ed/836.

Hern, Matt, Ed. *Everywhere All the Time: A New Deschooling Reader*. Oakland, Calif.: AK Press, 2008.

Holt, John. *Instead of Education*. New York: Dutton, 1976.

Hussar, William J., and Tabitha M. Bailey. "Projections of Education Statistics to 2018: Thirty-seventh Edition." National Center for Education Statistics. September 2009. http://nces.ed.gov/pubSearch/pubsinfo.asp?pubid=2009062

Iiyoshi, Toru and M. S. Vijay Kumar, eds. *Opening Up Education: The Collective Advancement of Education through Open Technology, Open Content, and Open Knowledge*. Cambridge, Mass.: MIT Press, 2008. Also available at http://mitpress.mit.edu/catalog/item/default. asp?ttype=2&tid=11309

Illich, Ivan. *Deschooling Society*. London: Marion Boyars, 1971.

Institute for College Access & Success. "Lowest Cost Colleges Are Hardest to Afford." Press release. 13 May 2009. www.projectonstudentdebt.org/pub_view.php?idx=452.

Jaschik, Scott. "Bucking the Tide on Private Loans." *Inside Higher Ed*, 16 July 2007. www.insidehighered.com/news/2007/07/16/barnard.

Jencks, Christopher. *The Academic Revolution*. Garden City, NY: Doubleday, 1969.

———. *Inequality: A Reassessment of the Effect of Family and Schooling in America*. New York: Harper, 1972.

Johnson, Lyndon. "Remarks at Southwest Texas State College Upon Signing the Higher Education Act of 1965." 8 November 1965. www.presidency.ucsb.edu/ws/index. php?pid=27356.

Johnson, Steven. *Everything Bad Is Good for You*. New York: Riverhead, 2005.

Kahlenberg, Richard D. *The Remedy: Class, Race, and Affirmative Action*. New York: Basic Books, 1996.

Kahn, Jeffery. "Ronald Reagan Launched Political Career Using the Berkeley Campus as a Target." UC Berkeley NewsCenter, 8 Jun 2004. http://berkeley.edu/news/media/ releases/2004/06/08_reagan.shtml.

Kamenetz, Anya. "Johnny Comes Marching Home to Loans." *Village Voice*, 21 June 2005. www.villagevoice.com/2005-06-21/nyc-life/ johnny-comes-marching-home-to-loans/.

———. "The Laws of Urban Energy." *Psychology Today* (July 2007). www.psychology today.com/articles/200706/the-laws-urban-energy.

———. "MyRichUncle Is Out of Cash." *Fast Company*, blog, 9 February 2009. www.fastcompany.com/blog/anya-kamenetz/green-day/myrichuncle-out-cash.

———. "The Profit Chase." *Slate*, 16 November 2005. www.slate.com/id/2130516/.

———. "Robbing Joe College to Pay Sallie Mae." *New York Times*, 12 December 2005. www.nytimes.com/2005/12/12/opinion/12kamenetz.html.

———. "A Sleeping Class: Young Americans Fight for Every Cause But Their Own. Wake Up, Already." *Village Voice*, 25 May 2004. www.villagevoice.com/2004-05-25/ news/a-sleeping-class/.

———. "Student Loans: MyRichUncle." *Fast Company*, February 2006. www.fast company.com/magazine/103/open_16-khan-garg.html.

———. "Universities Inc." *Fast Company*, December/January 2009. www.fastcompany .com/magazine/141/universities-inc.html.

Kantrowitz, Mark. "Would Forgiving Student Loans Stimulate the Economy?" Fastweb .com. 9 August 2009. www.fastweb.com/financial-aid/ articles/1447-would-forgiving-student-loans-stimulate-the-economy.

Keller, Josh. "At Transfer Time, Thousands of California Students Hit a Dead End." *Chronicle of Higher Education*. 5 October 2009. http://chronicle.com/article/At-Transfer-Time-Thousands-of/48678/.

Kerr, Clark. *The Uses of the University*. Cambridge, Mass.: Harvard College, 1963.

Kingsbury, Kathleen. "Go Western, Young Man," *Time*. 13 November 2008. www.time.com/time/magazine/article/0,9171,1858876,00.html.

Kirn, Walter. *Lost in the Meritocracy: The Undereducation of an Overachiever*. New York: Doubleday, 2009.

Kurlansky, Mark. *1968: The Year That Rocked the World*. New York: Random House, 2004.

LaMacchia, Joe, and Bridget Samburg. *Blue Collar and Proud of It*. Deerfield Beach, Fla.: Health Communications, 2009.

Lave, Jean, and Etienne Wenger. *Situated Learning: Legitimate Peripheral Participation*. Cambridge: Cambridge University Press, 1991.

Lazear, Edward. "Stimulus and the Jobless Recovery." *Wall Street Journal*. 1 November 2009. http://online.wsj.com/article/SB10001424052748703932904574509341078005538.html.

Lederman, Doug. "College Isn't Worth a Million Dollars." *Inside Higher Ed*. 7 April 2008. www.insidehighered.com/news/2008/04/07/miller.

Lee, Gordon C., ed. *Crusade Against Ignorance: Thomas Jefferson on Education*. New York: Bureau of Publications, Teachers College, Columbia University, 1961.

Lehman, Nicholas. *The Big Test*. New York: Farrar, Straus & Giroux, 1999.

Lerman, Robert I. "Widening the Scope of Standards through Work-Based Learning." Presentation at the Thirtieth Annual APPAM Research Conference, 6 November 2008. www.urban.org/events/upload/Lerman-Work-Standards6.pdf.

Lessig, Lawrence. *Remix: Making Art and Commerce Thrive in the Hybrid Economy*. New York: Penguin, 2008.

Levine, David O. *The American College and the Culture of Aspiration, 1915–1940*. Ithaca, NY: Cornell University Press, 1987.

Lew, Helen. "Audit to Determine if Cohort Default Rates Provide Sufficient Information on Defaults in the Title IV Loan Programs." Department of Education, 22 December 2003. www.ed.gov/about/offices/list/oig/auditreports/a03c0017.doc.

Lewin, Tamar. "Higher Education May Soon Be Unaffordable for Most Americans, Report Says." *New York Times*. 3 December 2008. www.nytimes.com/2008/12/03/education/03college.html.

Lips, Dan. "Reagan's ABCs." *National Review Online*. 22 May 2001. www.cato.org/pub_display.php?pub_id=4281.

Lombardi, John V. "The Next Big Thing: Crisis and Transformation in American Higher Education." *Inside Higher Ed*. 3 August 2009. www.insidehighered.com/blogs/reality_check/the_next_big_thing_crisis_and_transformation_in_american_higher_education2.

Loonin, Deanne, et al. "Paying the Price: The High Cost of Private Student Loans and the Dangers for Student Borrowers." National Consumer Law Center, March 2008. www.studentloanborrowerassistance.org/legal-policy/.

Lucas, Christopher J. *American Higher Education: A History*. New York: Palgrave Macmillan, 1996.

Martin, Gary. "A Portrait of the Youth Labor Market in 13 Countries, 1980–2007." Bureau of Labor Statistics, Monthly Labor Review. July 2009. www.bls.gov/opub/ted/2009/ted_20090804.htm.

McGuire, Ronald B. "The Struggle at CUNY: Open Admissions and Civil Rights." Leftspot Blog. 3 November 2006 (originally published in 1992). http://leftspot.com/blog/?q=cunystruggle.

Means, Barbara, et al. *Evaluation of Evidence-Based Practices in Online Learning: A Meta-Analysis and Review of Online Learning Studies*. U.S. Department of Education, Office of Planning, Evaluation, and Policy Development, 2009. www.ed.gov/rschstat/eval/tech/evidence-based-practices/finalreport.pdf.

Mears, Bill. "Sotomayor Says She Was 'Perfect Affirmative Action Baby'." CNN.com. 11 June 2009. www.cnn.com/2009/POLITICS/06/11/sotomayor.affirmative.action/index.html.

Meyer, John, et al. "Higher Education as an Institution." Stanford Center on Democracy, Development, and the Rule of Law. Working Paper no. 57, May 2006. http://cddrl.stanford.edu/publications/higher_education_as_an_institution/.

"Michelle Obama: Barack's Book Sales Paid off Our Student Loans." Associated Press, 9 April 2008. www.foxnews.com/politics/elections/2008/04/09/michelle-obama-baracks-book-sales-paid-off-our-student-loans/.

Middle Class Task Force. "Financing the Dream: Securing College Affordability for the Middle Class." Staff Report, Office of the Vice President of the United States. April 2009. www.whitehouse.gov/strongmiddleclass/reports.

Morris, Steven. "Father Delivers Baby Son after Watching YouTube Childbirth Clips." *The Guardian*. 30 April 2009. www.guardian.co.uk/profile/stevenmorris.

National Center for Education Statistics. *The Condition of Education 2004*. 2004. http://nces.ed.gov/programs/coe/.

———. *The Condition of Education 2006*. 2006. http://nces.ed.gov/programs/coe/.

———. *The Condition of Education 2009*. 2009. http://nces.ed.gov/programs/coe/.

———. "High School Dropout and Completion Rates in the United States: 2007." 2007. http://nces.ed.gov/PUBSEARCH/pubsinfo.asp?pubid=2009064.

———. "On Track to Complete? A Taxonomy of Beginning Community College Students and Their Outcomes 3 Years After Enrolling: 2003–04 through 2006." July 2009. http://nces.ed.gov/pubSearch/pubsinfo.asp?pubid=2009152.

National Center for Public Policy and Higher Education. "Measuring Up 2008." 2008. http://measuringup2008.highereducation.org/.

Nelson, Libby. "Students at For-Profit Colleges Are Most Likely to Default on Loans, Report Says." *Chronicle of Higher Education*. 21 September 2009. http://chronicle.com/article/Students-at-For-Profit/48552/.

New York Daily News. "Howard Stern in Virgin Territory." 9 September 2008.

Obama, Barack. "Remarks of President Barack Obama—Address to Joint Session of Congress." White House Press Office. 24 February 2009. www.whitehouse.gov/the_press_office/remarks-of-president-barack-obama-address-to-joint-session-of-congress/

O'Hara, K. et al., eds. *Public and Situated Displays: Social and Interactional Aspects of Shared Display Technologies*. Norwell, Mass.: Kluwer Academic Publishers, 2003.

Organization for Economic Cooperation and Development. *Education at a Glance 2008*. www.oecd.org/document/9/0,3343,en_2649_39263238_41266761_1_1_1_1,00.html.

Ornstein, Allan. *Class Counts: Education Inequality, and the Shrinking Middle Class*. New York: Rowman & Littlefield, 2007.

Owston, James M. "Survival of the Fittest? The Rebranding of West Virginia Higher Education." PhD diss., Marshall University. 2007. www.newriver.net/AAUA/owston-aaua.pps.

Padawer, Ruth. "Keeping Up with Being Kept." *New York Times Magazine*. 10 April 2009. www.nytimes.com/2009/04/12/magazine/12sugardaddies-t.html.

Parry, Mark. "Utah State U.'s OpenCourseWare Closes Because of Budget Woes." The Wired Campus, *Chronicle of Higher Education*. 3 September 2009. http://chronicle.com/blogPost/Utah-State-Us-OpenCourseWare/7913/.

Pope, Justin. "For-Profit Colleges Boost Lending." Associated Press. 14 August 2009. http://abcnews.go.com/US/wireStory?id=8330001.

Project on Student Debt. "Student Debt and the Class of 2008." December 2009. http://projectonstudentdebt.org/files/pub/classof2008.pdf.

Rosenbaum, James. *Beyond College for All: Career Paths for the Forgotten Half.* New York: Russell Sage Foundation Publications, 2001.

Rosenfeld, Seth. "Reagan, Hoover, and the UC Red Scare." *San Francisco Chronicle.* 9 June 2002. www.sfgate.com/cgi-bin/article.cgi?f=/c/a/2002/06/09/MNCFINTRO.DTL

Rothstein, Richard. "How Can Colleges Help Graduates Pursue a Career?" *National Journal Online.* 13 July 2009. http://education.nationaljournal.com/2009/07/how-can-we-help-college-gradua.php.

———. "Supply, Demand, Wages and Myth." *New York Times,* 1 November 2000. www.epi.org/publications/entry/webfeat_lessons20001101/.

Rucker, Wes. "Neyland Stadium Renovations Cost University of Tennessee Plenty." *Chattanooga Times Free Press.* 18 July 2008. www.timesfreepress.com/news/2008/jul/18/neyland-stadium-renovations-cost-university-tennes/.

Rudolph, Frederick. *The American College and University: A History.* 1962. Reprint, with an essay and bibliography by John Thelin, Athens, Ga.: University of Georgia Press, 1990.

Santora, Mark. "For the Last Presidential Debate, a Nation's Eyes Will Turn to Hofstra." *New York Times.* 24 August 2008. www.nytimes.com/2008/08/25/nyregion/25hofstra.html.

Schofer, Evan, and John Meyer. "The World-Wide Expansion of Higher Education in the Twentieth Century." Working paper, Stanford University Center on Democracy, Development, and the Rule of Law, 2005. http://cos.sagepub.com/cgi/content/abstract/48/4/261.

ScienceDaily. "Aquaculture's Growth Seen as Continuing," 9 January 2009. www.sciencedaily.com/releases/2009/01/090102082248.htm.

Smith, Peter. *The Quiet Crisis: How Higher Education Is Failing America.* San Francisco: Jossey-Bass, 2008.

State Higher Education Executive Officers. "State Higher Education Finance FY 2008." 2009. www.sheeo.org/finance/shef_fy08.pdf.

Thelin, John R. *Higher Education and Its Useful Past.* Cambridge, Mass.: Schenkman, 1982.

———. *A History of American Higher Education.* Baltimore: Johns Hopkins University Press, 2004.

Thoreau, Henry David. *Walden.* New York: Dutton & Co., 1908.

Uchitelle, Louis. "Despite Recession, High Demand for Skilled Labor." *New York Times.* 23 June 2009. www.nytimes.com/2009/06/24/business/24jobs.html.

University of Phoenix. "2008 Academic Annual Report." 2008. www.phoenix.edu/about_us/publications/academic-annual-report.html.

U.S. Census Bureau, Current Population Survey (CPS), "March and Annual Social and Economic Supplement, 1996–2008." www.census.gov/apsd/techdoc/cps/cpsmar08.pdf.

U.S. Department of Education. "A Test of Leadership: Charting the Future of US Higher Education." A Report of the Commission Appointed by Secretary of Education Margaret Spellings. 2006. www.ed.gov/about/bdscomm/list/hiedfuture/reports/pre-pub-report.pdf.

U.S. National Archives and Records Administration. *Our Documents: 100 Milestone Documents from the National Archives*. www.ourdocuments.gov/content .php?flash=old&page=milestone.

Veblen, Thorstein. *The Higher Learning In America: A Memorandum On the Conduct of Universities By Business Men*. New York: B.W. Heubsch, 1918.

Vedder, Richard. *Going Broke by Degree: Why College Costs Too Much*. Washington, D.C.: AEI Press, 2004.

Wellman, Jane V., et al. "Trends in College Spending: Where Does the Money Come From? Where Does It Go?" Delta Cost Project, 2009. www.deltacostproject.org/ resources/pdf/trends_in_spending-report.pdfWells, H. G. *The Outline of History: Being a Plain History of Life and Mankind*. New York: The Review of Reviews Company Publishers, 1923.

Wieruszowski, Helene. *The Medieval University: Masters, Students, Learning*. Riverside, N.J.: Andrews McMeel Publishing, 1966.

Yoffe, Emily. "Seeking: How the Brain Hard-Wires Us to Love Google, Twitter, and Texting. And Why That's Dangerous." *Slate*. 12 August 2009. www.slate.com/ id/2224932/.

In addition to the resources listed above, the writing of this book was informed by personal interviews conducted by the author with:

Armstrong, Lloyd. 6 July 2009.
Arum, Richard. 15 June 2009.
Autor, David. 5 August 2009.
Babble, Meagan. 22 July 2009.
Baker, Judy. 1 June 2009.
Baum, Sandy. 7 July 2009.
Berger, Jeff. 25 June 2009.
Bischke, Jon. 8 July 2009.
Blackall, Leigh. 30 July 2009.
Blankenship, Laura. 8 June 2009.
Campbell, George. 16 June 2009.
Carnevale, Anthony. 3 June 2009.
Carson, Steve. 6 May 2009.
Casserly, Cathy. 11 May 2009.
Christen, Carol. 1 July 2009.
Crane, Kaileen. 9 July 2009.
Couros, Alec. 8 July 2009.
Cox, Geoff M. 26 June 2009.
Falik, Abigail. 21 July 2009.
Farley, Toni. 14 May 2009.
Gallagher, Dean. 25 June 2009.
Green, Casey. 28 May 2009.
Guidi, Jo. 5 June 2009.
Gunn, Linda. 25 June 2009.
Graves, William H. 25 April 2009.
Gray, Kenneth. 29 July 2009.
Hartle, Terry. 9 July 2009.
Hauptman, Arthur M. 9 June 2009.
Hine, Dougald. 5 May 2009.
Hirst, Tony. 4 June 2009.

Hochberg, Scott. 1 July 2009.
Hoffman, Nancy. 3 June 2009.
Horn, Michael. 7 May 2009.
Isaak, Larry. 28 May 2009.
Kanter, Martha. 1 June 2009.
Kaplan, Jeff. 29 July 2009.
King, James. 26 May 2009.
Kirwan, William E. 23 June 2009.
Lamb, Brian. 26 May 2009.
Lane, Andy. 18 May 2009.
LeBlanc, Paul. 30 June 2009.
Long, Bridget Terry. 13 July 2009.
Ludlow, Richard. 27 April 2009.
Lupton, Chris. 3 August 2009.
Marathe, Abhijit. 19 June 2009.
Matthews, Dewayne. 29 April 2009.
Mattoon, Rick. 13 July 2009.
Mendenhall, Robert W. 3 June 2009.
Meyer, John. 6 July 2009.
Nivi, Farbood. 30 June 2009.
Paharia, Neeru. 10 May 2009.
Patrick, Tarra. 22 July 2009.
Rouse, Cecilia E. 14 July 2009.
Schmidt, Philipp. 4 June 2009.
Schmitz, Paul. 3 August 2009.
Shireman, Robert. 8 July 2009.
Siemens, George. 30 July 2009.
Silverman, Harold. 2 July 2009.

ABOUT THE AUTHOR

Anya Kamenetz grew up in Baton Rouge and New Orleans, Louisiana, and graduated from Yale University in 2002. She covers technology, innovation, sustainability, and social entrepreneurship as a staff writer for *Fast Company* magazine. In 2005, when she was 24, the *Village Voice* nominated her for a Pulitzer Prize for the feature series and column Generation Debt, which led to a book of the same title published by Riverhead in 2006. *Generation Debt* drew national media attention and passionate online debate with its argument that young people are facing unique and unprecedented economic challenges.

With a growing awareness that we're living in a time of profound change, Kamenetz feels blessed to be engaged in the work of envisioning the future, connecting with others who are excited about change, and telling stories about the possibilities. As a national figure representing her generation, she has appeared in several documentaries including the "Generation Next" series on PBS, on media outlets including CNN's *Larry King Live*, ABC's *The View*, and NPR, has been featured as a "Yahoo! Finance Expert," and has submitted testimony to Congressional committees and state legislatures about student debt and college affordability.

She's published op-eds and additional online editorials in the *New York Times*. Her writing has appeared in a range of publications including the *Washington Post*, *New York* magazine, *Slate*, *Salon*, *The American Prospect*, and *The Nation*. She contributed an essay, "Mutual Aid Revisited," about her experiences with Hurricane Katrina and the power of community, to the anthology *Toward 2012: Perspectives on the Next Age* (Tarcher, 2008).

She speaks regularly on campuses and elsewhere across the country, blogs at Fastcompany.com, The Huffington Post, and anyakamenetz.blogspot.com, and Twitters at Anya1anya. She lives in Brooklyn with her husband and cat.

INDEX

the politics and practice of sustainable living

CHELSEA GREEN PUBLISHING

LIVING ABOVE THE STORE
Building a Business That Creates
Value, Inspires Change, and
Restores Land and Community
MARTIN MELAVER
Foreword by RAY ANDERSON
ISBN 9781603580854
Hardcover • $27.95

POISONED FOR PROFIT
How Toxins Are Making
Our Children Chronically Ill
PHILIP and ALICE SHABECOFF
ISBN 9781603582568
Paperback • $17.95

WAITING ON A TRAIN
The Embattled Future of
Passenger Rail Service
JAMES MCCOMMONS
ISBN 9781603580649
Paperback • $17.95

THE END OF MONEY
AND THE FUTURE OF CIVILIZATION
THOMAS GRECO, JR.
ISBN 9781603580786
Paperback • $19.95

CHELSEA
GREEN
PUBLISHING
the politics and practice of sustainable living

For more information or to request a catalog,
visit **www.chelseagreen.com** or
call toll-free **(800) 639-4099**.